Tony Bove and Cheryl Rhodes, co-editors of a monthly newsletter, *Desktop Publishing: Bove and Rhodes Inside Report,* founded, edited, and published *Desktop Publishing,* the magazine now known as *Publish.* They are the authors of the well-received *The Art of Desktop Publishing* and have written several other books on personal computers. Bove and Rhodes are contributing editors to *Publish* and columnists for *Computer Currents* and other computer magazines, as well as independent consultants.

Bove and Rhodes first collaborated at Data General Corporation in the late seventies. They established a partnership in 1981 and founded and published *User's Guide* (a magazine for CP/M computer users) and copublished *Datacast Magazine* (for software and telecommunications users) with Computer Faire Inc.

THE WELL-CONNECTED MACINTOSH

THE WELL-CONNECTED MACINTOSH

MACINTOSH

An Overview of Desktop Communications

Tony Bove
Cheryl Rhodes

HARCOURT BRACE JOVANOVICH, PUBLISHERS
Boston   San Diego   New York

Printed in the United States of America

Library of Congress Cataloging-in-Publication Data

Bove, Tony, 1955-
The well-connected Macintosh.

Includes index.
1. Macintosh (Computer)   2. Local area networks
(Computer networks)   I. Rhodes, Cheryl.   II. Title.
QA76.8.M3B68 1987   004.165   87-21115
ISBN 0-15-195610-3
ISBN 0-15-695666-7 (pbk.)

First edition
A   B   C   D   E

Trademarks

3+, 3+Mail, 3+Share, and 3Server3 are trademarks of 3Com Corporation.
4th Dimension is a trademark of Acius Inc.
Apple, Apple File Exchange, AppleLine, Apple Personal Modem, AppleShare and AppleTalk PC Card are trademarks of Apple Computer Inc.
AlisaTalk is a trademark of Alisa Systems Inc.
BLAST is a trademark of Communications Research Group
CompuServe is a trademark of CompuServe Information Services
ComServe is a trademark of Infosphere
Crosstalk is a registered trademark of Digital Communications Associates, Inc.
C-Server is a trademark of Solana Electronics
DaynaFile is a trademark of Dayna Communications, Inc.
dBASE II is a registered trademark of Ashton-Tate Corp.
Desktop Express is a trademark of Apple/Dow Jones & Company, Inc.
Dialog is a registered trademark of Dialog Information Services, Inc.
DiskFit is a trademark of SuperMac Software
Dow Jones News/Retrieval is a trademark of Dow Jones & Company, Inc.
EtherPort SE and EtherSC are trademarks of Kinetics, Inc.
EtherTalk is a trademark of Apple Computer Corp.
FastPath 3 is a trademark of Kinetics, Inc.
GEnie is a trademark of General Electric Information Services
Glue is a trademark of Solutions, Inc.
Hercules is a trademark of Hercules Computer Technology
Hewlett-Packard is a registered trademark of Hewlett-Packard Corp.
HyperNet is a trademark of General Computer
IBM is a registered trademark of International Business Machines Corp.
InBox is a trademark of Think Technologies, Inc.
InTalk is a trademark of Palantir Software
InterBridge is a trademark of Hayes Microcomputer Products, Inc.
InterMail is a trademark of Internet
K-Spool is a trademark of Kinetics
LaserServe is a trademark of Infosphere
LaserServer is a trademark of DataSpace Corp.
LaserShare, LaserWriter and LaserWriter Plus are trademarks of Apple Computer, Inc.
LaserSpeed is a trademark of Think Technologies
Linotronic is a trademark of The Linotype Corp.
Lotus and 1-2-3 are registered trademarks of Lotus Development Corp.
MacDraw, MacPaint and MacWrite are trademarks of Apple Computer, Inc.
Macintosh is a trademark of McIntosh Laboratories, Inc. and is licensed to Apple Computer, Inc.
Mac86 and Mac286 are trademarks of AST Research
MacBuffer LW is a trademark of Ergotron Corp.
MacDasher is a trademark of Kaz Business Systems
MacLink Plus is a trademark of DataViz, Inc.
MacMainFrame is a trademark of Avatar Technologies
MacMover is a trademark of Tri-Data
MacTerminal is a trademark of Apple Computer
MacServe is a trademark of Infosphere
MacWindows 3270 is a trademark of Tri-Data
Maxwell is a trademark of Racal-Vadic
MCI Mail is a trademark of MCI
MicroPhone is a trademark of Software Ventures Corp.
Microsoft and MS-DOS are registered trademarks of Microsoft Corp.
Microsoft Word is a trademark of Microsoft Corp.
Mockwrite is a trademark of CE Software
ModemShare is a trademark of Mirror Technologies, Inc.
MultiMate is a registered trademark of MultiMate International Corp., an Ashton-Tate Company
MultiMate Advantage is a trademark of Ashton-Tate Corp.
MultiTalk is a trademark of Abaton Technology
NetModem is a trademark of Shiva Corp.
Netway is a trademark of Tri-Data
Network DiskFit is a trademark of SuperMac Software
OfficeTalk is a trademark of OfficeTalk Inc.
Omninet is a trademark of Corvus Systems, Inc.
Omnis 3 Plus is a trademark of Blyth Software
PacerPrint and pcLink are trademarks of Pacer Software, Inc.
PageMaker is a registered trademark of Aldus Corp.
PC AT is a trademark of International Business Machines Corp.
PC MacBridge is a trademark of Tangent Technologies, Limited
PC Talk III is a trademark of Headlands Press
PhoneNET is a trademark of Farallon Computing
Pocket Modem is a trademark of Migent
PostScript is a trademark of Adobe Systems, Inc.
ProComm is a trademark of PIL Software Systems
Smartcom II is a trademark of Hayes Microcomputer Products, Inc.
Smartmodem is a registered trademark of Hayes Microcomputer Products, Inc.
The Source is a trademark of Source Telecomputing
SuperLaserSpool is a trademark of SuperMac Software
Symphony is a registered trademark of Lotus Development Corp.
Telescape is a trademark of Mainstay
TOPS is a registered trademark of TOPS, a Sun Microsystems company
TOPS Network and TOPS PRINT are trademarks of TOPS
Trailblazer is a trademark of Telebit Corp.
VersaTerm Pro is a trademark of Peripherals Computers & Supplies
WordStar and MicroPro are registered trademarks of MicroPro International Corp.

Contents

Acknowledgements

We gratefully acknowledge the following for their gracious support, especially in helping us make this book as accurate as possible:

Bob Denny and Suzanne Young of Alisa Systems; Mimi Cook-Hall, Peter Friedman, Jean-Louis Gasseé, Marie Hedman, Peter Hirschberg, Ric Jones, Jahna Michaelson, Sharon Morgan, Scott Schnell, John Scull, John Sculley, Gursharan Sidhu, Martha Steffen, and Keri Walker of Apple Computer; Ray Robideaux and Dave Troup of AST Research; Neal Checkoway and Bob Van Andel of Avatar Technologies; John Abbott of Data General Corp.; Russ Hall of GTE; Sharon O'Brien and John Hall of Hayes Microcomputer Products; Lenny Schafer of ImageSet; Steve Nelson of Kinetics; Janet and Sanjay Sakhuja of Krishna Copy Center; Stacey Byrnes and Laurie McLean of McLean Public Relations; Kevin D. O'Neill of Pacer Software; Janel Hopper of Regis McKenna; Gary Cosimini of The New York Times; Tom Reilly of SuperMac Technology; Guy Mariande of Tangent Technologies; Jack Hodgson of Think Technologies; Derek Brown and Elaine Hansen of 3-Com Corporation; Kim Criswell and Nat Goldhaber of TOPS; Alex Gernert of Tri-Data; and Hugh Daniel, John Gnu Gilmore, Troy Soult, and Paul Winternitz. Special thanks to John Duhring of SuperMac Software for suggesting the title.

We also would like to thank the editors of Harcourt Brace Jovanovich, especially Susan J. McCulley and Alice Peters, for their unflagging enthusiasm and patience through all the schedule slips. We also thank Bill Gladstone.

Preface

John Sculley, President of Apple Computer, has described our transition out of the Industrial Age and into the Information Age as an opportunity to implement many ideas that would bring about a better standard of living, such as reducing our dependence on nonrenewable energy and saving our forests from extinction. Mr. Sculley believes that time and space compress with the availability of better communications.

One giant step in this direction, designed to link Macintosh and other computer users worldwide, is the AppleTalk Network System of protocols, for communicating among users in a local-area network, and with many local-area networks in a wide-area network, no matter what kinds of computers are used. In the foreseeable future, networks will help us share the information we need to make this planet healthy again.

At a very early stage of the history of computers, scientists believed that one large computer could house all of the information in the world, and that smaller laboratory computers could have access to that information. Then, as now, computer users wanted most of all to share information. Yet, in the past, communications has been a large black hole of ambiguities, incompatible data formats, and complex, expensive solutions.

Computing power is today distributed around the world on desktop computers, with the larger mainframes and minicomputer systems acting as departmental repositories of information. One evolutionary step in computing was the introduction of the local-area network, used to link desktop computers, and share information more productively than the more costly mainframes or minicomputer systems with terminals. Desktop computers now communicate with mainframes and minicomputers as peers, requesting and supplying information, not merely as terminal emulating slaves, for typing commands while a master computer does all of the work.

The Macintosh is the easiest desktop computer to learn and use for communications. Apple has become one of the most important innovators in the market, offering a technology for sharing files and devices between computers, without requiring costly connections and extensive training.

Since 1976, we have progressed from using "primitive" Apple //, CP/M, and PC communication programs, to using the Macintosh for our telecommunications, and AppleTalk networks for sharing information. This book grew from that experience and the belief that communications could bring more people into computer literacy than any other phenomenon. We all want electronic mail, right?

The goal of this book is to introduce new users to the world of communication and information-sharing technology. The organization provides both an introduction and overview of desktop communications, and descriptions of communication offerings in the commercial and public domain.

Chapter 1 explains why you would want to connect your Macintosh to communication products, and how you could share information and computing resources. The Macintosh filing system, and conventions for using the mouse, windows, desk accessories, the Control Panel, and the Chooser are described. These tools are necessary for sharing information over networks and transmitting or receiving data to or from information services. Finally, the chapter explains the various ways to expand your Macintosh.

Chapter 2 introduces communicating over telephone lines using a modem, and describes a range of hardware and software products for communicating with electronic mail carriers, such as MCI Mail, and information services, including

Dow Jones and CompuServe. You can also use these products to communicate with other types of computers.

Chapter 3 explains communication between Macintosh and IBM PC computers, including the PS/2 models. This chapter details the nuances of Macintosh-PC connectivity, including the differences in files, using cables and modems, transferring files by disk, and using different types of networks to share files between PCs, PS/2 computers, and Macintosh computers. TOPS, AppleShare PC file sharing software, PC MacBridge, and InBox/PC for electronic mail are profiled. The chapter concludes with a description of methods for translating files from one format to another.

Chapter 4 explores the physical aspects of AppleTalk local-area and wide-area networks, cabling options, bridge devices, and the use of another network, such as Ethernet or Token Ring, as a backbone for the AppleTalk Network System. Cable options include using fiber optic or coaxial cable, or a PBX (private branch exchange) phone system.

Chapter 5 describes the file sharing, device sharing, and electronic mail services available for an AppleTalk network. Print spooling, private electronic mail over several linked networks, dedicated and distributed file sharing, setting up privileged file access and protection mechanisms, and how to use network-aware programs are explained.

Chapter 6 shows how AppleTalk networks and Macintosh computers can communicate effectively, as peers or as terminals, with IBM mainframes and a variety of minicomputer systems, including computers from Digital Equipment Corporation, Wang Laboratories, and Sun Microsystems. The products described enable Macintosh computers to share information with virtually any type of computer on the planet.

The last chapter provides a connection checklist for determining your communication needs, and descriptions of real world applications of desktop communications. It also shows a practical example of sharing information over modems and networks. The chapter also provides a glimpse of the future, with electronic voicemail, integrated voice/data digital networks, truly distributed information sharing, and more.

Appendix A describes the various file format translations available with Macintosh software, and how to convert files from one format to another. Appendix B explains cabling options, including SCSI (Small Computer Systems Interface) cabling instructions, and pin diagrams for serial connectors.

Appendix C lists the products mentioned in this book alphabetically with pricing information and company names, and lists the companies alphabetically with addresses and phone numbers. The book concludes with a complete index.

This book has been a joy to produce now that desktop publishing tools have matured. We used Macintosh computers and Microsoft Word for writing and editing, Adobe Illustrator, SuperPaint, and GraphicWorks for creating and editing graphics, and PageMaker for page makeup. We used an Apple LaserWriter for page printing (for proofs and copies), and a Linotype Linotronic imagesetter for final camera-ready pages. Products were tested and screen shots produced, on Macintosh Plus, SE and II computers, using AppleTalk networks and bridge devices, Apple, SuperMac Technology, and Jasmine Technology hard disks, and various modems and network cabling methods.

We hope you have as much fun reading this book as we had researching, writing, and producing it.

Tony Bove & Cheryl Rhodes
Woodside, California

Foreword

As I sit down to write, I am reminded that I don't like forewords. Somehow Bret Harte's remark that "It's time to cut out the cackle and get to the hosses" keeps coming to mind. Yet, when a book is written on a subject that has been the focus of my intense and undivided attention for the last five years, the temptation to add to it a few of my own thoughts is irresistible.

Most readers will readily grasp the importance of LANs for allowing the sharing of expensive peripherals among several computers. However, in my opinion there is a much more compelling reason for paying special attention to this technology. Perhaps the most bedevilling difficulty with computers is that there are so many different kinds, each with its own operating systems, file formats, disk formats, etc. And, these systems are all essentially incompatible. It is not easy for the user of an MS-DOS computer to take a file or a disk from that machine and read it on a Unix computer. Application programs written for one machine will not run on a machine of a different ilk. However, quite unavoidably organizations own machines of various types. Computer networks offer one of the best hopes for allowing interoperation between the different computers of such a mixed environment, and therein lies their true importance.

Unfortunately, many different computer network systems have been developed, each using its own internal languages of interaction, known as protocols. This is quite similar to the many different languages used by people, such as Swahili, English, French, Pidgin, etc. The same difficulties, symbolized by the metaphorical "Tower of Babel" and experienced by people with regard to natural languages, apply to the world of computer networks and their multiple protocol families. This has provided ample grist for the press, and analysts have speculated and commented at length on how protocol standards will emerge and somehow there will be one single uniform protocol family that all computers will speak. This is a promising if somewhat confusing picture; the difficulty is that there are so many protocols that claim to be "standards" and the poor computer user is dragged through more confusion and nervousness. But should we expect a single standard for protocols to emerge any more than the emergence of a single uniform natural language spoken by all humans on the globe?

The point, of course, is that all these discussions of important esoterica divert attention from the basic issue of providing true end-user value on computer network systems. Users do not want to be dragged through a welter of technical discussion; they want to use computers for realizing their everyday life and professional activities more efficiently and more enjoyably.

We at Apple Computer have, for the last five years, been involved in the development of a comprehensive computer network system, known as AppleTalk, for the Macintosh and Apple-II personal computer families. As the pioneering company in the field of personal computing, our goal has been to extend this to interpersonal computing. For, people do not work in isolation.

A network system such as AppleTalk is composed of various components, all of which have to work in harmony to provide the end user with the necessary services in a consistent fashion. The development of these components occurs over a period of several years and in fact never ends as the system continues to evolve and change to keep pace with technology and user needs. The consistency and harmonious operation of such a sophisticated system throughout its evolution is best ensured by using an underlying framework model as the embodiment of guiding principles and architectural constructs. At Apple we have followed what we refer to as Apple's Communications Framework (ACF).

ACF consists of several conceptual building blocks and the technical principles that govern their interoperation. Key among these is the Macintosh personal computer which is the point of contact of a user with the network system. There are several technologies that give the Macintosh its special enticing and empowering characteristics; to name a few, the use of a bit-mapped high-resolution display screen, the Mouse, and QuickDraw. The second key component of the ACF is the AppleTalk protocol architecture, a suite of network interaction protocols used by all devices connected to an AppleTalk network system. Printing technology forms a third component of the ACF, especially the use of PostScript. The confluence of the Macintosh, the AppleTalk network protocols, and the PostScript-based LaserWriter was the basis on which desktop publishing emerged, starting in 1985.

More recently we have introduced other portions of the framework. In particular, Internetworking and Information Sharing. The first of these allows the user to build large network systems consisting of many AppleTalk networks of different sorts all connected to each other by means of bridging devices which operate according to the internetworking rules of the ACF. The Information Sharing portion of the ACF is specified in the form of a standard protocol known as the AppleTalk Filing Protocol. On the basis of AFP, we developed the AppleShare file server, which provides a standard platform for the development of workgroup productivity applications to support the sharing activities of a group of users. AFP and AppleShare start making fundamental contributions to the mixed environment interoperation potential of LAN technology referred to above. In fact, AppleShare currently allows Macintosh, MS-DOS and Apple-II computers to share information through the AppleShare file server. This building block is extensible and should be expected to grow to encompass other systems, including Unix.

My overriding objective as the chief architect of the ACF and the AppleTalk system has been very straightforward. We have chosen to sidestep the widespread bickering over technical minutiae and focus on providing end-user value. It has been an exciting challenge to build a network system which extends the very powerful yet friendly and immediate soul of the Macintosh out through the network system. This has been an exercise that has appealed in a very direct way to admiration of elegance and aesthetics. We have strived for elegance in our designs through simplicity.

The AppleTalk system now consists of a string of related products, including various connectivity options with differing price-performance points, and a variety of servers and services. All of these components attempt to provide enjoyable and very directly useful capability through access of remote resources in the simplest manner possible. It is through such value that the "year of LAN" might eventually come to pass, not through protestations of technical detail.

"The Well-Connected Macintosh" discusses most of the products that make up this system. Tony Bove and Cheryl Rhodes have made a signal contribution by examining these as they relate to the end user's needs and interests rather than to the technical underpinnings. As experienced end users of this system they are amply qualified and this becomes very evident throughout this book.

Gursharan S. Sidhu, Manager,
Network Systems Development,
Apple Computer, Inc.

1 Preparing For Macintosh Communications

I'd love to turn you on. — John Lennon/Paul McCartney

Everyone communicates with many different people to exchange information. In fact, communication with certain individuals and organizations is the most important part of many businesses and professions.

A Macintosh computer can be an extension of yourself, making you more productive by letting you exchange information with many different types of computers, such as IBM PCs and compatibles or larger computers ("minicomputers" and "mainframes"). You can take information from these other computers, and inspired by the graphics and text styles offered by the Macintosh, prepare a business report or commercial publication using a Macintosh.

The Macintosh is an excellent computer for sharing data because it has a powerful, easy-to-learn method for making requests (the "human interface"). It also has software to help you organize your information and automate your typical operations (the "operating system").

For example, the operating system displays folders that you can use to keep files of data together under a single topic name. The idea of having a folder of files you can open, close, and copy to disks is just as powerful as the traditional method of grouping information in directories, but folders are easier to open, close, and copy and easier for a layperson to understand. You don't have to be a computer scientist or wizard to learn how to use a mouse to point, select, and move folders across an electronic desktop (see Figures 1-1 and 1-2).

Text and·Pages

The system also displays graphic icons that represent programs and files. The names of these files and their folders can be very descriptive. It is easy to use a mouse to select a file, and the system automatically runs the program associated with that file.

The Macintosh method of selecting and manipulating files, folders, and programs, which has been imitated in other personal computer systems, is also the best method for selecting and reading today's electronic mail, or running a file conversion operation.

Macintosh application programs tend to look like other Macintosh programs because they mostly use the same menu conventions. The Macintosh system provides the display of pull-down menus and the mechanism for selecting commands and options from menus. The system also provides the display of dialog boxes (see Figure 1-3) with settings such as Drive (to switch drives) and Eject (to eject a disk), and the OK and Cancel buttons.

Nearly all Macintosh programs use these conventions, such as having the Open, Close, and Quit commands in the drop-down File menu, so that you are not completely lost when you start up a new program for the first time.

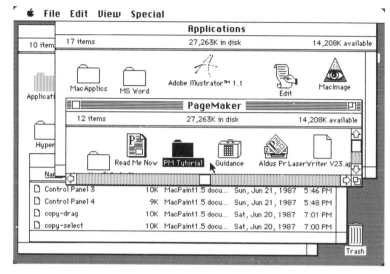

Figure
1-1

A typical Macintosh desktop with folders containing files — you select a folder or file by moving the pointer with a mouse, then clicking the mouse button.

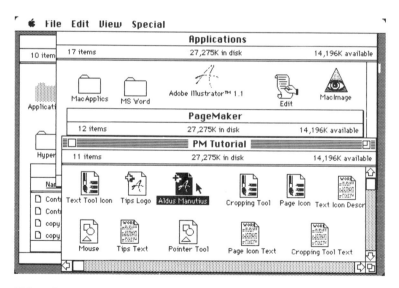

Figure
1-2

Either choose the Open command from the File menu, or click the folder twice, to open it and display its contents (which could be other folders as well as files and programs).

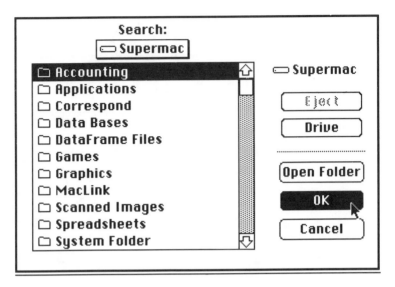

Figure
1-3

The typical Macintosh dialog box lets you pick selections for an operation, such as searching, then gives you two buttons: OK (go ahead) or Cancel (don't do it).

Figure
1-4

Copying the highlighted information from a financial wire service to the Macintosh Clipboard.

Another feature of nearly all Macintosh applications is the ability to copy or cut an object (consisting of text and graphics) from one file and paste it into another via the Macintosh Clipboard (provided with every system). The Clipboard and the Copy (or Cut) and Paste commands in the Edit menu make it possible for you to take information from one source, and quickly and easily, deposit that information in a file on your disk, or vice-versa. You can also copy portions of one message or document and use them in another message or document. Imagine being able to copy financial information from a mainframe computer and paste it into a document on your Macintosh disk, then produce a report using the information (see Figures 1-4 and 1-5).

From our experience with primitive electronic mail and communications systems, we know that communicating from the desktop computer was much harder in the days before computers had graphic icons and drop-down menus activated by pointing devices (such as a mouse). Today, communication is nearly effortless — you can transfer files from Macintoshes to IBM PCs and compatibles, and back to Macintoshes, very quickly and sometimes with automatic conversion so that you don't have to think about it.

Of course, we want you to think about all the possibilities using communications and the Macintosh. You could set up electronic mail between members of a work group, which could include the ability to exchange documents and graphics. You could share large data bases and devices such as laser printers, high-speed printers, and typesetters among several different kinds of computers.

You can also use a *modem* (short for modulator-demodulator, which is a device that converts digital computer information into analog telephone signals and back again to digital) with a regular telephone line or a special leased line in order to connect with a network of information services. You can do research, compile reports, communicate with colleagues in other geographic areas, or even make airline reservations and

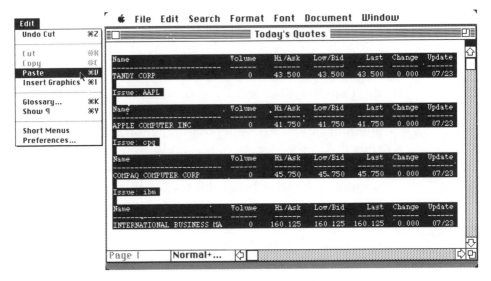

Figure
1-5

Pasting the information from the example in Figure 1-4 into a Microsoft Word document on your Macintosh.

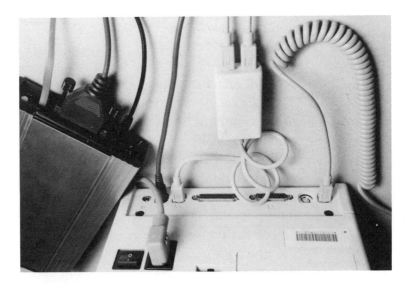

The Macintosh Plus with a Hayes Smartmodem connected to one port and the AppleTalk Personal Network connected to another port. The keyboard is connected to the port on the far left, and the mouse is connected to the keyboard (not shown).

purchase the tickets with these services, which are described in Chapter 2.

The possibilities are endless, and they all start with equipment you can buy in a retail store, some of which you may already have on your desk: a Macintosh, an AppleTalk network cable, and a modem.

The Macintosh already has all the connectors (called *ports*) you'll need to get started in the world of desktop communications (see Figures 1-6 to 1-8). There are icons above the ports that identify them for you:

The modem port is used to attach one modem or any serial device that uses an RS-232 signal. Modems are described in Chapter 2.

The AppleTalk or printer port is used to attach either an AppleTalk Personal Network cable (for connecting

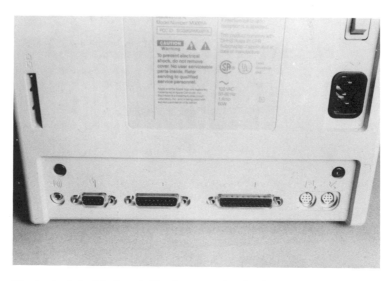

*Figure
1-6*

The back of the Macintosh Plus has ports for the AppleTalk Personal Network (or a printer), a modem (or other serial device), a SCSI device or chain of devices, a floppy disk drive, a mouse, and an audio device (the keyboard plugs into the front).

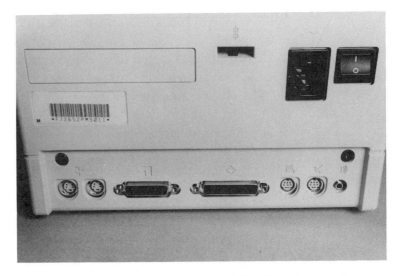

Figure
1-7

The back of the Macintosh SE has two Apple DeskTop Bus ports for input devices like a keyboard and mouse (there are additional ports on the keyboard), plus the ports for the AppleTalk Personal Network (or a printer), a modem (or other serial device), a SCSI device or chain of devices, a floppy disk drive, and an audio device.

Figure
1-8

The back of the Macintosh II has the same ports as the Macintosh SE in Figure 1-7, plus additional slots for add-in boards that can have their own ports.

one or more laser printers and other Macintosh computers in a network), or an ImageWriter cable. AppleTalk networking is described in sections of Chapters 3 and all of Chapter 4.

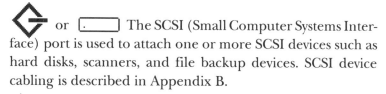 or ☐ The SCSI (Small Computer Systems Interface) port is used to attach one or more SCSI devices such as hard disks, scanners, and file backup devices. SCSI device cabling is described in Appendix B.

The mouse port is used to attach the mouse (Plus only).

The keyboard port (in the front under the display) is used to attach the Macintosh keyboard (Plus only).

The Apple DeskTop port is used to attach any Macintosh SE or II keyboard, mouse, or input device. You can use one DeskTop connector to attach the keyboard, and you can then attach the mouse to one of the keyboard's port, leaving the other DeskTop ports free for other input devices such as a drawing tablet.

The external disk drive port is used to attach an external floppy disk drive (not a SCSI drive).

The audio port is used to attach audio equipment for listening to Macintosh-generated sound.

As we write this book, both our Macintosh Plus computers are connected through these ports to various devices. We have several portable hard disks (the DataFrame XP40 from Super-Mac, the Jasmine 20, and the Apple HD-SCSI 20) connected to the SCSI ports. We also have a Datacopy Model 730 scanner and a Dest PC Scan scanner attached as SCSI devices. We need a lot of disk space available while we write because graphics and scanned images take up a lot of space, as do publication files produced from page makeup programs.

9

Both computers are attached to an AppleTalk network, which connects them to a LaserWriter Plus. Our Macintosh SE and II computers are also connected to our AppleTalk network, sharing the laser printer. We can transfer files to and from the other computers instantly using the Centram TOPS network system, or we can dedicate one of the computers to act as a library of files using AppleShare (both are described in detail in Chapter 4).

Both computers also have modems attached — the Hayes Smartmodem 1200 on one, and the Hayes Smartmodem 2400 on the other. We use the modems to call services such as CompuServe and MCI Mail and to call research libraries such as Lockheed's Dialog and Apple's AppleLink. These are described in Chapter 2.

Frankly, we'd feel hampered if we did not have the ability to communicate with other services and other computers, and to expand disk space and functional capabilities (such as performing daily backups of all disks and scanning paper images and text to create electronic files). Writing is much more than simply typing sentences (doing "word processing") — most of the time is spent organizing information from various sources. This task is best served by a computer that can communicate with many sources and retrieve information without hassles. The Macintosh line of computers has served this purpose well.

Reasons for Connecting

Why should you consider connecting a Macintosh to another disk drive or computer, either directly, through a modem, or over a network? For one thing, you may want to share information, such as reports, budgets, or data base records, with other workers. For another, you may want to share expensive devices, such as high-capacity disk drives and tape backup devices, high-speed laser printers, and typesetters.

Why would you want to share electronic information with

other users by connecting computers to other computers and devices? Here are three good reasons:

1. Sharing information in folders. Just as you would pass a folder to a colleague in the next office, you can pass electronic folders to numerous colleagues in nearby offices or even remote locations. You can, in fact, share files with people who are in different countries. The information would not have to be retyped; charts and graphs would not have to be redrawn; spread sheets can be edited and added to; documents from various writers and editors can be edited and produced without retyping or dealing with paper.

2. Controlled information sharing with many users. You can't always afford to equip all of your Macintoshes with high-capacity storage devices, but many users need access to a lot of information at once. The desired information has typically been collected and managed with a mainframe computer or minicomputer, and the idea is to connect personal computers to the mainframe or mini. However, haphazard access to this information is not what you want — you want controlled access with built-in protections so that unauthorized people can't gain access to sensitive information. The appropriate network and communication software gives you that control.

3. Integrating and enhancing information from other sources. Large repositories of information, such as corporate data bases and inventory management systems, do not usually have the software for making presentations or producing publications. Besides, time on the large computers is already much in demand, and bottlenecks are probably already occurring. You will be more productive if you use your Macintosh, which can be outfitted with sophisticated presentation and publishing software. You can also offload the task of enhancing and integrating information to communication specialists who are using Macintoshes or other personal computers.

This reasonable question could be asked by anyone who already has a mainframe or minicomputer: why use personal computers for information management with multiple users?

There are many reasons, but here are two general ones:

1. To replace old terminals with personal computers that can double as desktop productivity tools. Terminals can't produce spread sheets, text files, graphic representations, and data base listings by themselves, but desktop computers can do those things and much more, while at the same time providing access to minicomputers and mainframes. In other words, desktop computers make better "terminals" than terminals, and they may in fact be less expensive.

2. An information management system is usually bottle-necked if it has to perform all the functions of information management for a large group of users. Communication and local area networks can help alleviate this situation by transferring some of the processing activities to desktop computers.

Let's look at information sharing from another angle: who sends the information and who receives it.

Sharing Information

The most popular form of information sharing — electronic mail and file exchange — is characterized by the need of individuals to occasionally pass information to each other, with also the ability to ignore communications and work on the information at hand. Similar to communications over telephones, you can make a call only when you need to, and you need not spend all your time on the phone.

Electronic mail (with file exchange) can occur without your being disturbed — as if a phone answering machine was set up to give all the information needed and process your requests, without your intervention. An electronic mail system offers this type of information sharing among a small work group, across a very large organization, or across the world (using a service such as MCI Mail or CompuServe).

In such a system, a person sends a message and perhaps a file, such as a spread sheet, to another person's electronic mailbox. The mailbox is checked only when the other person wants to, and no one is disturbed by the communication, although an alert message can appear on the screen if the other person wants to have such an option. We call this type of access sender-directed since it occurs only when a sender wants to send something. Electronic mail vendors such as MCI and CompuServe use mail systems to link individuals all over the world.

The next level of information sharing is the use of a *file server:* a disk that holds files available for sharing. Senders put files on this server disk (or in a server area of a high-capacity disk), and receivers actively search the server for these files when they need them. This type of access is receiver-directed because it occurs only when receivers need information (senders of information post the information once and are not disturbed by continual access). Again, communication is passive, not disturbing either party.

The next higher level of information access is when users share a program and its information simultaneously. Communication in this fashion is active — both parties are aware and are actively communicating. They may be sharing a publication or data base and making changes so that the other party can see the updated information immediately.

The simplest form of this type of communication would be two users sharing a common document, and perhaps sharing a document style sheet to prepare other documents in the same style. A more complex form would be several users sharing an inventory/parts list data base and placing orders that update the data base immediately, so that other users know immediately what parts are in stock and what parts have to be backordered.

You can share files by simply swapping disks with other computer users. When swapping is impractical (over long distances, or when people would rather work than be disturbed by disk copying, or when files are too large for floppy disks), you will want to use a communication system that lets you transfer complete files from one computer to another, either through a cable or through a modem and the phone network.

There are many ways to communicate, and tradeoffs with each one. Sharing disks can be impractical but economical. A direct link to a PC-compatible computer may be effective for file transfers, but it would not be enough for electronic mail. A network can be tightly controlled or liberal about file access, depending on how you implement the network control software. On a network you can store all files on one dedicated file server computer or distribute the shared files over several computers without having to dedicate one as a server. When you gain access to mainframes and minicomputers, you can decide whether you want simple terminal emulation, or more sophisticated emulation and file transfer, or even more sophisticated communication. These tradeoffs are discussed in more detail in later chapters.

Sharing Devices

It seems like a good idea to share expensive devices among many computers if you can implement the plan without a lot of expense and training. Many businesses and departments of large companies would like to share devices that are too expensive to attach to every computer. There are a variety of ways of sharing devices and controlling access to them.

Apple provides an easy way to share laser printers and dot matrix printers with several computers — the AppleTalk Personal Network. Apple has delivered the potential for an AppleTalk network in every LaserWriter and in every Mac, thereby making it feasible to buy the computer without making a decision about whether to buy the network.

You can start with one Macintosh and one ImageWriter, then add an AppleTalk Personal Network cable and a LaserWriter. You can connect up to 32 devices using AppleTalk Personal Network cable, including LaserWriters, Macintosh computers, and PCs (as described in Chapter 3).

Although Apple Computer offers an inexpensive solution with the AppleTalk Personal Network cable, you can set up an AppleTalk network with other types of cable. For example, you can substitute a higher-speed cable, such as DuPont's fiber optic cable, or an existing wiring scheme, such as Northern Telecom's PBX or Farallon Computing's PhoneNET (both of which use ordinary telephone wire) to build an AppleTalk network that has more than 32 devices spread throughout a building. The adjective "AppleTalk" is used to describe networks that use the same communication protocols, regardless of what cabling system is used. You can substitute other kinds of cabling systems, or establish an AppleTalk network using another type of network as a *backbone*, such as Ethernet, so that the AppleTalk system of communications runs on top (network operations are the same,but faster). You can also link AppleTalk networks into an *internetwork* (a network of networks) using a bridge device such as the Hayes InterBridge. All these AppleTalk network scenarios are in Chapter 4.

Even with one Macintosh, one LaserWriter, and the inexpensive AppleTalk cable, you can enjoy the benefits of *print spooling* — sending output to a spooler program that handles the printing task while you go back to work in your application program. Spoolers can save time by freeing your computer to run the application program.

With spoolers you also have many choices and tradeoffs. With some, your Macintosh runs both the spooler and your program simultaneously (which is called *background spooling*); the benefit is that you can get spooling from your Macintosh without involving other computers. This is also called *client spooling* by Apple and direct spooling by others, since it works directly from one computer to the printer.

With another type of spooler you can ship the document off to another computer that runs the spooler. Called a *server* spooler and implemented in Apple's LaserShare (described in Chapter 4), the spooler runs on a Macintosh or other computer that is a dedicated file server, allowing it to act as a spooler performing print jobs for every computer on the network. It is also possible to have spoolers reside on several computers and share the work of spooling print jobs without disturbing the users of those computers.

The approach for handling many computers may be to establish a print server in the departmental minicomputer or mainframe. There are several products that let you connect AppleTalk to IBM and Digital Equipment Corporation computers and enable those computers to perform as file servers and print servers while also doing their regular chores. We describe such print servers in Chapter 5.

A high-speed modem can be shared in a similar fashion using various modem-sharing products on an AppleTalk network (described in Chapter 2). Each user on the network can have access to the high-speed modem for special communication tasks. Another way to share a high-speed modem is to use a network similar to one offered by 3Com (described in Chapter 4). In 3Com's Ethernet-based network, you have a dedicated file server that can handle communication with other networks if the server has one or more modems attached to it.

Learning to Use the Mouse

To use the Macintosh and most Macintosh applications, you must become familiar with the mouse. There are basically five actions to perform with a mouse:

Point. When you move the mouse, a pointer moves across the display. You perform this action all the time.

Click. You click a point on the display by quickly pressing and releasing the mouse button. You do this to establish an insertion point in a text file, to establish a point in an image, or to select a cell in a spread sheet.

Double-click. You double-click a point (such as a file or program icon) by quickly pressing and releasing the mouse button twice. By double-clicking a file or application program, you automatically run the program associated with that file.

Drag. You drag something (such as a graphic object, block of text, or icon) by pointing the mouse, holding down the mouse button, and moving the mouse so that the pointer (or object) moves to a new position, then releasing the button.

Select. To select a menu option or command, drag down a menu (which drops down to show you the options or commands) until the command or option you want is highlighted, then release the mouse button. To select text, double-click a word or drag across one or more words or paragraphs.

The Macintosh employs drag-down menus and displays dialog boxes after you select a command or option. In the dialog boxes you can select items by clicking boxes or buttons displayed on the screen, and sometimes there are scroll bars for scrolling items in a small window. To operate the scroll bar, click below the white box in the gray area, or click the up or down arrow, or drag the white box up or down. Dialog boxes

Empty Folder

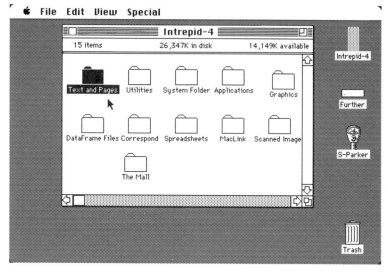

Figure 1-9

The Macintosh desktop displays an icon for each disk drive, each program, each file, and each folder, but usually files are hidden inside folders. Here, the folder "Text and Pages" is selected but not yet opened.

17

often have text boxes for typing numbers or text, and every dialog box has an OK and a Cancel button.

Nearly every menu command can be activated by typing a key while holding down the Command key (the key with a cloverleaf icon). For example, we describe below how to use the New Folder command, which is in the File menu. This command can be activated by dragging down the File menu and releasing the mouse on the New Folder command. However, you can also select this command quickly by typing a shortcut: hold down the Command key and type an *N*. Whenever we refer to a key sequence of this type, we call it "Command-N." Similar to function keys on a PC, these Command key combinations make it possible to run programs entirely from the keyboard without using a mouse.

Files and Folders

The secret to successful information management is the ability to properly organize files into folders. The Macintosh desktop displays icons for both files and folders, but many users put all files within folders so that all you see on the desktop are folders along with icons for the disks (Figure 1-9).

To create a folder, you drag down the File menu and release the mouse on the New Folder command (you can also select this command by typing a shortcut: Command-N). A folder appears, named Empty Folder, and you can change its name by typing a new name immediately, or by first selecting the name (or part of the name) by dragging across the name, then typing new characters to replace the selected characters (Figure 1-10).

The folder is now ready to hold files. You can place already-created files into the folder by dragging the file icons. You can select more than one file icon at a time by first clicking one icon, and then holding down the Shift key while clicking subsequent icons. Another way to select several files at once is to drag diagonally across the area of the window containing

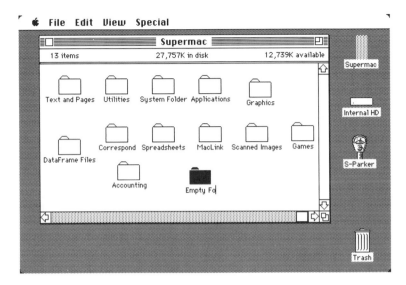

Figure 1-10

After creating a new folder (which has the name Empty Folder until you change it), rename the folder by dragging across all or part of the old name and typing new characters to replace the selected characters.

the files, drawing a selection rectangle (Figure 1-11). After selecting several files at once, you can drag all of them to a folder to place them inside the folder. For example, Figure 1-12 shows how you would drag the selected files into a folder. By the way, you can use descriptive names for files and folders, including spaces, digits, and any symbols (except colons). You can use up to 25 characters.

To open a folder, you can click the mouse twice while pointing to the folder, or click once and select the Open command from the File menu. The contents are then displayed, and you can select another file or folder (Figure 1-13).

Using commands in the View menu, you can display the file and folder names of the contents of a folder either by icon (Figure 1-14) or alphabetically by name (Figure 1-15). The Macintosh also keeps track of the last time and date the file was changed, so you can display the files by date, with the file most recently worked on at the top (Figure 1-16) and the rest sorted by date of the last modification.

The Well-Connected Macintosh

You can use a different display type for each folder — when you reopen a folder it remembers what display type you were using the last time it was opened. We use the date-sorted display in our text file folders so that we can make backup copies quickly by copying only the recently changed files. With a regular backup schedule we never miss a file. We use the name-sorted display for folders of reference documents. We use the icon display for a folder consisting mostly of other folders and for folders holding very few files. You can switch from one type of display to another using the View menu.

The Macintosh provides an easy-to-learn mechanism for adding comments about a particular file, for checking the date it was created and modified, and for controlling access: the Get Info command. To use it, select a file by pointing and clicking its icon once, then either choose the Get Info command from the File menu, or hold down the Command and *I* keys (abbreviated Command-I).

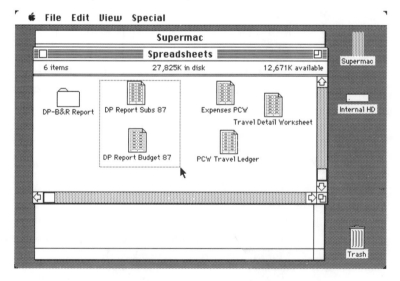

Figure 1-11

Selecting more than one file at a time by dragging diagonally across the window area, drawing a selection rectangle.

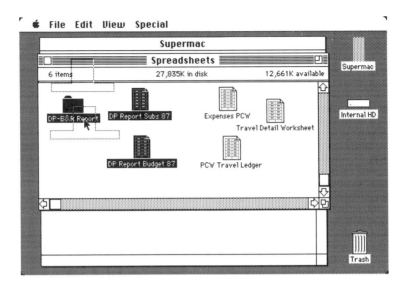

Figure 1-12

Dragging the selected files into the folder DP-B&R Report.

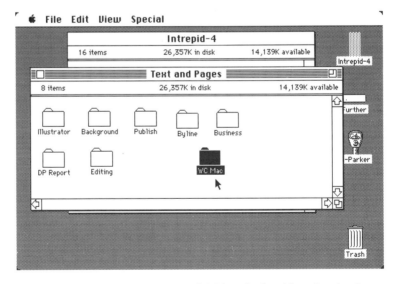

Figure 1-13

The contents of the "Text and Pages" folder, displayed by using the Open command in the File menu, or by double-clicking the icon of the folder. The "WC Mac" folder, which resides in the "Text and Pages" folder, is then selected.

21

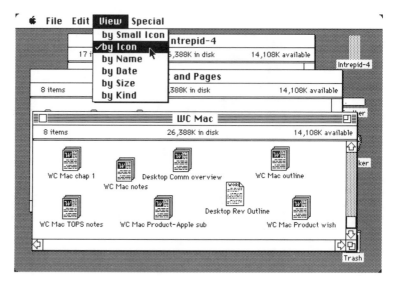

Figure
1-14

Displaying the files in a folder by icon, which is the default setting for Macintosh folders.

Figure 1-17 shows the Get Info window that appears after you use the command. It gives you a lot of useful information: where and when the file was created, when it was last modified, how big it is, and the type of file (either the file is an application program, or it is a data file or document used with an application program). Get Info also works with folders — it tells you the size of the folder, which includes all the files within that folder, and it lets you add a comment describing its contents.

Figure 1-18 shows how you can type a comment to describe the file, and Figure 1-19 shows how you can check the file's Locked box if you don't want the file to be changed by anyone (including yourself). To change or get rid of a locked file, you have to first open the Get Info window and then click the Locked box so that the X mark disappears.

The folder window that shows its contents can be resized in many ways to keep other icons and folders visible on the desktop. Click the bottom right corner of the window and drag (hold down the mouse button while moving) the corner

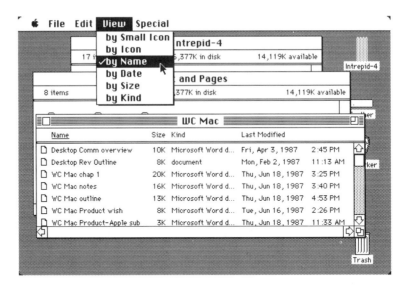

Figure
1-15

Displaying the files in a folder alphabetically.

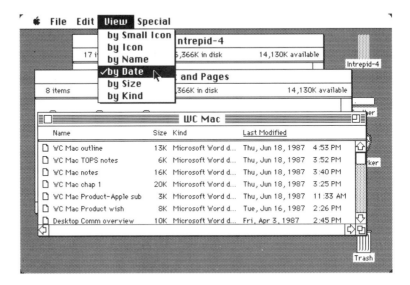

Figure
1-16

Displaying the files in a folder by date, so that the file most recently changed is at the top and the rest are listed by the date and time of their last modification.

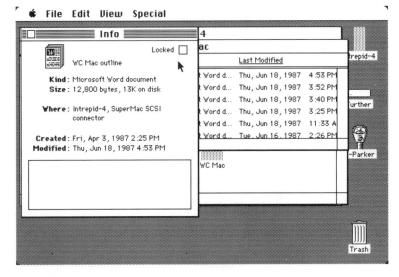

Figure 1-17

The Get Info command in the File menu (also Command-I) displays a window of information about a file, including the date it was created and the disk drive or folder in which it resides, the date of last modification, and the file's size.

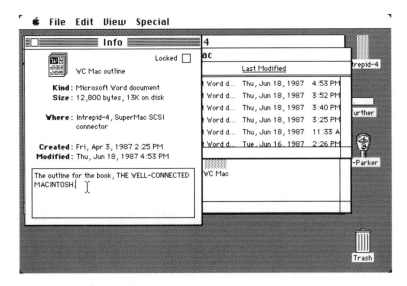

Figure 1-18

Adding a comment to the Get Info window for a particular file.

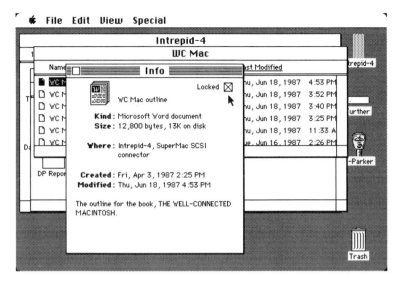

Figure
1-19

Marking the Locked box to lockout any changes to the file (this also changes the display of the comment, so that you can't change the comment unless you first unlock the file).

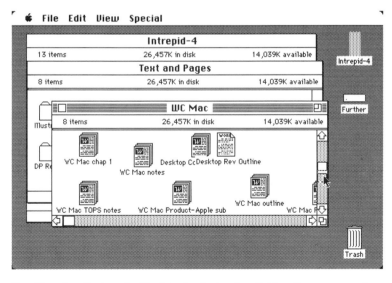

*Figure
1-20*

Scrolling the display of a Macintosh window by clicking the arrows, or by dragging the scroll box, or by clicking above or below the scroll box.

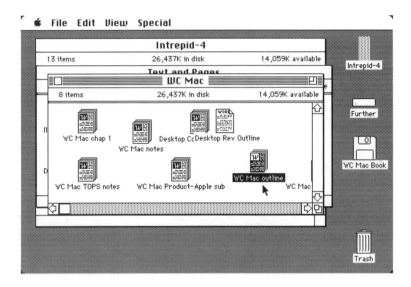

Figure
1-21

Selecting a file to copy onto a disk.

to a new location. You can scroll the display of the folder's contents by dragging the scroll box in the scroll bar, or clicking above or below the box in the scroll bar, or by clicking the arrows at the top and bottom of the scroll bar (shown in Figure 1-20).

Files and folders can be moved around on the desktop by selecting and then dragging them. You can move a file into a folder by dragging it into the folder. This is also the way you make copies of files on different disks: first select the file or folder (Figure 1-21), then drag it on top of the disk icon until the disk icon changes color or turns black (as shown in Figure 1-22).

The Macintosh can automatically make a duplicate file of an existing file on the same disk with the Duplicate command in the File menu. It creates a new file automatically and uses the same file name but with the words "Copy of" added. However, this method, which is fine for making a duplicate file, is not used for making backups on different disks. You

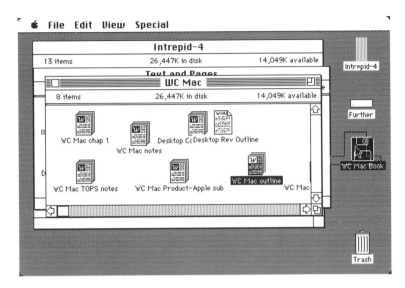

Figure
1-22

Dragging the file's outline to the disk icon; when the disk icon changes color, you can let go of the mouse button.

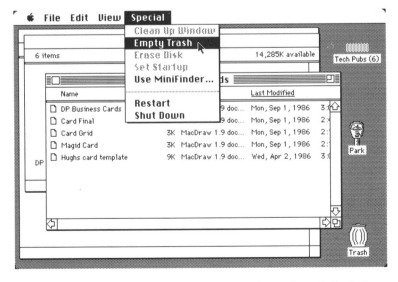

Figure
1-23

After dragging a file or folder to the trash can, the can has a bulge in it, which means that you can still retrieve the file or folder from the can.

simply drag the original file to the other disk, and the Macintosh makes a copy (using the same name) on the other disk, leaving the original alone.

The only way to get rid of a file or folder is to drag it to the trash can icon and let it go in (the same way you drag a file to another disk). The can will look like it has a bulge in it, which means the file is still retrievable (Figure 1-23); in fact, you can retrieve it by simply double-clicking the trash can (which is a special folder) and dragging the file or folder to a disk or folder. To actually get rid of the file and reclaim the disk space, use the Empty Trash command in the Special menu. This "empty trash" function happens automatically when you start an application or copy a file to another disk.

An interesting feature of the Macintosh Finder (the part of the system that displays a desktop of files and folders and responds to your menu requests) is that you can drag a file out of its folder and onto the gray-shaded desktop (the gray shade can be changed to some other pattern or no pattern, as described later). Sometimes you will want to drag some files out onto the desktop so that they appear automatically when you first start the computer from that disk. On the other hand, you may want to put such a file back into its folder. The Put Away command in the File menu sends the file or folder back to its original folder.

Finding Information

Although file folders help you organize information by topic or any other nomenclature, what happens when several other hard disk icons — possibly from file servers in other parts of the network — appear on your desktop? How can you quickly search through all the folders in all the disk drives?

The Macintosh System has room for you to store miniprograms, called desk accessories, that perform special operations while you are running one or more programs. Desk accessories are similar to pop-up memory-resident programs

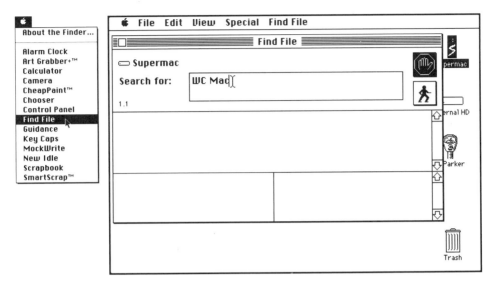

Figure
1-24
The Find File dialog box in which you can type the full or partial name of a file, and search all disk drives and folders for any matches.

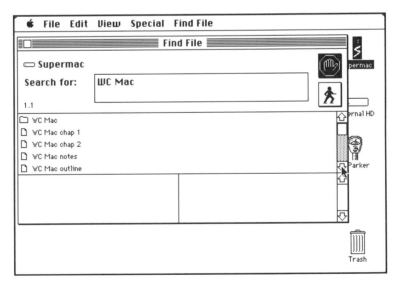

Figure
1-25
Find File displays a list of files that contain the words you typed.

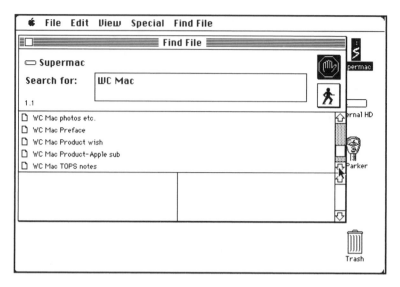

Figure
1-26

Clicking the up or down arrows in the scroll bar to scroll the list of file
names in the Find File dialog box.

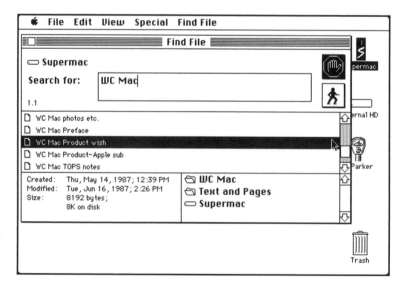

Figure
1-27

Find File displays file information and the route of folders to open in
order to access a particular file.

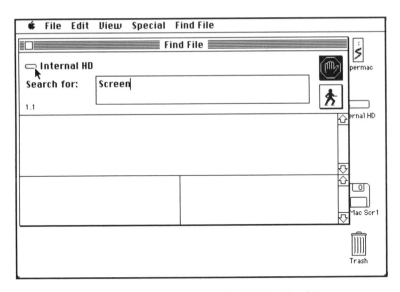

*Figure
1-28*

You can start the search on another drive by clicking the drive name,
which automatically changes to the next drive found on the desktop.

on PCs, except that they occupy memory only when you use
them. You may have already used the Alarm Clock or Calculator desk accessory by dragging down the System menu (click
the Apple logo to see the System menu) and letting go on the
accessory's name.

One desk accessory supplied with the System file (in addition to Alarm Clock, Calendar, Notepad, Scrapbook, Control
Panel, Chooser, and others) is Find File. This remarkable
accessory will search folders on multiple disk drives and display file information and the route through disks and folders
to gain access to that file. You can run it during an application
session and find a file before using the application's Open
command to open the file.

Find File is easy to use: simply drag down the Apple System
menu and release the mouse on Find File, to display the Find
File dialog box, and type the full or partial name of a file (Figure 1-24). Find File finds all file names that contain the word
or words you typed and displays them in a list (Figure 1-25).

31

Scroll through the list to find the exact file (shown in Figure 1-26). When you click the name you want, Find File displays file information on the left side of the screen, and a list of folders you have to open to get to the file (Figure 1-27).

The search is limited to one disk drive at a time, to avoid long delays while the computer searches all available disk drives and servers on a network. Find File is designed to work in a network of drives that may appear on your desktop as icons with names. When Find File detects several disk drives, it displays the name of the drive holding the active System Folder first (as in the previous examples). You can change the drive being searched by clicking the name of the drive in the Find File dialog box (in the upper left corner); it changes automatically to the next drive it finds (Figure 1-28). You can continue to click the drive name to select another drive.

You can also limit the search to one folder (which itself may contain many folders) on a drive. Find File displays a special menu from which you can select the Search Here command (Figure 1-29), which displays a list of folders on the drive

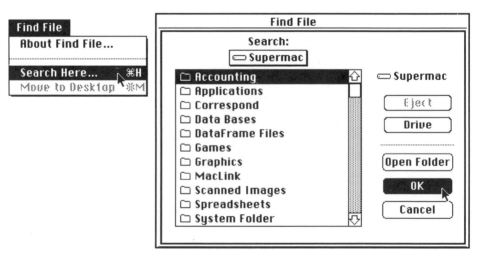

Figure 1-29

Limiting a Find File search to a single folder on a drive (the folder may contain many folders).

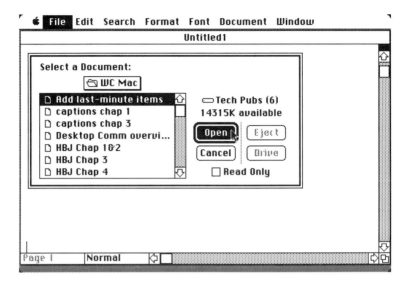

Figure 1-30

In an application, when you open a file you see this dialog box, which displays the active folder and its contents.

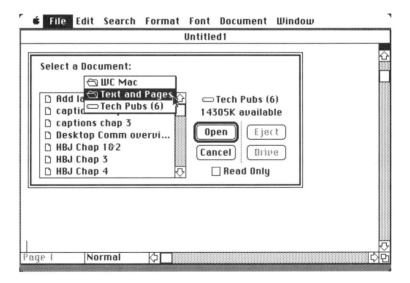

Figure 1-31

You can select files from another folder by clicking the active folder name to see a list of folders, and dragging down to select a higher level folder.

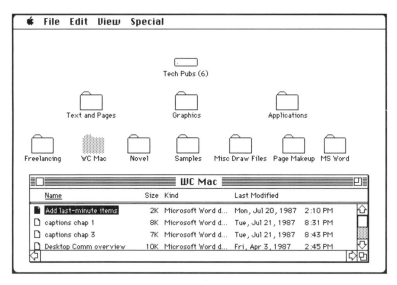

Figure
1-32

Keep a visual reference of your folder arrangement, such as this tree structure, to remind yourself how to find specific folders.

selected. You can also use the Eject button to eject a floppy disk and search another.

You can stop a search by clicking the Stop symbol. Also, you don't have to wait for the search to be completed to select a file or folder and display information. Find File will continue to search while you select files and display information, and will sound a beep when it finishes the search.

Creating and Saving Files

Files are usually created by application programs, either from scratch or by using another file as a template — a file used without data to carry on the same format in a new file that will contain new data. For example, you might start a memo using MacWrite and a blank page, or you might start a business report in MacWrite by opening the file of an older report, deleting the old data, and typing the new data.

The two commands that give you the ability to create files, and which are found in nearly every application in the File

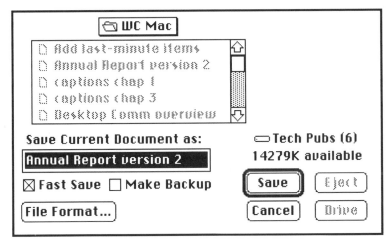

Figure 1-33

The same type of dialog box appears when you use the Save As command (or the Save command with a newly created unnamed file).

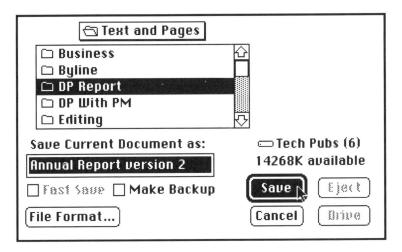

Figure 1-34

After switching to another folder, click the Save button to save the file in that folder.

menu, are the Save and Save As commands. The Save command saves the file you are working on, replacing the older contents of that file. You can use the Save As command to save another version of the file under a new name or save the file with a new format (such as the format for the PC version of Microsoft Word).

When you use any command that needs to find a file or establish a place for storing a file (such as Open to open an existing file, or Save and Save As to save a file), you get a dialog box such as the Open dialog box in Figure 1-30. The active folder and its contents are displayed, and you can pick a file by clicking its name and clicking the Open button, or you can pick a folder within the active folder in the same manner. The scroll bar next to the list of names lets you scroll up or down the list. You can also select another folder by clicking the folder name and dragging downward (Figure 1-31), displaying a list of files and folders that are in that particular folder.

The folder icon is displayed next to each folder name, with a disk icon next to the last name, "Tech Pubs" — this last one is the disk itself, which is actually the base "folder" that contains all other folders. Think of folder arrangements as a tree structure (Figure 1-32) in which the disk itself is the root (as in the PC world you have a "root directory"), and all folders on a disk grow from that point. You may have to switch back to the disk (the root) in order to move up another branch of the tree to a specific folder.

The same type of dialog box appears when you use the Save As command (or the Save command with a newly created file that has no name yet). You select a folder to place the saved file in the same manner: either open a folder that is within the active folder, or change folders by clicking the folder name and dragging downward (Figure 1-33). When you've switched to the folder in which you want to place the file, you can then click the Save button (Figure 1-34).

Files and Folders in Communications

These methods of accessing files and folders are used also in communication and network management. For example, a disk on a network appears on your desktop as a normal disk

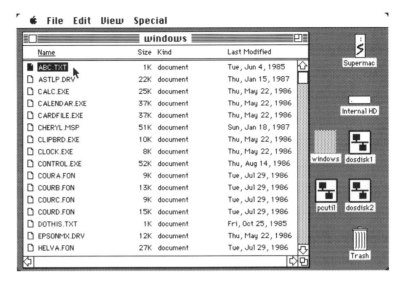

*Figure
1-35*

The desktop displays an icon for a disk drive that is actually on the network, not attached directly to your Macintosh but made "public" using Centram's TOPS file server software (as described in Chapters 3 and 4); you can manipulate files and folders on this disk just like any disk attached to your Macintosh.

*Figure
1-36*

The dialog box for printing a document from MacWrite on the Laser-Writer.

*Figure
1-37*

The dialog box for printing on the ImageWriter from MacPaint.

dosdisk1

icon (Figure 1-35). You can open the disk and display a folder and its contents, as long as you have clearance to open the folder. You can copy files from your disks to the network disk by dragging their icons to the network disk icon, or copy files from the network disk to your disks, in the same way described earlier — selecting the icon, then dragging. You can also select several files and drag them to a disk that is on the network.

Of course, the manuals supplied with the Macintosh adequately explain all the system commands, options, shortcuts, and methods for manipulating files and folders, which are managed by the System and Finder programs in the System Folder. For a complete tutorial on how to use the Macintosh System and Finder, see the Macintosh Plus, Macintosh SE, or Macintosh II manual.

You can also watch an animated training cartoon, created using the Videoworks program from MacroMind, to learn how to open and close folders, move files and folders around the desktop, scroll the window display, resize windows, and get

File	
New	⌘N
Open...	⌘O
Close	⌘W
Save	⌘S
Save As...	
Delete...	
Page Preview...	
Print Merge...	
Page Setup...	
Print...	⌘P
Quit	⌘Q

Page Setup

Paper: ⦿ US Letter ◯ A4 Letter
◯ US Legal ◯ International Fanfold

Orientation: ⦿ Tall ◯ Wide

[**OK**]

[Cancel]

Paper Width: `8.5in` Height: `11 in`

[Set Default]

Margins: Top: `1 in` Left: `1.25in` ☐ Facing Pages

Bottom: `1 in` Right: `1.25in` Gutter: `      `

Default Tab Stops: `0.5in` ☒ Widow Control

Footnotes at: ⦿ Bottom of Page ◯ Beneath Text ◯ Endnotes

☒ Restart Numbering   Start Footnote Numbers at: `1`

Start Page Numbers at: `1`   Line Numbers at: `1`

Next File: `                    `

Figure 1-38

The Page setup dialog box for setting up the page layout in Microsoft Word.

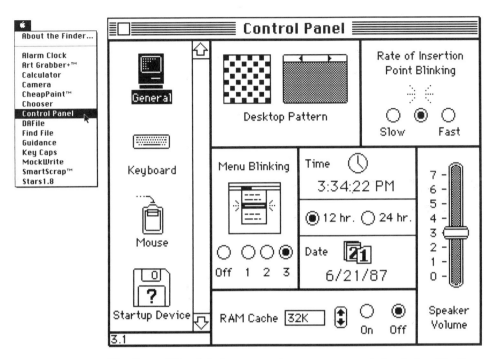

Figure
1-39

The Control Panel desk accessory lets you set controls for devices like the mouse, the keyboard, the display device, and the Macintosh built-in features like the clock and speaker.

information about files and folders. The cartoon is supplied on the Apple Tour disk and can be activated by starting your Macintosh with that disk as the boot disk (containing the System folder for starting up the computer).

Setting Up Devices

The Macintosh has easy-to-use methods for giving you control over devices. When you use the Print command in the File menu to print a document, the system uses the application program's print function (as long as you have the application program on the disk at that time).

Each application controls the printer using either Apple's LaserWriter (Figure 1-36) or ImageWriter (Figure 1-37) print

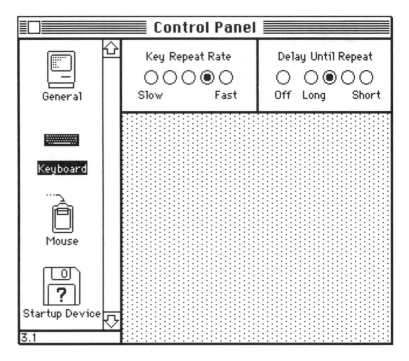

Figure
1-40

Setting the keyboard controls (repeat rates) using the Control Panel desk accessory.

dialog box. You can also set the page layout in some programs using the Page Setup command (Figure 1-38).

The Macintosh provides two desk accessories that give you control over the devices:

• *Chooser* for choosing an output device or zone in a network.

• *Control Panel* for controlling the characteristics of your keyboard, mouse, and display devices.

Both are located in the System menu along with other desk accessories (such as Find File, described earlier).

Control Panel

To run the Control Panel desk accessory, open the Apple System menu and select Control Panel. Icons for devices

40

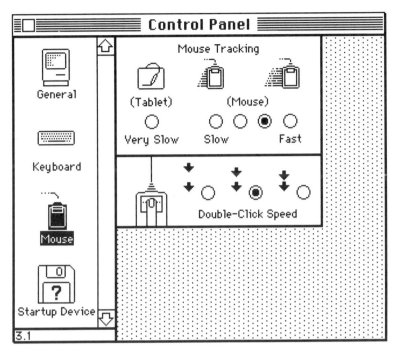

*Figure
1-41*

Setting the mouse or drawing pad controls using the Control Panel desk
accessory.

appear in the left column, and a control panel window takes
up most of the rest of the display. The window changes
according to the device icon selected; when you first open the
Control Panel, it displays a window of controls for the Macintosh itself (Figure 1-39). You can set the speed of the blinking
for the insertion point and for menu selection, the volume of
the speaker, the desktop pattern, the time, the date, and the
amount of memory (RAM) used as a *disk cache* (a holding area
for disk data) to speed up disk operations.

Icons for other devices appear below the General icon for
the Macintosh. Select the Keyboard icon to control the rate at
which a character will be repeated if you hold down the key
(the key repeat rate), and the delay before repeating a key
(Figure 1-40). Select the mouse icon to control the speed of
the mouse tracking and double-clicking (Figure 1-41), and to

41

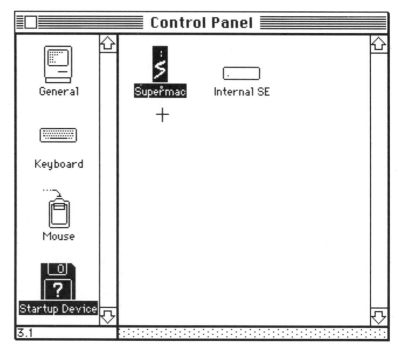

*Figure
1-42*

Selecting the Startup Device — the disk to use for starting the system — using the Control Panel desk accessory.

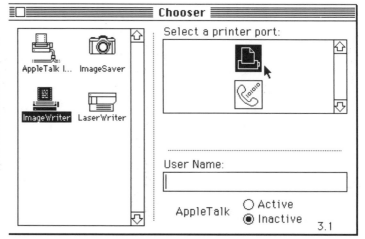

*Figure
1-43*

Using the Chooser to select an ImageWriter for either the modem or printer port, with the AppleTalk network connection inactive.

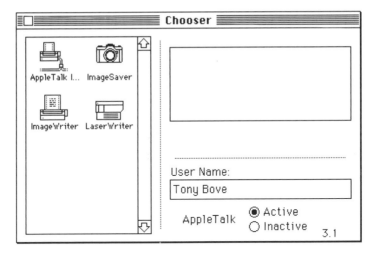

Figure
1-44

Using the Chooser, with the AppleTalk network active, to type your user name to identify your Macintosh to others on the network.

control a drawing tablet, which should be set to a very slow tracking speed.

Select the Startup Device icon to designate one disk drive as the drive to use for starting the computer and operating the system (Figure 1-42). The Macintosh usually starts the system by first looking for a disk in the lower internal drive, then in the upper drive, then in any non-SCSI hard disk drives connected to the disk drive port, and then in the internal SCSI or external SCSI disk drives (according to SCSI number, the highest first). You can change the order by selecting a specific startup disk.

Chooser

The Chooser, another desk accessory supplied with every Macintosh, displays a dialog box that lets you choose devices for output, and lets you control whether the AppleTalk network is active or inactive. The Chooser's dialog box (with the AppleTalk network disconnected) lets you choose an ImageWriter for either the modem or printer port (Figure 1-43).

43

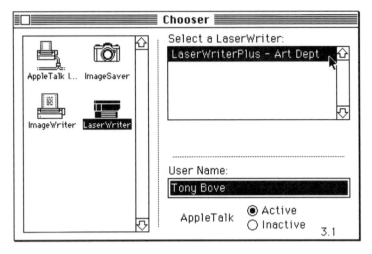

Figure
1-45

Using the Chooser to select a specific LaserWriter (with the AppleTalk Personal Network active and connected).

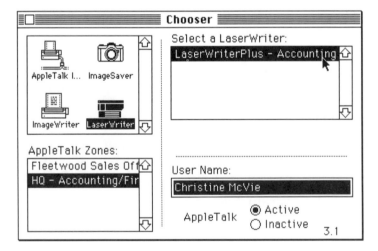

Figure
1-46

Using the Chooser to select a LaserWriter in another zone (with the AppleTalk Personal Network active and connected).

The Chooser plays an important role in the well-connected Macintosh. With the AppleTalk network connected, you can choose one of many LaserWriters (if they are also connected), file servers (when using AppleShare, described in Chapter 3 and 4), and other AppleTalk-compatible devices.

Your user name in the Chooser window identifies your Macintosh on the network (Figure 1-44). As you will learn in Chapter 4, it helps to have descriptive names for users and LaserWriters on a network, so that everyone knows exactly what they mean. Each user and LaserWriter on a network should have a unique name. User names are set with the Chooser. LaserWriter names are set when you first install the LaserWriter software and fonts, and you can change them whenever you like with the Namer utility supplied with the LaserWriter utility programs.

To select a LaserWriter on the AppleTalk network, make sure AppleTalk is connected (always connect cables with machines turned off), and make sure it is set to active in the Chooser dialog box, then select the LaserWriter icon in the left column, and select a specific LaserWriter by its name in the right window (Figure 1-45).

You can link several AppleTalk networks together and share devices on all of them. The Chooser lets you choose servers and devices in other AppleTalk zones (logical groupings of interlinked networks) if networks are connected by InterBridge devices. Zones and the InterBridge are described in Chapter 4. You use the Chooser to select a zone first, then a device by name (Figure 1-46). The list of device names changes with each zone you select. Chapter 4 explains AppleTalk zones in more detail.

Expanding Your Macintosh

Every Macintosh has a built-in AppleTalk Personal Network port for connecting it to a network, and a SCSI (Small Computer System Interface) port for connecting SCSI devices (in addition to a disk drive port for connecting external floppy disk drives). SCSI cabling information is provided in Appendix B, including a description of how to use terminators.

45

In addition, the Macintosh SE has an expansion connector that lets you add a circuit card from Apple or a third party. Popular add-in cards include the AST Mac86, which lets you run standard MS-DOS (Microsoft's DOS for PCs) on the Macintosh SE. Another is the SuperView full-page monitor from Supermac Technology, which lets you display two full-sized pages at actual size when using a program such as Page-Maker. You can also add light pens, drawing tablets, hand controls, joysticks, and special keyboards to the DeskTop Bus ports.

The Macintosh II has six expansion slots for adding various cards, although at least one slot is usually taken up with a card for the monitor. The Macintosh II, with its NuBus architecture, can sense the characteristics of cards that are designed for it, so that you don't have to understand expansion issues or use dip switch settings — the system takes care of establishing connection. The Macintosh II also has all the ports that are on the Macintosh SE.

You can use the modem port to expand your capabilities with a modem, as described in the next chapter. The AppleTalk-printer port is used to connect with an AppleTalk Personal Network or an Imagewriter printer (or similar device). Together with the SCSI interface and the expansion slots for the Macintosh SE and II, these ports to different devices and circuits put the Macintosh product line at the hub of a flexible, fast-growing network.

2   Modems and Services

Without going out of your door you can know all things on earth.
— George Harrison

A tiny device, about the size of a Macintosh mouse, can
connect your Macintosh to the worldwide telephone network.
You can use this type of connection to send and receive
messages to and from other computer users (using an electronic mail service such as MCI Mail), and to use information
services such as CompuServe, Dow Jones, The Source, and
GEnie.

This tiny device, called a *modem* (short for modulator-
demodulator), is the Apple Personal Modem. You can also
buy modems from other vendors that range from the same
size to boxes that are larger than breadbaskets.

A modem connects to the modem port on your Macintosh
with a serial cable designed for the modem. The Apple
Personal Modem requires the Apple System Peripheral-8
Cable (with the mini circular-8 connector), which is available
from any Apple dealer (Figure 2-1).

Other modems, such as the popular Hayes Smartmodem 1200 or 2400, connects to the modem port of the Macintosh and has a DB-25 connector on the other end to connect to the modem. You can get the proper modem cable from your Apple dealer to connect a Hayes Smartmodem or other third-party modem directly to a Macintosh Plus; or you can attach

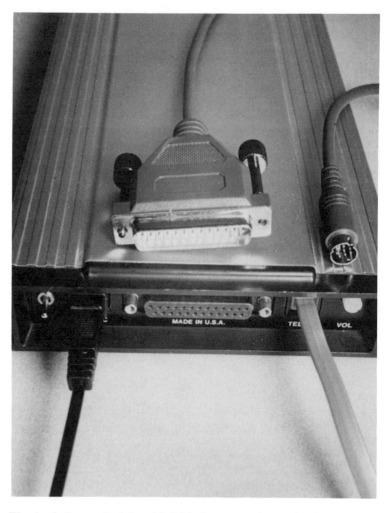

Figure
2-1

48

The Apple System Peripheral-8 Cable for connecting an Apple Personal Modem to the modem (serial RS-232) port on your Macintosh.

the cable supplied with the modem to the Macintosh Plus
Peripheral Adapter Cable (this is a cable that connects to a
Macintosh Plus and presents a Macintosh 128 or 512 connec-
tor to the third-party cable).

You then connect the Apple or third-party modem to a
telephone line using a standard telephone modular cable

Figure
2-2

To connect a Hayes Smartmodem to the phone line, use a standard
phone cable with modular RJ11 or RJ14 connectors.

49

with an RJ11 or RJ14 connector (Figure 2-2). High-speed modems are sometimes connected in a special fashion to leased lines, but the modular telephone cable is the most common connection.

Modems are essential for communicating over phone lines. The modem acts as translator, converting digital information into telephone audio tones (when it is sending) and converting the audio tones back to digital information (when it is receiving). The modems we'll be discussing are *direct-connect* modems that attach directly to the phone line and can perform such functions as automatic dialing of phone numbers. Another type of modem, called an *acoustic coupler*, attaches to the handset of a telephone rather than directly to the line, and sends or receives audio tones. Acoustic couplers are not in use much because they are susceptible to bad reception and noise and do not offer features such as automatic dialing and answering, but they are handy for use with public pay phones and hotel/motel phones that are wired directly into the wall and provide no access for direct-connect modems. Another choice, however, for using the more reliable direct-connect modems with hard-to-connect phones is to use a mouthpiece connector cable available from electronics stores that can connect a modular telephone cable to the mouthpiece of almost any telephone.

The terminology used to describe modem functions is particularly confusing because it encompasses both telephone and computer technology, but there are numerous telecommunications directories in print, many of which contain helpful Bibliographies and glossaries.

The first measure of a modem is the speed at which information is transmitted and received. One absolute measure, *bits per second*, counts information in bits. Usually a character of information occupies eight bits, or one *byte*. However, your communication may include special control bits, or information that is compressed into fewer than eight bits per character, so bits per second (bps) may not tell you exactly how fast a file transfer will occur. Another measure, *baud rate*, counts the number of modulations per second the modem performs while sending or receiving information. At low speeds, bps and baud are nearly the same number because one bit accounts for one modulation. The terms have been used synonymously to describe speed. However, higher speeds are sometimes achieved by sending or receiving more bits per modulation. Bps is the correct term for describing information flow in bits.

Speed is perhaps the central issue when buying a modem. While computer users have been content with 300 bps and 1200 bps modems, faster modems are now available for a higher price. The standard modem (such as the Apple Personal Modem or the Hayes Smartmodem 1200) has a top speed of 1200 bps, which can send or receive about 120 characters (bytes) per second. Modems that can run at 2400 bps are now becoming available — they are twice as fast, but not twice as expensive in most cases. The next step are high-speed modems that operate at 9600 bps or 19,200 bps, which are considerably more expensive. Some of these modems can also reduce the speed to 300 bps when communication is hampered by noise on the telephone line.

How do you choose the right modem? If you are paying for the time you use an information service or mainframe, the higher speed modems might appear to be worth the extra expense. However, some information services add a surcharge for using higher speed modems that, together with the incompatible communication methods used with high-speed modems (there is no guarantee that modems from different vendors will communicate), almost completely wipes out the incentive. At 300 bps, 1200 bps, and 2400 bps, there are standard communication methods that guarantee compatibility.

Determine first what applications you have for the modem. If you are checking electronic mail and occasionally sending and receiving files, a 1200 or 2400 bps modem is most likely the best buy. If you are relying on modems to send and receive critical information in a time-sensitive manner, and you want to be most productive in using your time and your computer's time, you may want to spring for the expensive high-speed modems. You also have options in this choice: you can share a high-speed modem among several users in a variety of ways, thereby spreading its cost among several users.

Reasons for Using Modems

Modems are also useful for communicating to and from your home and office. Imagine you have a lot of data on your office computer (which could be Macintosh, a PC, a minicomputer, or a mainframe), and you want to access it from your Macintosh at home over the weekend. You would leave your office modem in *answer mode* (ready to answer a phone line) and set up your office computer for answering the phone and handling your data processing requests. You could then call the office computer at any time from your home computer and request information.

Individual users and professionals can use modems to connect with the world of electronic mail, teleconferencing (holding conferences in which individual conference members type messages that are read by all), data base searching (for retrieving article abstracts, company profiles, or technical information), stock market services (like Dow Jones), news wire services (like NewsNet), teleshopping (like CompuShop on CompuServe), and telecommuting (using the office computer from home).

Corporate users and small businesses can make use of modems for all these reasons, but they can also use them for interoffice communications, such as sending sales reports and accounting information back to the home office. The information is secure because it is not deposited in a public electronic data base, but transferred directly from one modem to another. The information can be encrypted so that even if your competitors tried illegal phone tapping to obtain your records, they would not be able to decode the information. You could also lease private telephone lines for sensitive data transfer.

One of the benefits of using a modem is that you can transfer information from one type of computer to another (as long as the other computer also has a modem). For example, using a modem with each computer, you can transfer a text file from a Macintosh to a PC, or from a PC to a Macintosh (as described in Chapter 3). We've used modems to transfer data to and from CP/M systems and a Macintosh, as well as minicomputers, mainframes, and personal computers from Commodore, Atari, and Radio Shack.

One essential ingredient for using a modem is the software to control the modem. Modems handle the task of making the phone line a useful connection, but it is the communication program, running on your Macintosh and the other computer, that prepares and sends information to the modem and receives information from the modem (Figure 2-3).

You can choose from dozens of communication programs for the Macintosh. Some programs are designed for personal communication with electronic mail and information ser-

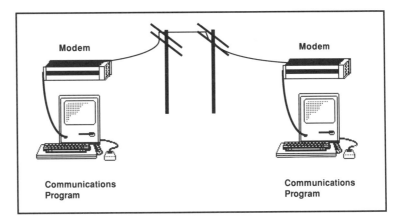

Figure 2-3

A communication program sending information, via modems and a phone line, to another communication program.

vices. Others are designed for calling into mainframes and minicomputers — they turn your Macintosh into a terminal on the larger computers.

The features to look for in personal communication software include automatic dialing, originate and answer modes, Hayes compatibility (for use with modems that are Hayes-compatible), and the ability to use error-checking protocols in your text transfers. These features are described in this chapter. Communication software for accessing minicomputers and mainframes is described in Chapter 5.

Communication Protocols

An important consideration when buying a modem is whether the modem will function properly with other modems that are already in use. For two modems to communicate, they must be set to the same speed and transmission protocols (a *protocol* is a prescribed method for one modem's telling the other modem how to communicate with it). Most modems follow the Bell standards: the Bell 103 protocol for 300 bps, and the Bell 212A protocol for 1200 bps. The Apple Personal Modem and the Hayes Smartmodem 1200 both use these protocols, as do most information services such as MCI Mail and CompuServe.

For 2400 bps modems, the standard protocol is the CCITT V.22bis protocol (created by the Consultative Committee on International Telegraph and Telephone, an advisory organization). High-speed modems offer many standards — 9600 bps modems can use the CCITT V.32 protocol or a special version of the CCITT V.29 protocol, or a proprietary protocol (in which case you must use modems from the same manufacturer).

High-speed modems that can also communicate at low speeds using standard protocols are a better buy than proprietary modems that do not use standard protocols, because they can communicate with more than one type of modem.

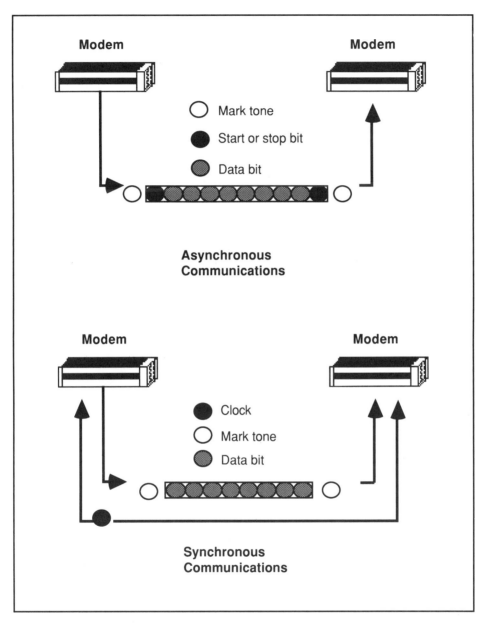

Modem   Modem

○ Mark tone

● Start or stop bit

◎ Data bit

**Asynchronous
Communications**

Modem   Modem

● Clock

○ Mark tone

◎ Data bit

**Synchronous
Communications**

*Figure
2-4*
How a modem communicates with another modem asynchronously: first the modems recognize the phone line protocol, then the software in the sending computer sends data with start and stop bits which are recognized by the receiving computer's software.

Synchronizing

These protocols are "phone line handshake" protocols because they describe how signals are interpreted from the phone lines. Once the modems know how to interpret the signals, the next step is for them to synchronize themselves so that the receiving modem is translating frequencies into the same bits that the sending modem translated into frequencies (Figure 2-4).

There are two ways to send information so that a receiving modem interprets it correctly: asynchronously and synchronously. Asynchronous transmission is common among personal computer modems — there is no need for a clock signal to synchronize transmission. Instead, one modem sends start and stop bits surrounding each byte (character) to the other modem, which can then understand and interpret each byte.

In synchronous transmission, a clock signal synchronizes the sending and receiving modems so that start and stop bits are not used. The synchronous communication method is used in older modems and between mainframes or minicomputers for high-speed transfers. With personal computer communications, and communication between a personal computer or terminal and a minicomputer or mainframe, you use asynchronous modems.

Error Checking

Another type of protocol, generally referred to as an *error-checking and correcting* protocol, is essential for file transfers. Electromagnetic interference and rain can cause *glitches* (receipt of different characters than the ones that were sent). Error checking is not necessary for electronic mail or for emulating a terminal on a mainframe or minicomputer — glitches will not harm most electronic mail messages, article abstracts, news reports, and other textual data. But glitches can be fatal to financial data, spread sheets, data base programs, graphics files, page makeup files, and programs.

Error-checking protocols are built into some high-speed modems, but some require that you use the same or a similar modem at both ends. With 300, 1200, and 2400 bps modems, the typical case is that the error-checking protocols are employed in the communication programs used at both ends.

Many communication programs offer well-known error-checking protocols that work with other communication programs. Some programs, such as MacLink Plus (Dataviz, $195, described in Chapter 3), provide an error-checking protocol requiring use of the same program on both ends. Usually such a program also offers other protocols as options, so that you can use it to communicate with computers that don't run the same program. However, in every case you will need to use the *same protocol* to communicate between two communication programs.

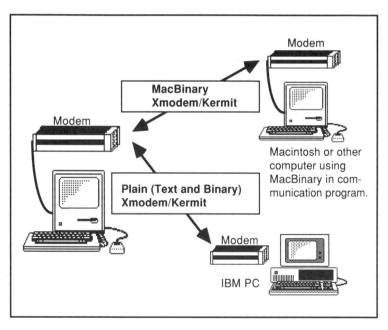

Figure 2-5

With error-checking transfers you can send or receive the Macintosh file including its resource fork using MacBinary, or just transfer the data fork (all that is needed for text files) by skipping MacBinary.

In addition to an error-checking protocol, you may also need to encapsulate the file in a special format for transferring and receiving all of the information properly. A file encapsulation standard called MacBinary was developed to be used along with an error-checking protocol (Figure 2-5). MacBinary, developed by Dennis F. Brothers and refined by a work group of Macintosh developers, is usually offered as a menu option in your communication program that you use *in addition to* the transfer protocol.

With the MacBinary encapsulation method, you can send or receive the Macintosh file including its resource fork, which contains the file's icon (if the file is a program, it also contains menu commands and other elements of the program that are necessary for running on a Macintosh). MacBinary or a similar encapsulation method (such as BinHex, available from user group public domain libraries) is necessary for transferring Macintosh files with complete accuracy to other computers and then back to a Macintosh. MacBinary is the preferred method which is also used by CompuServe. MCI Mail uses Desktop Express for encapsulating Macintosh files, which is described later.

Transferring non-Macintosh files (files that originated on other computers) and simple text files does not require MacBinary or other methods — you need only use an error-checking protocol such as Xmodem or Kermit. If you are transferring Macintosh text files, you can skip MacBinary and still have error checking; if, however, you want to transfer files that include fonts, formatting, and graphics, you must select MacBinary as well as Xmodem or Kermit. Usually, the choice of MacBinary in a program is tied to a choice of Xmodem.

With the Xmodem protocol (developed by Ward Christensen and Keith Petersen and placed in the public domain), a program first performs a handshake with the other end using acknowledgment signals, then it sends a block of information through the modem to the other modem and the other program. If the block is transferred without errors, the receiving program sends a confirmation signal back to the sending program, telling it to go ahead and send the next block. If there are errors, the receiver sends back a negative confirmation message, and the sender resends the block (Figure 2-6).

Xmodem lets you transfer a file without glitches caused by noisy lines; however, if the lines are very noisy, or if the receiving computer can't keep up with the sending computer, or if the distance is so large that the sender can't wait long enough to hear the confirmation, then Xmodem breaks down. It is also not very good for high-speed transfers because the process of confirming slows down the entire process. But

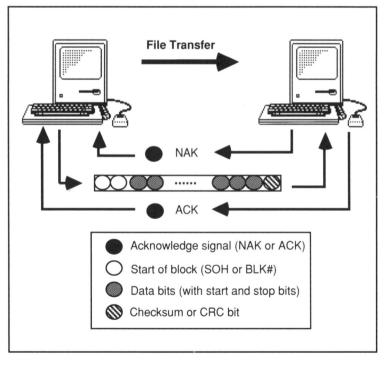

Figure
2-6

How the Xmodem protocol works: after sending a block of data, the program waits for confirmation; the receiving program checks for errors, then either sends back confirmation or sends back a message to resend the block because an error occurred.

Xmodem is convenient for PC to Mac and Mac to PC transfers as well as transfers between other personal computers.

The Xmodem without MacBinary option on many program menus, which is sometimes called the Text Xmodem or plain Xmodem option, can use one of two methods to check for errors in the transmission: the CRC (cyclic redundancy check) or the Checksum algorithm. Programs usually offer a choice between these settings, but CRC is generally regarded as more reliable.

Xmodem is popular with programs that run on an IBM PC, PC XT, PC AT, PS/2, or a compatible; it is also useful for Apple // computers, CP/M systems, UNIX systems, Digital Equipment Corporation minicomputers, and other types of computers. Almost every communication program for IBM PC-compatible computers offers the Xmodem protocol, including PC Talk III (Headlands Press), Crosstalk Mk.4 (Digital Communications Associates, Inc.), Relay (VMPC), Pro-Comm (PIL Software Systems), MaxiMITE (Mycroft Labs), and public domain programs such as Qmodem.

Kermit is an alternative protocol (developed at Columbia University and widespread in the developer community) that works much like Xmodem but lets you control the size of the block of information (called a *packet*) transferred from modem to modem. Kermit is also used on minicomputers such as Digital Equipment Corporation's VAX, and is available for systems that run the UNIX operating system from Bell Labs, as well as for IBM VM systems.

The Xmodem and Kermit protocols are generally implemented in the communication programs, not in the modems. The programs send one block or packet of data at a time, always waiting for confirmation from the receiving modem before sending the next block. This mode of communication is *half-duplex,* meaning that although communication can occur both ways, it can only occur one way at a time.

Other protocols include X.25, X.PC, BLAST, and Ymodem (a derivative of Xmodem). Another high-speed protocol that is growing in acceptance is the MNP (Microcom Network Protocol).

When considering the relative merits of error-checking protocols that are available in communication programs, remember that you may need more than one program for different types of communication. We use Desktop Express (Apple/Dow Jones, $149) for checking electronic mail on the MCI Mail network and for accessing the Dow Jones service. The protocol used by Desktop Express works with Lotus Express for PCs, but is, at the time of this writing, only offered for use with MCI Mail and Dow Jones services. We use Micro-Phone (Software Ventures, $75) for calling CompuServe, The Source, and modems on PCs and other personal computers, because it offers MacBinary used with Xmodem. The other programs and services use Xmodem, and some also use MacBinary with it. We show file transfer examples later in this chapter.

Modem Features Checklist

Modems come in varying shapes and sizes, but most have an array of lights that indicate whether the modem's power is on, whether it is connected to a computer, and whether it is detecting a modem at the other end of the line. If your modem is "talking" to the other computer successfully, a carrier-detect light (or message on your display) should be on. If you are sending data out through the phone line, the send-data light should flash; if you are receiving data from another modem, the receive-data light should flash. There may also be an answer-mode light if the modem can answer the phone.

The essential features you want in almost any 300, 1200, or 2400 bps modem are the following:

Bell 103 and 212A compatibility for 300 bps and 1200 bps. This compatibility is essential for normal communication with information services such as CompuServe and Dow Jones, or electronic mail services such as MCI Mail.

CCITT V.22bis compatibility for 2400 bps communication.

Asynchronous communication. This is necessary for communicating with information services such as CompuServe and Dow Jones, or electronic mail services such as MCI Mail, or with other personal computers, or with mainframes and minicomputers that are set up for asynchronous communication. Synchronous communication is usually reserved for high-speed communication between mainframes.

Full- as well as half-duplex operation. Some modems offer only full-duplex, which is fine; the communication programs handling Xmodem or Kermit transfers will still be communicating in half-duplex, but full-duplex is possible with other protocols.

Flow control with software-based XON/XOFF or RTS/CTS. Information flow can be temporarily halted during disk access or if you want to read something before it scrolls away, either by using the XON/XOFF method in the communication program, or the RTS/CTS method in the hardware of the modem, whichever is used by the other system. CompuServe and MCI Mail use the XON/XOFF method, but you should have the choice. This feature is usually found in the communication program as well and may not be necessary in the modem.

Hayes compatibility. Many communication programs already know how to control a Hayes Smartmodem, so most of the personal computer modems emulate a Hayes (see command sets below). Be sure that the communication program you buy will work with your modem.

Auto-dialing. This is an essential feature of any direct-connect modem (a modem that connects directly to the phone line rather than acoustically through the mouthpiece and earpiece). The modem must be able to dial numbers automatically, even using codes for a private branch exchange (PBX) or a long-distance carrier. Sometimes the capability to use PBX or long-distance carrier codes is implemented in the communication program, not in the modem.

Auto-answering. This feature lets a modem answer a call; with most modems you can set the number of rings before answering.

Error-checking protocol. Error-checking protocols let you transfer information with the secure feeling that there will be no errors placed in the data from noisy telephone lines or other electromagnetic interference. Most 300 bps, 1200 bps, and 2400 bps modems do not include a protocol, but you can use one that is implemented in the communication software. High-speed modems may have proprietary error-checking protocols that do not have to be available in the communication software.

Dynamic speed adjustment. The lower speed modems usually do not have this feature — you have to set the speed first, then start communicating (usually you set the speed in the communication software which controls the modem). A high-speed modem often can adjust its speed by handshaking with the other modem and agreeing on the highest possible speed for both modems.

Command set. Many modems can be programmed using a set of commands that can be typed using a communication program that is emulating a terminal (described later in this chapter). Most of these programmable modems emulate the Hayes Smartmodem and incorporate the Hayes commands in their command sets.

Speaker. It is useful to be able to hear the dialing of the phone and the receiving modem's answer to be sure that you are calling a modem and not waking a person up in the middle of the night.

We recommend the Hayes Smartmodem ($599, 300/1200 bps; $899, 300/1200/2400 bps) or the Apple Personal Modem ($429, 300/1200 bps). Other 2400/1200/300 bps modems recommended for a Macintosh include the Migent Pocket Modem ($259, 1200 bps), the Novation Professional 2400 ($795, 2400 bps), and the Racal-Vadic Maxwell 1200VP ($295, 300/1200 bps). You can use any of these modems and communicate with other modems that use the standard Bell protocols for 1200 and 300 bps (or the CCITT V.22bis protocol for 2400 bps).

We can recommend several high-speed modems for use with the Macintosh. The fastest modem is the Telebit Trailblazer ($1445, top speed 19,200 bps), but it offers only half-duplex operation (which at that speed is not a big drawback). The Codex 2260 is slower ($3495, top speed 9600 bps) and considerably more expensive, but it offers full-duplex operation, as does the Telcor Accelerator ($995, top speed 9600 bps). Although the Telcor may seem more attractive at the lower price, the Codex offers a special connection for leased lines and line-quality monitoring with an external oscilloscope.

The Microcom AX/9624c ($1799, top speed 9600 bps) uses the MNP class 5, which includes a data compression algorithm for faster transmission, and operates in half duplex. The Fastcomm 2496 ($999, top speed 9600 bps) offers nearly all the same features as the Microcom but without MNP and without data compression. The Racal-Vadic Maxwell 9600VP ($1495, top speed 9600 bps) also offers the same features including an MNP superset.

Sharing Modems in a Network

A high-speed modem can be too expensive to justify for use with one computer, but it may not be too expensive if shared by a network of computers. A modem server is hardware or software that acts as a traffic controller, routing calls from different computers on a network to one or more modems, effectively sharing the modems over the network.

The NetModem V1200 ($599, Shiva Corp.) lets each user on an AppleTalk Personal Network make calls by sharing a modem. The Shiva NetModem connects directly to the AppleTalk network, and users can choose the device using the Chooser desk accessory described in Chapter 1. Once the modem is chosen, your communication program works with it as if it were attached to your Macintosh. If you try to use the modem when someone else is using it, you receive a message that includes the name of the other user, so that you can contact that user if you have priority. The NetModem provides call monitoring by sending the usually audible tones of the modem back over the network to your Macintosh so that you can still hear them as if the modem were connected to your Macintosh.

ComServe from InfoShare works much the same way — after you select the modem's icon in the Chooser, you can use communication programs as if the modem were attached to your Macintosh. If someone is using the modem when you try to access it, the modem server returns a "device busy" message to your Macintosh.

ModemShare from Mirror Technologies is another modem server that works much the same way but uses a different stream protocol for AppleTalk transmission (the serial protocol is a method of passing single characters through an AppleTalk network, which regularly passes packets of information rather than single characters).

Another way to share a high-speed modem is to use a hardware server such as the C-Server (Solana Electronics, $595), which attaches directly to the AppleTalk cable and has three serial ports for high-speed (up to 19,200 bps) modems, or MultiTalk (Abaton Technology, $699), which has three ports for 9600 bps modems.

In some cases a modem server can also act as a device that lets a Macintosh call in from a remote location and connect to an AppleTalk network as if it were directly connected. These types of devices, called bridges, are described in Chapter 4.

These methods for sharing modems use the AppleTalk network. Another type of network, such as 3Com's 3+ network (described in Chapter 4), can make use of a dedicated server with modems attached that can handle communications with other networks.

Communication Software

Communicating with modems can be a productive experience or a frustrating one, depending on the quality of the software controlling the modem. Modems can be controlled with simple programs that act as terminal emulators, but then you have to learn the modem's command set and keep phone numbers and electronic mail addresses handy. The best communication programs let you communicate without having to learn a new set of obscure commands to make or receive phone calls and transfer data. The best programs also provide mechanisms for setting up automatic phone dialing and message transfer.

There are basically two kinds of programs for communications: general-purpose, which are for all types of communications, and special-purpose, which are for specific information service or mainframe-minicomputer linkup.

General-purpose programs can communicate with almost any other type of computer that is running any general-purpose program. They do not require the same program on both ends because they use standard file transfer protocols for error-checking.

Special-purpose programs typically offer a proprietary file transfer protocol (one that works only with that specific program), which requires that both ends use the same program (or complementary programs, as in the case of mainframe communications). There are also special-purpose programs for use with particular information services, usually sold by those services — for example, Dow Jones sells Desktop Express, which works only with Dow Jones and MCI Mail.

We use both types of programs, because the programs are not expensive and they complement each other to make us more productive in managing communications.

For PC to Macintosh or Macintosh to PC transfers over telephone lines or directly through a modem cable, we use MacLink Plus which is supplied with the appropriate cable and also offers file conversion. MacLink Plus is an example of a special-purpose program (for PC file transfers and conversion) that has some general-purpose characteristics, like the ability to use a modem. We also use Desktop Express, which is a special-purpose program for calling MCI Mail or Dow Jones. For a general purpose program, we use MicroPhone, which works with almost any program operating at the other end (including MacTerminal, a popular general-purpose program).

We describe, briefly, the capabilities of Desktop Express, MacTerminal, and MicroPhone in this chapter, and give demonstrations. MacLink Plus is described in more detail in Chapter 3.

Desktop Express and Glue

The MCI Mail electronic mail service has been in use for a long time, but until recently the capability of sending and receiving programs, spread sheets, and other types of files besides text was extremely limited. Most MCI Mail users sent and received

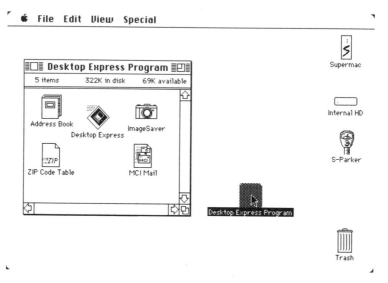

Figure 2-7   Desktop Express: a special-purpose program for MCI Mail and Dow Jones services.

text messages without fonts, graphics, or special characters.

Desktop Express for the Macintosh and Lotus Express for the PC add the capability to send and receive any type of file, including executable programs, page makeup files, word processing files formatted with fonts, spread sheet files, and data base files. In addition, Desktop Express includes the Glue ImageSaver utility that lets you send graphics and images of the screen. MCI Mail has installed hundreds of Apple Laser-Writers across the country so that you can send an image or word processing file to anyone in the world, letting MCI Mail do the laser printing for you.

MCI Mail's other services are described in more detail later in this chapter. This section shows how Desktop Express works with MCI Mail to manage electronic mail activities.

Desktop Express (Figure 2-7) is supplied with several files including an empty Address Book for storing addresses of mail recipients, the ImageSaver utility, a ZIP Code Table for preparing mail for hand (postal) delivery, and MCI Mail, with a file containing the preferred phone numbers and your password for your MCI Mail account.

The ImageSaver program (part of the Glue package that is sold separately by Solutions, Inc.) acts as a substitute for the printing software so that you can save a disk file holding the printed version — first you choose ImageSaver as if it were a printing device (Figure 2-8), then you use the Print command in the application for that file. ImageSaver creates a disk file holding the printed image. You can send this file to someone who doesn't have the application program it was created with, and they can use the Glue Viewer program to print the file. This makes it possible for you to send a PageMaker publication file to a print service that does not have PageMaker, or to MCI Mail's LaserWriter for printing and distribution through regular mail.

To start Desktop Express, double-click the Desktop Express icon. The program presents a dialog box for typing your account name, password, first-choice phone number, second-

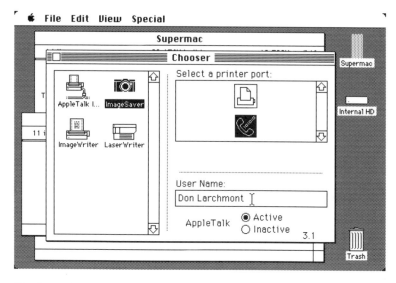

*Figure
2-8*

The ImageSaver program (part of the Glue package) acts as a printer driver but instead saves a disk file; you can then transfer that file to someone who does not have the application for the file, and that person can use Glue to print the file.

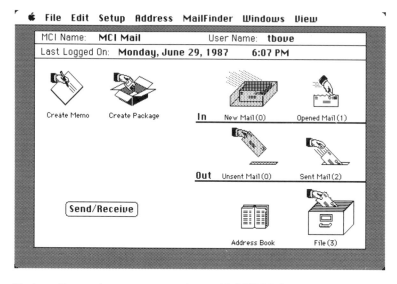

*Figure
2-9*

Desktop Express lets you communicate with MCI Mail using icons and menu commands.

69

choice number (if the first number is busy), and selections for calling through the Tymnet service (a carrier of several information services including MCI Mail). Phone numbers can have commas inserted for placing pauses in the dialing for calling out using an access number. (The second-choice number is filled in with the toll-free 800 number, but MCI charges you an extra $0.15 per minute for using it. You will save money by using a local MCI Mail or Tymnet phone number.) Another setting you can change is the type of phone line — either touch-tone (the default setting) or pulse.

After filling out the dialog box information and clicking the Save button, Desktop Express presents the communication desktop (Figure 2-9). From this command post you can send electronic mail messages, check and read your mail, create and edit memos (messages), create a "package" for a recipient, and transfer any Macintosh files and graphics (the program uses a special-purpose error-checking protocol).

Before sending a message, you should add the recipient's address to your Address Book. After double-clicking the

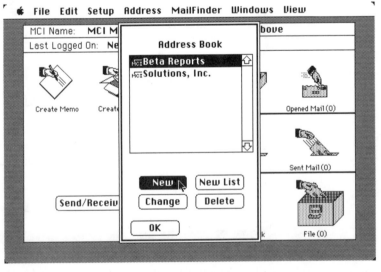

Figure 2-10

Selecting the new address function in the Desktop Express address book.

Address Book icon, Desktop Express presents a list of names and buttons to select, such as the New button to create a new address (Figure 2-10). After clicking the New button, the

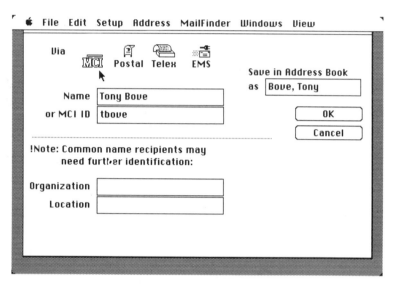

Figure
2-11

Adding a new address to the Desktop Express address book.

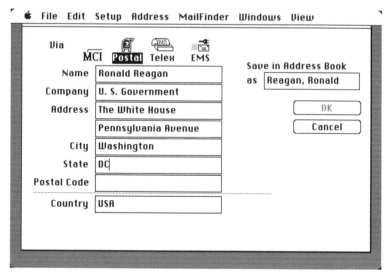

Figure
2-12

Adding a postal address for hand delivery via regular mail.

program displays a dialog box for typing a new MCI Mail address (Figure 2-11). You can add a postal address for hand delivery through the regular mail system (Figure 2-12), and you can add a Telex address for sending a Telex message to any Telex recipient in the world (Figure 2-13). You can also add an address for a recipient who is on another electronic mail system, such as CompuServe's EasyPlex mail system (Figure 2-14).

The next step is to create a message. Desktop Express lets you type and edit a message because it has a built-in text editor (Figure 2-15). The text editor is very similar to MockWrite (a desk accessory for writing that has no formatting capabilities) and lets you use Cut/Copy and Paste commands with other messages.

When you are finished editing the message, click the Address button to display the Address Envelope dialog box (Figure 2-16). In the dialog box, you select a name to copy over to the envelope list. You can send a message to many mail-

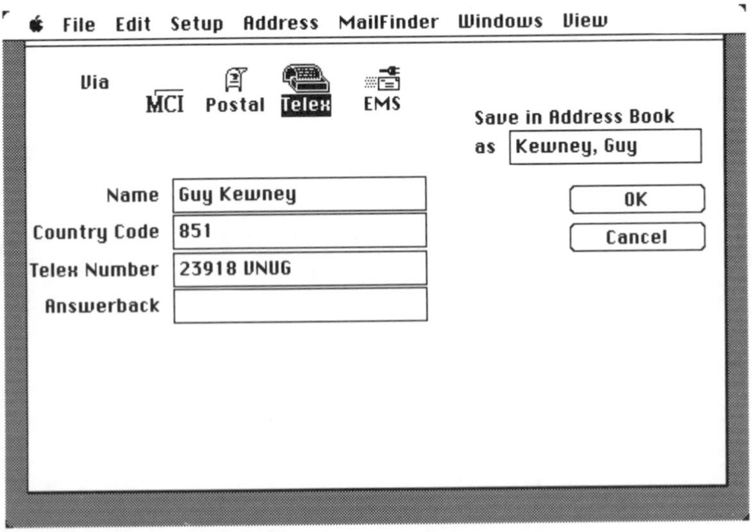

Figure
2-13

Adding a Telex address for sending a Telex message.

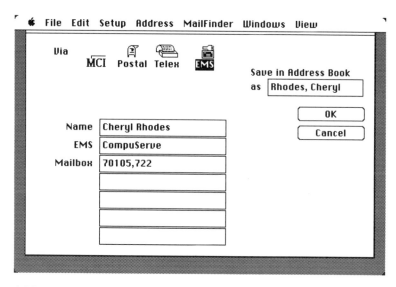

Figure
2-14

Adding a CompuServe EasyPlex mail address to the Desktop Express Address Book.

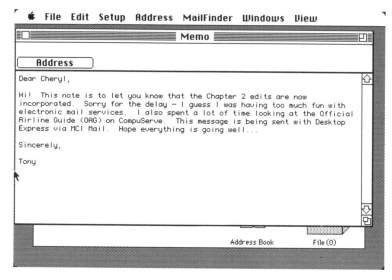

Figure
2-15

Using the text editor in Desktop Express to type a message before connecting to the service and sending the message.

boxes at the same time, and click the blank box next to any
name if you want the name to appear in a "cc:" (courtesy copy)
list rather than in the "To:" list. You can also add a new address

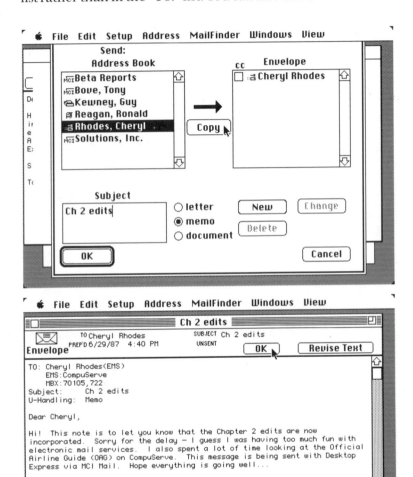

Figure
2-16

The dialog box for addressing an electronic envelope using Desktop
Express; you can prepare many messages for mailing before connecting
to the service.

if your Address Book does not contain the address you want, or change an address already stored in the Book. The subject description you type in this dialog box becomes the name of the file.

After clicking OK, Desktop Express displays an icon for the envelope, and the memo itself, allowing you another chance to revise the text before preparing it for delivery. Click OK again to return to the command desktop. The Unsent Mail icon should now show one piece of unsent mail (Figure 2-17).

You can also prepare a Macintosh file, such as a spread sheet, as a package to be sent to another MCI Mail subscriber who retrieves mail with Desktop Express. To prepare a package such as an Excel spread sheet, first double-click the Create Package icon. The program displays a list of file names in the currently opened folder that match the icon (Text, Image, or Any) below the list. Select Any to see a list of all the files in the folder (see Figure 2-18), and select the file you want to transfer. Click the Address button, and copy the address to the en-

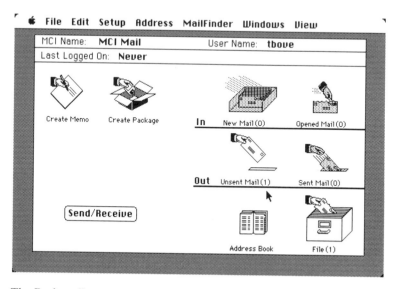

*Figure
2-17*

The Desktop Express command center is ready to send one piece of mail when you connect to MCI Mail.

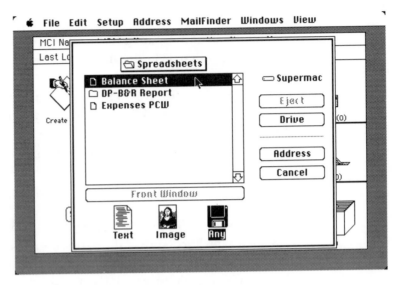

*Figure
2-18*

Selecting a spread sheet file to transfer to MCI Mail using the Create
Package command of Desktop Express.

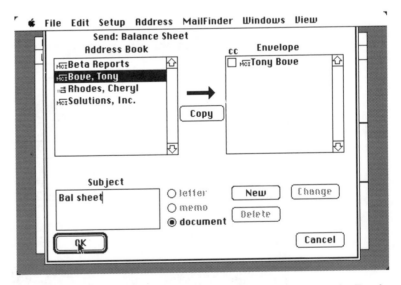

*Figure
2-19*

Addressing the envelope for the electronic package containing the Excel
spread sheet file.

velope as before (Figure 2-19). Click OK, and the program returns you to the command center, showing two unsent mail messages ready to be sent.

To send or receive messages from MCI Mail, click the Send/Receive button. Desktop Express displays the dialog box for selecting which messages to send and receive. You can select to send all new messages or only those selected. You can also select to receive all new messages sent to you or just the selected ones (Figure 2-20).

You click the Go Ahead button, and Desktop Express calls MCI Mail (Figure 2-21) using your first-choice phone number and your name and password (Figure 2-22), then it immediately starts sending the messages (Figure 2-23). If you select to also receive all messages addressed to you, Desktop Express automatically transfers them to your computer and lets you choose where to store them on disk (Figure 2-24).

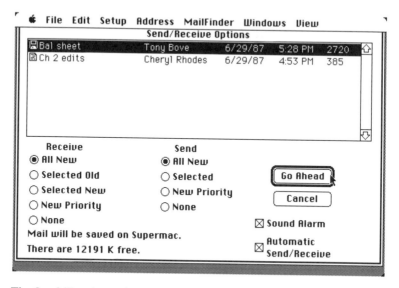

Figure 2-20

The Send/Receive options with Desktop Express, which lets you automatically send and receive all or selected messages.

If you want to reply to the message, you can see incoming mail by double-clicking the New Mail icon, and clicking the Answer button (Figure 2-25).

Desktop Express provides message-file management in a

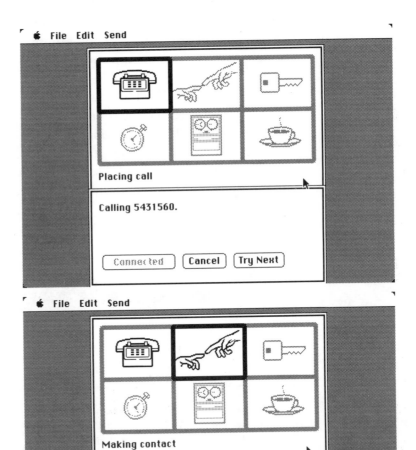

Figure
2-21

Desktop Express automatically places the call, using your name and password to log into the MCI Mail service.

menu called MailFinder, which you can use to copy or delete messages, move them to other folders, and create new folders. Desktop Express also displays the time and date of your last MCI Mail log-on.

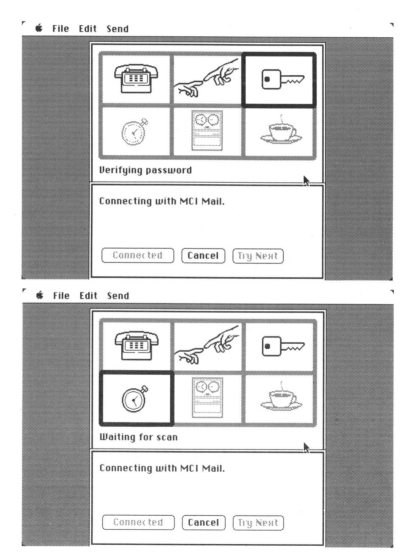

Figure 2-22

Desktop Express also automatically looks for any MCI Mail messages addressed to you.

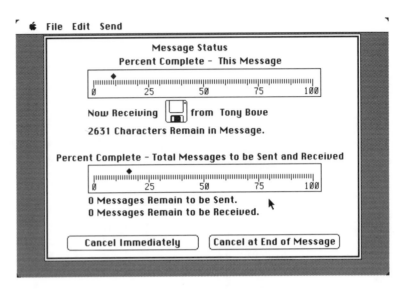

Figure
2-23

If there is mail addressed to you, Desktop Express first starts receiving it and storing it on disk.

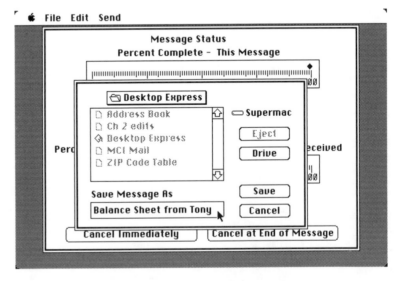

Figure
2-24

When automatically receiving mail, Desktop Express stores it on your disk; when you turn off the automatic feature, Desktop Express asks for a new name and location for the received message or file.

Desktop Express is perhaps the easiest communication program to learn how to use, because it hides most of the technical details of using MCI Mail and setting up your modem. The special-purpose program only handles access to MCI Mail and Dow Jones at the time of this writing (although you can send mail to users of other services and to Telex users, as well as to anyone with a postal address). You can also exchange files with PC users who are using Lotus Express.

There are other programs that can call MCI Mail and Dow Jones, and these other programs give you a measure of control over MCI Mail and Dow Jones operations that are more difficult with Desktop Express. If you like Desktop Express, we still recommend that you get another communication program as well. Desktop Express is excellent for automatic file and message transfers because it can handle them without getting you involved.

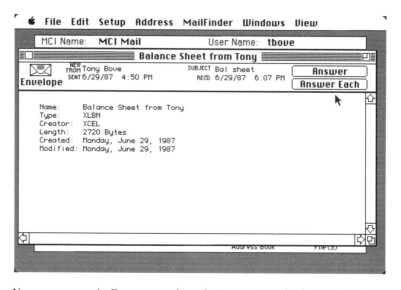

Figure
2-25

You can automatically start a reply to the message sender by opening the New Mail and using the Answer button.

The Glue package, included with Desktop Express, can also be purchased separately ($60, Solutions Inc.), and is bundled with other communication programs, notably MicroPhone, which is described later in this chapter.

MacTerminal

At the other end of the ease-of-use spectrum is MacTerminal (Apple; version 2.0, $125), a bare-bones communication program that can emulate a variety of terminals and establish a link with call-up services. MacTerminal does not offer a full slate of features, but it does emulate popular terminals to make it useful for connecting to mainframe systems. This aspect of MacTerminal is described in Chapter 5.

A demonstration of MacTerminal is useful for showing what MCI Mail looks like to other communication programs. MacTerminal is supplied with documents that contain proto-

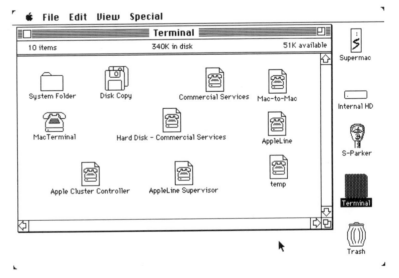

Figure 2-26

MacTerminal comes with documents containing appropriate settings for protocols used with different services; double-click a document to start MacTerminal with those settings.

col settings for different types of communication (see Figure 2-26). You can start MacTerminal by double-clicking one of the supplied documents in order to start with those settings, or you can start by double-clicking the MacTerminal icon and set up a new document with new settings.

To set up communication with MacTerminal, either start with a supplied document (and change its settings if necessary), or start MacTerminal and create a new document with the New command in the File menu. The most important settings are in the Settings menu, starting with the Terminal emulation settings (Figure 2-27). The best terminal to emulate for MCI Mail or CompuServe is a VT100 (Digital Equipment Corp. terminal) at the ANSI setting. These are the default settings — they are preset automatically every time you start MacTerminal without a document.

You can change the shape of the blinking cursor, change the line width of the display (80 columns is the normal amount), and change other features such as local echo,

File
New
Open...
Close
Save
Save As...
Send File...
Receive File...
Page Setup...
Print Selection...
Quit

Settings
Terminal...
Compatibility...
File Transfer...
Answerback Message...
Show Tab Ruler

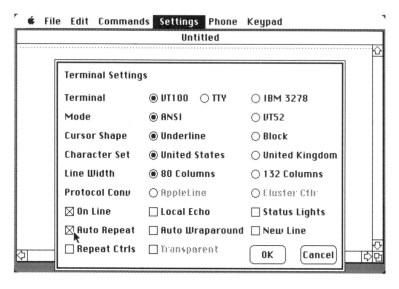

Terminal Settings

Terminal	⦿ VT100 ○ TTY	○ IBM 3278
Mode	⦿ ANSI	○ VT52
Cursor Shape	⦿ Underline	○ Block
Character Set	⦿ United States	○ United Kingdom
Line Width	⦿ 80 Columns	○ 132 Columns
Protocol Conv	○ AppleLine	○ Cluster Ctlr

☒ On Line ☐ Local Echo ☐ Status Lights
☒ Auto Repeat ☐ Auto Wraparound ☐ New Line
☐ Repeat Ctrls ☐ Transparent [OK] [Cancel]

Figure 2-27

The terminal settings possible in MacTerminal; the default settings are shown here, which are useful for communicating with MCI Mail.

83

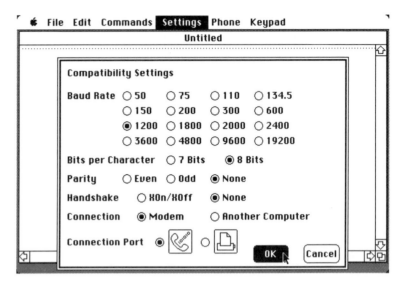

*Figure
2-28*

The compatibility settings control some of the protocols for modem-to-modem communications.

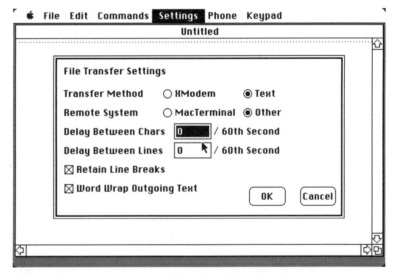

*Figure
2-29*

The file transfer settings control use of protocols for file transfer, including a special MacTerminal Xmodem protocol for transferring complete Macintosh files.

automatic wraparound, and so forth. These features are described in the software checklist later in this chapter.

The compatibility settings (Figure 2-28) control some, but not all, of the protocols necessary for modem-to-modem communication, including the speed and the line compatibility settings. The file transfer protocol settings (Figure 2-29) let you choose between the Xmodem protocol for error checking during file transfers, or text file transfers (with no error checking). You can also select either a Macintosh running MacTerminal or another type of computer as the remote computer; with a Macintosh running MacTerminal you can transfer complete Macintosh files including their icons. For text transfers you can also set a delay between each character and at the end of each line to slow down transmission so that the remote computer (sometimes called the "host" computer in IBM terminology) can keep pace with your modem.

MacTerminal stores one phone number per document file, so it makes sense to create a different document for each service you use. The Phone Settings dialog box (Figure 2-30) lets you set which kind of phone line (including a mixed tone and pulse line), which type of modem you are using (Hayes-compatible modems are compatible with the Apple 1200, which has since been replaced by the Apple Personal Modem), and the number of rings before MacTerminal will answer the phone. You set MacTerminal to answer the phone by selecting the Wait for Call option in the Phone menu.

After creating settings for your service, save the document with the Save command in the File menu. You can start MacTerminal with these settings the next time by double-clicking the icon for the document. You can also copy this document to other disks and give it to other users who need the same communication settings.

A session with MacTerminal is a lot different than a session with Desktop Express. For example, calling MCI Mail is easy to do, but you have to type the log-on sequence, and you see MCI Mail's service the way other computers see it — as a terminal

that lets you type commands, but not as a Macintosh that lets
you drag graphic objects. You can use Desktop Express in this
manner if you use the Call MCI Interactive command in the
File menu; you can also use MicroPhone in this manner, but
with some preprogrammed functions to make access easier.

The other settings in MacTerminal have to do with emulating a terminal when connecting to a mainframe ("host")
system, described in Chapter 5.

MicroPhone and Glue

MicroPhone (Software Ventures, $75) is one of the most
popular communication programs because it combines the
powerful features of mainframe terminal emulation programs with the capabilities to make mail service easy to use,
with push-button convenience. MicroPhone is supplied with
the Glue package and sample settings documents (Figure 2-
31) so that you can send printable versions of graphics and

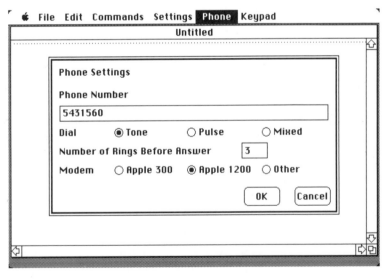

*Figure
2-30*

MacTerminal's Phone dialog box can only store one number, but you
can set the number of rings before MacTerminal will answer the phone.

publication files to persons who do not have applications to print the files, but do have the Viewer utility in Glue to both display and print the files.

MicroPhone can act like MacTerminal in saving the settings for a particular service in a separate document file, which you can launch by double-clicking that document rather than the program itself (double-clicking the program brings up default settings, as with MacTerminal). MicroPhone's Settings menu lets you change the default settings for communications (Figure 2-32) and terminal emulation (Figure 2-33) with an answer-back message that displays when MicroPhone answers the phone.

The file transfer protocol settings (Figure 2-34) let you customize a document for a particular service that either needs delays built into text transfers, or needs you to wait until the service displays a prompt character (such as a colon or question mark) before sending text. You can also control the wrapping of words to the next line (the default is 80 columns), which lets you transfer a MacWrite or Word text file without

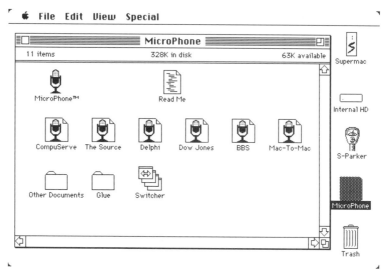

*Figure
2-31*

MicroPhone is supplied with Glue and with sample settings documents.

The Well-Connected Macintosh

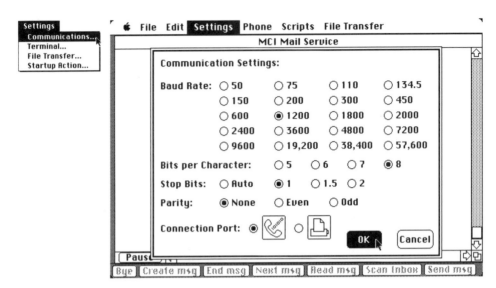

Figure 2-32

MicroPhone's dialog box for communications settings.

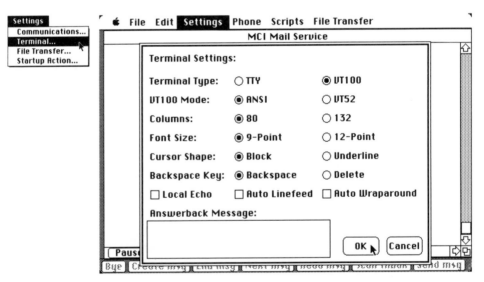

Figure 2-33

MicroPhone's dialog box for terminal emulation settings, which includes the font size for displaying text (nine-point lets you display 132 columns on the Macintosh screen).

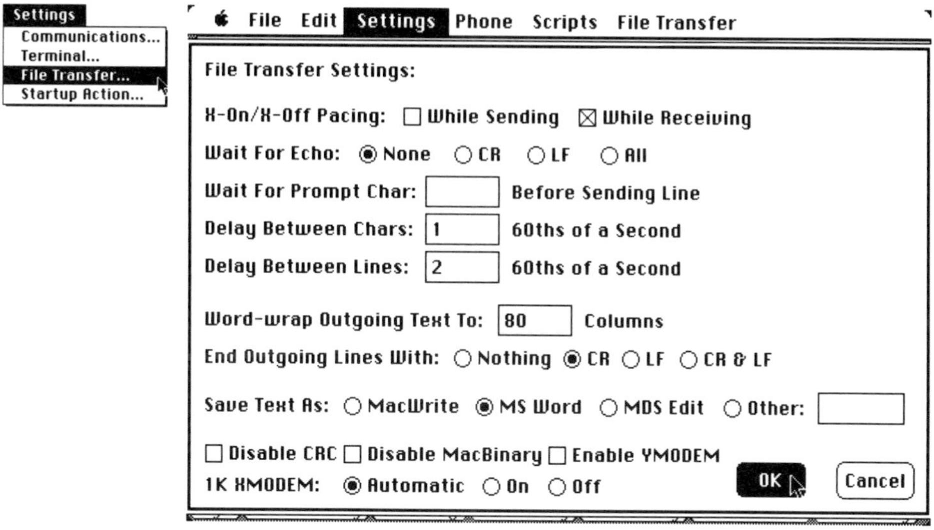

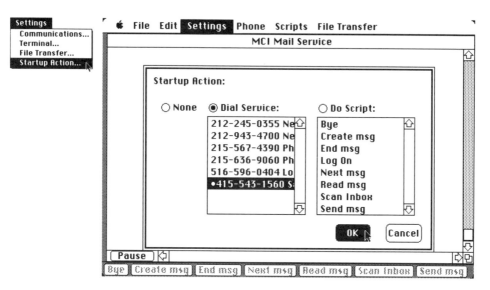

Figure 2-34

MicroPhone's file transfer protocol settings, which includes a wait function before sending text as well as the ability to save text in MacWrite or Microsoft Word formats, and the ability to control the Xmodem and Ymodem protocols.

Figure 2-35

MicroPhone's startup action dialog box lets you set up an automatic call and log-on sequence: after setting up phone services and scripts, you can tell MicroPhone to automatically dial a service and perform an operation.

worrying about line endings, and you can force lines to end with a control character such as a carriage return (CR) or line feed (LF). You can disable the MacBinary protocol and use raw Xmodem, or enable MacBinary with Xmodem for full Macintosh file transfers — the word "MacBinary" appears in the File Transfer menu next to "Xmodem" if you've enabled it. You can also enable the faster "1K" version of Xmodem, which creates blocks of 1024 bytes each rather than 128 bytes each, or use Ymodem rather than Xmodem.

If you enjoy having a measure of control over your communication sessions, you'll like using MicroPhone's script language. A script language lets you automate any operation you can perform by typing commands. MicroPhone has a "watch me" function that enables MicroPhone to remember every command you type, save it in a script file, and present the sequence of commands as a menu choice and as an on-screen push-button.

To use scripts for completely automated operation, Micro-Phone lets you choose a startup action to occur automatically

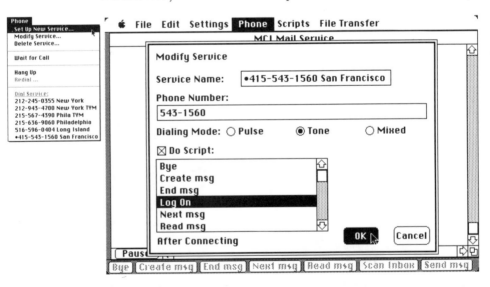

Figure
2-36

MicroPhone lets you assign several phone numbers to a document, and in the phone setup dialog box you can set up an automatic log-on sequence to occur when you select that particular number to dial.

when you launch the program from this document. We have already created several phone numbers (called "services) and scripts, so we can set a startup action to dial a particular service phone number and perform an operation controlled by a script (Figure 2-35). The next time you launch MicroPhone by double-clicking this document (which we call MCI Mail Service), it will automatically call the number and log-on to the service.

MicroPhone lets you assign several service phone numbers to a document. When you set up a new service number (Figure 2-36), you can also create an automatic log-on operation by assigning a script, such as the "Log On" script, to that number so that when you call that number, the script is automatically performed.

Scripts can appear as menu items in the Scripts menu, or as buttons at the bottom of your display, or as both. You can also assign a Command-key sequence to a script. In the scripts dialog box (Figure 2-37), you can use script commands,

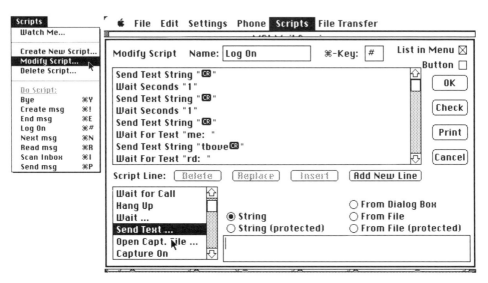

Figure 2-37

MicroPhone's scripts dialog box lets you build a script from scratch in the upper window using script commands in the lower window; you can then assign the script to a button and a menu selection as well as a Command-key sequence.

displayed in the lower window, to create a script (shown in the upper window) that lets you send text, wait for time to pass (one second) or for one or more prompt characters to be displayed by the service, and to control the modem (hang up, wait for call, etc.). The scripts can be listed in the Scripts menu and displayed as buttons at the bottom of your display, which you can activate by clicking once.

Figure 2-38 shows the beginning of an MCI Mail session in which MicroPhone dialed the service, performed the log-on sequence, and displayed MCI Mail's startup message and command line. You can then use the scripts in the buttons at the bottom of the display to check the mail, read messages, and create and send messages (using the Create msg button, the Send Text command in the File Transfer menu, the End msg button, and the Send msg button). We also show in this example how you can click the Pause button to stop the scrolling display, and the button turns into the Resume button, which you click to continue scrolling. After reading

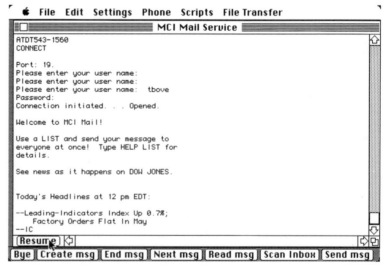

Figure 2-38

MicroPhone can call the service, automatically perform a log-on sequence, and leave you in control of MCI Mail, with buttons displayed for the MCI Mail functions (for which scripts were written).

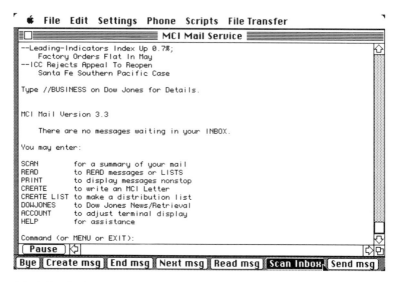

Figure 2-39

We defined a Scan Inbox button to scan our inbox (messages addressed to us).

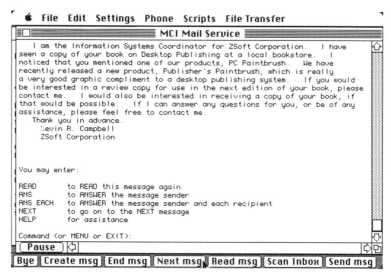

Figure 2-40

During an MCI Mail session, after reading a message, we can use our Next msg button to continue reading mail, or the Bye button to log off the service.

*Figure
2-41*

A MicroPhone document with settings for CompuServe, calling Compu-
Serve and performing an automatic log-on sequence.

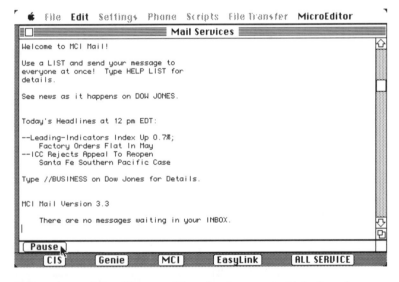

*Figure
2-42*

Using a master MicroPhone multi-service document with buttons for
each service; click a button and it displays a new set of buttons for that
service.

the initial display, we use the Scan Inbox button to see our mail (Figure 2-39).

Figure 2-40 shows the mail session after reading the first message — we can use our Next msg button to continue reading mail, or log off the service using the Bye button. You could also type those MCI Mail commands yourself, or define buttons for them.

MicroPhone lets you set up as many documents for different services as you need. Figure 2-41 shows a document set up for CompuServe access. Note that the button scripts have almost the same names as the MCI Mail scripts, allowing you to teach someone how to access several different services using the same button names, cutting down on training time. You can also create one document for all your services that uses a master script to call up a series of scripts for each service (Figure 2-42).

MicroPhone also has a built-in text editor which is available as a desk accessory. You can call up this text editor at any time while using MicroPhone (especially if you are not connected to a service), and use it to write or edit messages, then use the MicroEditor menu to save the messages as normal text files. You can also use the Cut, Copy, and Paste commands to copy sections of your communication session to a text file. You can use the scroll bar that is always displayed along the right side of your session.

MicroPhone has the most robust set of features of any communication program for the Macintosh. It has all the features of MacTerminal, plus the ability to create powerful push-button operations to automate your communications. With Glue as part of the package, you can transfer images, graphic files, and publication files to other Macintosh users (via the Xmodem MacBinary protocol) who can use them even if they do not have the application program.

The combination of the faster 1K version of Xmodem (or Ymodem), the text file send and receive protocols (XON/

XOFF and special delay settings), and the script language make MicroPhone the best buy for communication software as of this writing.

Software Features Checklist

Communication programs are constantly being improved and new ones are appearing frequently. Our favorite Macintosh communication programs, as of this writing, are Micro-Phone (Software Ventures, $75), Smartcom II (Hayes, $149), Red Ryder (FreeSoft, $40), Desktop Express (Apple/Dow Jones, $149, for use with MCI Mail and Dow Jones services only), and InTalk (Palantir, $195). Although MacTerminal (Apple, $125) is not our favorite, it is easy to get and many people use it.

Now that you have seen some of these programs in action, we can explain some of the features that are common among them. Rather than list the features of each program (which can become an incomplete list as soon as the program is revised), we provide the following checklist of features you should be looking for in such programs:

Error-checking file transfer protocols. This is number one on the list because it is essential for Macintosh file transfer. Error-checking protocols let you transfer information with the secure feeling that there will be no errors placed in the data from noisy telephone lines or other electromagnetic interference. Most 300 bps, 1200 bps, and 2400 bps modems do not include a protocol, so you need to have this feature in your software.

As described earlier, the most widely used protocols are Xmodem and Kermit, which are used along with the MacBinary file encapsulation standard to transfer Macintosh files to another Macintosh. MacTerminal uses a modified Xmodem protocol, so your program should also be able to transfer files with the MacTerminal Xmodem as well as regular and MacBinary Xmodem protocols. MicroPhone lets you transfer files to

MacTerminal using MacTerminal's protocol, and it also has Xmodem (or Ymodem) with the MacBinary protocol. Desktop Express, on the other hand, uses a proprietary protocol that works only with MCI Mail.

Support for popular modems and baud/bps rates. The program should be able to control a Hayes Smartmodem or Hayes-compatible modem (such as the Apple Personal Modem). Some programs will also support nonstandard modems such as the Telebit Trailblazer at top speed. Others can't handle the high speeds and therefore can only be used at low speeds with high-speed modems. If you are planning to connect computers directly by cable (without using modems), you need a program that supports high speed transfer (9600 bps or higher).

Ability to set number of bits per character, and start, stop, and parity bits. Most programs let you control the number of bits per byte (character), which can be either seven (for text-only files) or eight (for text and all other types of files). In the same menu they offer the ability to set the number of start and stop bits to use with asynchronous modems. Some services want two stop bits, others want one stop bit (depending on the speed you select). The *parity bit* is usually the eighth bit of a data or control byte that is added for some services and mainframe communications that use the parity bit to determine whether a data character was transferred correctly. You want to be able to set the parity bit to even, odd, space, mark, or none (depending on the service you are calling).

Terminal emulation. Many programs can emulate a Digital Equipment Corporation VT100 terminal or a standard ANSI X3.64 terminal, so that when you use the program to log onto a mainframe or minicomputer, your Macintosh can act as a terminal on the remote system. VT100 emulation will help you act as a terminal on almost any system (you can also use terminal emulation mode to type modem commands to do special operations with the modem). Along with terminal emulation should come functions such as the ability to send a "break" signal (these terminals have a Break key but your Macintosh does not), and the ability to display what you type (local echo) even if the characters were not received by the receiving computer. For more on terminal emulation, see Chapter 5.

Text receiving (without error-checking protocols). The features to look for include the ability to save text received as a MacWrite or Microsoft Word file (as in MicroPhone), and the ability to set the XON/XOFF protocol (this lets you pause the receiving of text in order to store the text on disk and do other operations, such as changing folders). This feature is also implemented as a "capture" function that saves everything typed or displayed to a text file on your disk. This feature is helpful for saving entire communication sessions, and for saving electronic mail while reading it.

Text sending (without error-checking protocols). You need to be able to set delays in the text sending operation — at least a delay between characters and at the ends of lines. MicroPhone also lets you set the program up to wait for a prompt character to be displayed by the service before sending text, and the program will automatically end each line with the appropriate control character, as well as wrap words around to the next line (some services require that lines end with a carriage return and that lines not exceed 80 characters in length).

Scripts, macros, or autopilot language. Sophisticated programs such as MicroPhone and Red Ryder let you automate all or part of your communication session with information services or mainframes. A simple script would be an automatic *log-on* sequence so that you don't have to type your name and password every time you call the service — the program recalls the script and types it for you.

A more complex script could be defined so that your program calls a service in the middle of the night while you're asleep, checks your electronic mail, retrieves information about a particular stock, saves both the information and your latest mail on your disk, and signs off the service and hangs up the phone. The test is to see if you can write such a complex script without too much trouble.

Automatic number dialing and redialing. Most communication programs will automatically dial a number (as long as your modem can perform the dialing function); some let you store several numbers in one settings document (Micro-Phone), and others let you store only one number per document (MacTerminal). Most programs will let you redial the same number over and over if the line is busy, and Desktop Express will try a second number automatically if the first one is busy. All programs let you hang up the phone, and some programs can answer the phone and display an answer-back message.

Built-in text editor. Programs such as Desktop Express and MicroPhone have built-in text editors for writing and editing messages. In both cases you can disconnect from the service (i.e., not paying access charges) while writing and editing, then reconnect to send or receive messages. Also, in both programs you can use Cut or Copy and Paste commands to move sections of text from one message to another, or from your communication session to the message you are editing. For example, if you write a message to someone who already sent you a message, you can use the Copy and Paste commands to copy the sender's address to your message.

Using Information Services

Information services are your gateway to research libraries, electronic shopping and banking, teleconferencing, airline schedules and reservations, and electronic mail with the rest of the world (not just your office or your corporation). Some also provide free programs (public domain software and shareware — software for which you pay a donation), user group bulletin boards filled with pertinent technical information, and up-to-date stock information.

One common feature of all information services is that you are charged for using them in some way, in addition to the actual phone call charges. Some charge by the minute (or second, or hour), some charge by the message (such as $1 a message for electronic mail), and some charge both — especially if they offer both an electronic mail service and data bases for searching. Shopping services usually charge a surcharge, as do airline reservation systems. Research libraries and services such as the OAG (Official Airline Guide for tracking schedules and fares) surcharge by the minute in addition to the charges incurred by using the parent service. For example, CompuServe offers both research libraries and the OAG, and you pay for both CompuServe's time and time spent in the OAG (although the charges are reasonable). Some user group services, such as MAUG (Micronetworked Apple Users Group), are free to members, and anyone can join.

It may seem like a whirlwind of charges at first, but you can sort out the charges by requesting a fee summary from the service before joining. Most services require that you write or call first (by voice) in order to sign on, but some let you sign on for the first time by computer.

The largest service is CompuServe, which is also the largest commercial electronic mail network since it has so many users. MCI Mail, which offers mail service and *gateways* to CompuServe and Dow Jones (the ability to connect to these services through MCI Mail), is the second largest public electronic mail service. Other services such as The Source, GEnie, BIX, and OfficeNet offer a variety of special services as well as electronic mail.

CompuServe

CompuServe (CompuServe Information Service) offers electronic mail, forums for special interest groups (where interests range from cooking to music to Macintosh business computing), teleconferencing using a "CB radio simulator" to exchange comments with many people at once, news wire services (Associated Press, Executive News Service, the Washington Post, Online Today Electronic Edition, and Canadian and overseas wires), and an Electronic Mall and Comp-u-store for teleshopping.

Financial transaction services are available (from regional banks), as are a brokerage service (Quick & Reilly Inc.), a stock exchange information service (Max Ule & Co.), portfolio management (Unified Management Corporation), and American Express member services. Securities quotes are available, as well as commodities and earnings forecasts, mutual funds descriptions, the Disclosure II corporate data base, and Standard & Poor's summaries and ratings.

You can book a flight with the airline reservation system; make reservations for hotels, rental cars, tours, and cruises; and get foreign and domestic travel information.

For education, research libraries include the entire Grolier's Academic American Encyclopedia, IQuest (data bases from business, commerce, and industry), the College Press Service, The College Board, and Peterson's College Databases.

Other interesting data bases and services include Health-Net (discussions with physicians), Aviation Weather (for round-the-clock weather reports for pilots), SuperSite (a demographic retrieval and reporting system), Journalism and Public Relations, and a variety of data bases on computers, telecommunications, and data processing.

CompuServe starts by displaying its Top menu, from which you can select different services (Figure 2-43). From this level you can check your mail using the command Go Easy (for Easyplex, the mail system), or you can go to any CompuServe screen directly if you know its name. Use the directory selection to learn the names of the opening screens of the services you want to use. Use the Subscriber Assistance selection to display CompuServe's fees and surcharges.

One of CompuServe's major assets is the MAUG (Micronetworked Apple User's Group), which is a collection of technical information libraries, public domain software libraries, information bulletin boards, and a conferencing system. Macintosh users can especially benefit from the libraries of technical information and free advice dispensed by user group members. Figure 2-44 shows the opening dialog, and Figure 2-45 shows the opening dialog for the special forum (MAUG) devoted to business computing with the Macintosh.

As of this writing, the best times for accessing CompuServe are very late at night (or early morning) on the East Coast of the United States, and at night on the West Coast (when the time difference coincides with the least activity in other populous time zones). CompuServe can slow down when it is in heavy use, and remember — you're paying for time as if it's a running taxi. Use your time wisely, and learn about using the system from the printed manuals, not from the wordy on-line help messages that take a long time to appear.

Figure 2-43

CompuServe's opening menu (using a MicroPhone document in which we've defined button scripts for navigating CompuServe).

```
MAUG(TM)MacBiz

VISITOR'S MENU

 1 Membership Information
 2 Forum Administrators
 3 Instructions
 4 Visit MAUG(TM)MacBiz
 5 Join MAUG(TM)MacBiz

 0 Exit

Enter choice ! 1$
************************
|       M A U G
|
|   The Micronetworked
|
|   Apple Users' Group
|
************************
|      MEMBERSHIP
|      INFORMATION
************************
|
|(MAUG is a trademark of
|  the Micronetworked
|  Computer Users Inc.)
************************
```

Welcome to MAUG(tm)'s Macintosh Business User's
Forum! This Forum is dedicated to helping power
users find ever more powerful and exciting ways
to use the Macintosh in all fields of business.

Press <CR> for more :

All of MAUG's Forums are free of any surcharges and there are no membership fees.
But we consider MAUG to be a club, a real
online community. For that reason, our only
membership requirement is that you use your
real first and last name while on any of our
Forums.

To join the Forum simply choose option 5
from the Vistor Menu ("Join the Forum") and
you will be prompted for your name. To conform with our membership requirement please
answer with your real first and last name.
If you have already signed up with a
"handle" or just a first name please use the
CN command once within the Forum to change
to your full name. Thanks very much.

Enjoy MAUG -- "The Nicest Place Your Computer Can Take You!"

VISITOR'S MENU

  1 Membership Information
  2 Forum Administrators
  3 Instructions
  4 Visit MAUG(TM)MacBiz
  5 Join MAUG(TM)MacBiz

  0 Exit

Enter choice ! 5

Figure
2-44

The opening dialog from the MAUG (Micronetworked Apple User's
Group) on CompuServe.

```
***************************
Welcome to MAUG(TM)MacBiz, V. 4B(154)

Hello, Tony Bove
Last visit: 19-Jun-87 12:01:59

Forum messages:   4498 to   4745
Last message you've read:      0

Subtopic(s) Selected:
 All Accessible

No members are in conference.

Short bulletin:
****************************************************
Welcome to MAUG(tm): The Macintosh Business Forum
****************************************************

LOW PRIME TIME RATES PERMANENT!!
As of June 1, CompuServe rates are the same 24 hours a
day. GO RATES for details, and visit MAUG(tm) 24 hours a
day for the same lower rates.

ACIUS Conference transcript available in DL6 as ACIUS.CO.

-> NEW SYSTEM SOFTWARE AVAILABLE! <-
The new System 4.1 and Finder 5.5 and all associated
files are now in the DL8 area of our sister Forum, the
Apple Developer's Forum (GO APPDEV). A subset of these
files are also available here in DL12 and in MACUS DL3.
But the complete set of all files is only available in
AppDev.

Mac II and Mac SE Product Announcement files are in DL6!

FIRST TIME HERE?: A Few Handy Pointers:
LN command for Library Names. SN command for Subtopic
Names.
GO AOL (Apples OnLine) for in-depth help files
```

```
Remember: UPLOAD TIME IS FREE! Please share with us all.
Thanks!
And Always Remember: Address a message to SYSOP For help!
*****************************************
|MAUG(tm)(Micronetworked Apple Users|
|Group) is a trademark owned by MCU |
| Inc. (PO Box 520, Bethpage, NY    |
| 11714). Voice help line available |
|          516/735-6924             |
| daily _only_ from 7pm to 10pm EST |
*****************************************
```

Figure 2-45

The MAUG business forum (on CompuServe).

MCI Mail

MCI Mail is a complete electronic mail service that links over a million people together so that they can send and receive messages.

MCI Mail can be accessed with Desktop Express (Apple/ Dow Jones) as described earlier, or you can use MCI Mail commands by typing them while connected to the service using a communication program. MCI Mail lets you scan the message headers (sender and subject) in your mailbox, read messages with or without pauses between messages and page breaks, create messages and address them to electronic mailboxes or to actual street addresses for hand delivery (MCI Mail prints the message using either an Apple LaserWriter or some other laser printer, perhaps adding a digitized signature), and build a distribution list of addresses.

You can also use MCI Mail to access the Dow Jones News/ Retrieval service (type the DOWJONES command). Offerings on Dow Jones include current stock quotes; the latest business news from the *Wall Street Journal, Barron's,* and the Dow Jones News Service or ticker; the full 20-volume Academic American Encyclopedia; and consumer services such as airline schedules, discount shopping, sports, movie reviews, weather, and a constantly updated world news report. Dow Jones records your time and adds a surcharge to your MCI Mail bill.

MCI Mail can send messages for delivery immediately to an electronic mailbox, or within four hours or overnight for paper delivery to a street address. Paper delivery means your message is printed on MCI Mail's laser printers, and you can

```
Please enter your user name:
Please enter your user name:   tbove
Password:
Connection initiated. . . Opened.

Welcome to MCI Mail!

Use a LIST and send your message to
everyone at once!   Type HELP LIST for
details.

See news as it happens on DOW JONES.


Today's Headlines at 12 pm EDT:

—Leading-Indicators Index Up 0.7%;
    Factory Orders Flat In May
—ICC Rejects Appeal To Reopen
    Santa Fe Southern Pacific Case

Type //BUSINESS on Dow Jones for Details.


MCI Mail Version 3.3

    There are no messages waiting in your INBOX.
```

Figure 2-46

MCI Mail displays the day's news and then a short menu of commands before displaying the command prompt line.

optionally register a signature for digitizing and printing on the message. With Desktop Express you can also send graphics mixed with text in word processing files (with fonts), or files from graphics applications, or publication files created by page makeup programs, all of which can be printed on MCI Mail's printers and hand-delivered to street addresses.

The details of delivery services may have changed by the time you read this, so type HELP DELIVER for the current information. At the time of this writing, MCI Mail offered overnight and four-hour hand-delivery service depending on the time you post the message. For overnight hand-delivered paper messages, Monday through Thursday, you can post your message by 11 p.m. Eastern Time, and MCI Mail will deliver it by noon the next day. Overnight letters posted between 11:01 p.m. Thursday and 11:00 p.m. Friday are delivered by noon on Monday. Overnight letters posted between 11:01 p.m. Friday and 11 p.m. Sunday to the special four-hour zip codes are delivered by noon Monday. Four major metropolitan areas are, at the time of this writing, included in this service: New York, Los Angeles, Chicago, and Washington, D.C.

For four-hour delivery service, you can post your message between 6 a.m. and 6 p.m. (recipient's local time), on any business day, and MCI Mail will hand-deliver it within four hours on the same day in these major U.S. cities: Chicago, Los Angeles, New York, and Washington, D.C. Four-hour letters posted after 6 p.m. (recipient's time) are delivered by noon the next business day.

MCI Mail offers an advance service for an extra $10 a month. This service lets you use step-saving commands rather than menus, create mailing lists so that you can send one message to everyone on the list with one command, forward a message to share messages with others (including a cover letter), use forms for different types of messages (such as memos), register up to fifteen signatures and letterheads for different purposes, reserve storage space for up to fifty pages on the network (or more for additional fees), and post items on the bulletin board.

The bulletin board lets you broadcast information to the network, update your information quickly, and control who has access to the information. You can publish classified ads, job postings, newsletter announcements, prices, and so on, in one central location where it can be viewed by other MCI Mail users. You can control who reads your items, when the items should be posted and deleted, and what order to list them. For help with bulletin boards, type HELP BULLETIN BOARD.

Help is available on MCI Mail any time you see the MCI Mail prompt (Figure 2-46). If you're not sure what to do next, just type HELP and an explanation appears. If you still need assistance or you want to sign up for the advanced service options, call Customer Support at (800) 424-6677; in Washington DC. call 833-8484. For information and assistance with Dow Jones, call Dow Jones News/Retrieval Customer Service at (800) 257-5114; in New Jersey call (609) 452-1511.

Other Services

The Source (The Source Information Network) is a competitor to CompuServe, offering basically a similar set of features and an electronic mail system (SourceMail) you reach by typing MAIL.

In addition to special interest groups (SIGs) devoted to topics ranging from cooking to computing (plus a group dedicated to the Macintosh), The Source offers travel services, bulletin boards, news with weather and sports, investor services, educational data bases, and electronic shopping. Two unique features are Chat, a conferencing session in which people type comments and see other people's comments immediately (similar to CompuServe's CB Simulator), and Participate, a conferencing facility for holding ongoing business or club meetings, with discussions arranged by topic.

The Source charges a membership fee and per-minute fees

The Well-Connected Macintosh

```
*** WELCOME TO GEnie (tm) ***

    The General Electric
Network for Information Exchange

Welcome to GEnie, the information
service for Micro-computer enthusiasts
and professionals...like you!

GEnie international availability;

 1. U.S.A.
 2. Canada
Enter # of country where
you are located?

Genie features include:

*  World news, Weather, Sports
*  Business & Financial Information
*  Travel, Airline & Tour Information
*  Electronic Encyclopedias
*  GE Mail (TM) electronic mail
*  RoundTable (TM) Bulletin Boards
*  LiveWire (TM) CB Simulator
*  Real-Time Conferencing
*  RoundTable (TM) Software Libraries
*  PC Newsletters and Information
*  Multi-player Games

Equipment Required:

*  Any ASCII personal computer or terminal
*  A Modem (Full or Half-Duplex)
*  Communications software

To sign up for GEnie, you will be asked for:

*  Your Checking Account or Credit Card #
   (VISA, MasterCard, Sears Discover, or American Ex-
   press)
```

```
      and credit card expiration date
*  Your name & billing address
*  Your residence address
*  Your work and home telephone numbers
*  Your mother's maiden name
   (for security)


Please be sure to check Item #4 to locate the GEnie
access number nearest you.


GEnie                        Page 999
     GEnie Sampler and Sign-up


 1. Sign up on GEnie
 2. GEnie: Price Schedule
 3. GEnie: Service Agreement
 4. GEnie: Local Phone Numbers
 5. Logoff


Enter Item #, <P>revious, <S>ign Up,
   <T>op, or <H>elp?


GENIE SERVICE AVAILABILITY:
The many services of GEnie are available 24 hours per
day, 365 days per year, with occasional scheduled outages
for routine maintenance. You may use any modem speed up
to 1200 baud for the same basic rate. In addition, 2400
baud service is available in selected cities at a
surcharged rate.


SUBSCRIPTION FEE:
A one time subscription fee of $18.00 is charged to open
your GEnie account, and mail you a GEnie User Manual.


BASIC CONNECT RATE:
Non-prime time: $ 5.00 per hour
Prime time:     $35.00 per hour
```

Figure 2-47

You can subscribe to GEnie by calling an 800 number and typing a special code, then answering the questions until you've given GEnie your billing information.

that are higher for higher speeds (300, 1200, and 2400 bps). Special interest groups and data bases can add per-minute surcharges. For information, contact The Source by voice phone at (800) 336-3366; in Virginia call (703) 821-6666.

General Electric's GEnie (GE Information Services) is another competitor that offers similar services to The Source and CompuServe, including electronic mail (GE Mail), Roundtable special interest groups, LiveWire conferencing (similar to CB Simulator), American Airlines EAASY SABRE Travel Service, Grolier's Electronic Encyclopedia, and domestic and international news.

GEnie lets you join by calling and typing a special code (Figure 2-47). You then follow the dialog and answer the questions, until you've given GEnie all the information it needs to bill you. Call GEnie at (800) 638-9636.

OfficeTalk (OfficeTalk, Inc.) offers electronic mail, laser printing, and typesetting services for Macintosh and PC users. OfficeTalk provides you with a version of Apple's Desktop Express that lets you transfer files to and from OfficeTalk with error-checking protocols. You can send formatted text, graphics, publication files from page makeup programs, or even PostScript programs to OfficeTalk for printing or typesetting on PostScript devices. In 24 hours you receive the printed or typeset version of your file at the highest possible resolution, letter or legal size (also tabloid size for typesetting), using the LaserWriter Plus fonts and custom company logos. For more information about OfficeTalk, call (800) 345-0133; in Pennsylvania call (215) 664-7440.

3 Communicating With the IBM PC and PS/2

We can work it out. — John Lennon/Paul McCartney

Compatibility between different types of computers is difficult to achieve when the computers contain proprietary technology that is either difficult or illegal to clone. Although manufacturers of computers that run MS-DOS (an operating system derived from PC-DOS, the IBM PC and Personal System operating system) claim that their computers are compatible with IBM's, true 100 percent compatibility is impossible to achieve because IBM keeps part of the system proprietary and takes legal action if any manufacturer copies it directly.

What most "PC clone" manufacturers provide is approximately 99 percent or less compatibility, but the most important feature offered by "PC clone" manufacturers is the ability to run off-the-shelf software designed specifically for IBM PCs and Personal Systems.

Apple and IBM computers do not usually run the same software, unless you add an MS-DOS card to the Macintosh SE or Macintosh II, which provides the same level of compatibility offered by "PC clone" computers. Add-in cards that provide PC compatibility, such as the Mac86 and Mac286 packages from AST Research, are described later in this chapter.

However, most users do not need MS-DOS running in their Macintosh computers. They simply want to share information in a variety of ways between the Macintosh and any IBM PC or compatible computer (including PC XT and PC AT models), and Personal System/2 (PS/2) computers. They want to run Macintosh software on the Macintosh and PC software on the PC, and share the same data. Macintosh and PC data sharing is covered in detail in this chapter.

Macintosh and PC computers are more compatible than most people believe. Both share a propensity for ASCII (American Standard Code for Information Interchange) as the code for characters and symbols. Both use similar modem cables (with different connectors) for transferring data between the computer and modems (or other computers). Both are inclined to use PostScript, a popular page description language used to print high-quality fonts and graphics on different printers and typesetters, although for PCs PostScript is only one of many page description languages for printing. Both can handle PostScript descriptions of graphics, and both are well versed in the Xmodem protocol for error-checking while transferring data.

This means you can share spread sheets by translating them to file formats used by such programs as Lotus 1-2-3 (on the PC) and Microsoft Excel (on the Macintosh). You can share text files, even formatted text files, if you first translate them using one of several translation programs such as MacLink+ (Dataviz, $195). Data bases can be shared the same way.

There are two ways to share files between Macintosh computers and PCs (or PS/2 computers): by direct file transfer over cable or modem, and by file servers or disk servers that make files available to other computers on a network. We describe both methods briefly in this chapter, then describe networks in more detail in subsequent chapters.

Differences in Files

You may not be able to run Macintosh application programs on PCs or PC application programs on the Macintosh (without the MS-DOS add-on card), but your applications can share data. For example, Microsoft Excel can read Lotus 1-2-3 spread sheets and convert them to Excel spread sheets, and Microsoft Word on the Macintosh can read and convert files from Word on the PC.

There are only a few small barriers to overcome for smooth transfer of files. The highest barrier is the recording format — no matter which type of computer you use, each file's format is determined by its associated application program.

For example, dBASE III Plus saves a data base file in a specific format that must be converted to another data base format for use with another data base program. To transfer these types of files, you first use a *translation program* that converts files from one popular format to another.

There are a variety of translation programs and conversion methods you can use with Macintosh computers and applications. You may not be able to transfer a file between two PC applications (such as WordStar to Microsoft Word on the PC), but you can use the Macintosh as an intermediate step to act as a translator (WordStar to MacWrite on the Macintosh, then to Microsoft Word on the Macintosh, then over to Microsoft Word on the PC).

In addition to the file's format, there are some differences between the Macintosh system's file management and PC file management:

1. the format of file names and means of identifying their applications;

2. the method of specifying a folder (Macintosh) or subdirectory (PC);

3. the way such files are stored on disk.

There are easy ways to overcome these differences if you develop good file management habits.

Macintosh files can have descriptive file names with up to 31 characters counting spaces and symbols. For example, you can have a file named:

Profit/Loss Statement '87

You also know what application program is used with the file because the Macintosh system displays the appropriate icon. Also, with the Macintosh system you can double-click a file and thereby run the application program with that file.

A PC file, on the other hand, can have only eight characters in a file name, with three characters following a period to identify the application program for that file. Spaces and special characters are not allowed. For example, you might have a file named:

PROFIT87.WKS

The first eight characters describe the file, and the three-character extension tells you that the file is a worksheet for use with Lotus 1-2-3.

Macintosh files are organized into folders, which can be contained within other folders. You can arrange folders on your Macintosh desktop and move files from one folder to another, or out to the desktop, whenever you like. To gain access to the files in a folder, you select the folder and open it to display its contents; you then select the file in the display window. There usually isn't any requirement for placing files in a special folder (except system files in the System Folder), or to group files together in a folder, but some application programs require specially organized folders.

PC files are organized into *directories* and *subdirectories*. At the top, or desktop level, is the root directory, which contains all other directories. Within each of these directories can reside files or subdirectories containing more files and further subdirectories.

Since both organizations are tree-shaped, networks can map them into one tree structure where a folder is equal to a subdirectory (the top folders are equal to directories). The desktop icon of a Macintosh disk is the root directory of a PC disk.

However, if you are sharing files with PCs, you should use file and folder names on the Macintosh that are unique in the first eight characters (not counting spaces). For example, when using the TOPS file server on an AppleTalk network (described later), the Macintosh files have eight-character names when you try to access them from a PC:

Macintosh file or folder	PC file or directory
Profit Plan for 1987	PROFITPL
Chapter 6	CHAPTER6
Annual Report	ANNUALRE

Note that if you had two Macintosh files — one named "Profit Plan for 1987" and the other named "Profit Plan for 1986" — the PC would try to use the same file name for both files, causing an error. You should therefore make the first eight characters of your Macintosh file names unique to each file.

PC names, on the other hand, are carried over to the Macintosh display just as they are on the PC. You should not have any trouble using PC files.

Transferring Files Directly

You can use a variety of methods to transfer files between a Macintosh and various PC-compatible computers. One easy method is to buy the DaynaFile 5.25-inch disk drive (Dayna Communications Inc., $595), available for any Macintosh with a SCSI port. If you have a Macintosh SE or II, you could

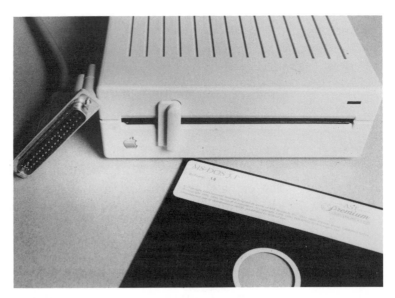

Figure
3-1

The Apple 5 1/4-inch PC-compatible floppy disk drive attaches to either an Apple disk drive controller card for the Macintosh SE or II, or to coprocessor cards such as the AST Mac86 and Mac286.

Figure
3-2

The Mac86 card for the Macintosh SE (installed by your dealer) provides MS-DOS and PC compatibility.

instead use the Apple PC 5.25 Drive ($399) to exchange 5.25-inch PC floppy disks (Figure 3-1). The Apple drive uses a standard DB-37 connector used with PCs, and attaches to a Macintosh SE or II controller card from Apple ($129), or to the MS-DOS add-in cards described next.

The 5.25-inch PC-compatible disks hold 360 kilobytes (roughly 360,000 characters). You can transfer information by copying files from one disk to another. Remember, however, that a single-sided Macintosh disk can hold 400K ("K" stands for kilobytes), and a double-sided Macintosh disk can hold 800K.

Using MS-DOS Cards

The MS-DOS cards for the Macintosh from AST Research provide MS-DOS (the PC operating system) and a level of PC compatibility that is as close as most clone manufacturers get. These cards come in two sizes: the Mac86 ($599) for the Macintosh SE (Figure 3-2), and the Mac286 ($1499) for the Macintosh II (Figure 3-3).

The MS-DOS cards from AST Research turn your Macintosh into a PC-compatible computer. The Mac86 card for the Macintosh SE provides PC XT performance; the Mac286 card for the Macintosh II provides PC AT performance. Both cards let the Macintosh keyboard, mouse, display, hard disk, and printer emulate MS-DOS counterparts (the mouse emulates a Microsoft Mouse).

Macintosh disks or folders now simulate DOS drives C, A, and B, and DOS applications run in a window on the Macintosh screen which can be scrolled and resized so that other windows also appear on the screen (Figure 3-4). The display can emulate the IBM Monochrome and IBM Color Graphics Adaptors (color on the II, black and white on the SE) and the Hercules monochrome adaptor.

Your ImageWriter or LaserWriter can emulate an Epson FX-80 printer, and DOS applications that output PostScript

119

The Well-Connected Macintosh

*Figure
3-3*

The Mac286 card set, installed in the Macintosh II, provides MS-DOS and PC compatibility.

```
 File  Edit  FKeys  Misc
══════════════════════ PC Hercules Display ══════════
Phoenix 80286 ROM BIOS Version 1.58
Copyright (c) 1985,1986 Phoenix Technologies Ltd
All Rights Reserved

Current date is Thu  4-23-1987
Enter new date (mm-dd-yy):
Current time is 14:43:12.17
Enter new time:

The IBM Personal Computer DOS
Version 3.10 (C)Copyright Interna         s Machines Corp 1981, 19
          (C)Copyright Microso            1985

C>_
```

Calculator
432.98

Caps | Num | Scrl | Func

*Figure
3-4*

Emulating a Hercules display, the Mac286 card runs a DOS application in one window while Macintosh applications occupy other windows; in this example, the Calculator desk accessory can be used on top of the DOS window.

120

for printing can use the LaserWriter's built-in PostScript features.

Copy-protected PC software can be run on the simulated drive C, although applications that use a parallel port for copy protection won't run because the Macintosh does not provide a parallel port.

You can transfer files to and from a Macintosh folder using the simulated drive D and the MS-DOS COPY command. Files stored on the simulated D drive can be accessed by the Macintosh Finder and System. You can transfer simple text files and use them with PC and Macintosh applications, or translate application files using MacLink Plus (described later in this chapter). You can also copy or cut data from one window, such as a Macintosh application, and paste the data into another window running a DOS application. You can also copy or cut data from a DOS window and paste it into a Macintosh application.

The Mac86 card uses an Intel 8086 processor, which is a high-performance version of the 8088 processor used in PC XT computers. The Mac286 card uses an Intel 80286 processor to provide compatibility with PC AT computers. The MS-DOS cards will not run software that requires any special PC Bus hardware, except floppy disk drives and the display adaptors supported by the card.

Cables and Modems

The least expensive way to connect a PC-compatible computer to a Macintosh is over the telephone using inexpensive modems, or directly using modem cable (without modems). This method is the only way to transfer files to and from any other computer (such as a Kaypro, Osborne, CP/M-based, Atari, and Commodore computers).

Modems are described in detail in Chapter 2. For cables, ask a Macintosh dealer or a computer software and hardware dealer for a standard Macintosh Plus or Macintosh 512 serial cable for connecting to a PC XT or PC AT serial port. The ports on a PC or AT are called COM1, COM2, and so on, and are directly addressable from the PC's operating system or from a communication program. Some programs, such as the PC version of MacLink Plus, come preset for the COM1 serial port because every PC has a COM1 port.

Most brands of PC XT-compatible computers, such as IBM, Compaq, and Leading Edge, have at least one serial port (with pins) that matches the 25-pin connector on a standard serial (sometimes called "RS-232") cable. Brands of PC AT-compatible computers have at least one serial port with pins that matches the 9-pin connector on standard AT serial cables; you can then use an AT adaptor cable that connects the 9-pin connector to the standard 25-pin connector.

Some PC XT-compatible or AT-compatible computers use a female serial port (with holes rather than pins); you then need to buy a gender-changer attachment that turns the port into a standard male port (with pins). Be sure to use a gender-changer (which transfers the signals straight through) rather than a similar-looking attachment called a *null modem* (which has crossovers in the connection). A null modem is used to connect two computers of the same type using a standard serial cable without a modem — the attachment simulates a modem connection.

A serial cable used to attach to the Macintosh (with a circular 8-pin connector for the Macintosh Plus, SE, or II phone or printer port, or a 9-pin connector for a Macintosh 512) will have either a 25-pin connector at one end to attach to a PC, or a 9-pin connector to attach to an AT. Alternatively for an AT, you can use a PC serial cable with an adaptor cable for the AT's 9-pin port. (MacLink Plus is supplied with the proper cable that can be used with a Macintosh 512 or with a Macintosh Plus, SE, or II by first connecting it to a Macintosh Plus Peripheral Adaptor Cable available from any Macintosh dealer.)

For an electronic diagram of Macintosh-to-PC cabling, see Appendix B.

Communication Software

With a serial cable or a modem-to-modem connection you can use a communication or transfer program such as MacLink Plus (Dataviz, $195). The MacLink Plus package includes a cable that plugs into an asynchronous port on the PC-compatible computer and into the modem port on the Macintosh, plus PC and Macintosh software to enable the machines to communicate.

As described in Chapter 2, error-checking protocols are essential to any file transfer method. MacLink Plus provides a special-purpose protocol for transferring files with PCs that are running the MacLink Plus PC software.

Other communication programs will also work with a cable link-up as if modems were involved in the process, even though modems are not being used. Communication programs such as MicroPhone and MacTerminal can be used for transferring to and from any PC communication program that uses the Xmodem protocol (described in Chapter 2). You must use the same protocol in the programs running on both computers.

As described in Chapter 2, you can use the Xmodem protocol to transfer files to PCs from Macintosh computers, and to Macs from PCs, and from both types of computers to CP/M, Apple //, and other computers and back again, without loss of data integrity. Almost every communication program for PC-compatible computers offers the Xmodem protocol, including PC Talk III (Headlands Press), Crosstalk Mk.4 (Digital Communications Associates, Inc.), Relay (VMPC), ProComm (PIL Software Systems), MaxiMITE (Mycroft Labs), and public domain programs such as QMODEM.

Transferring Files Over a Network

A popular method for managing the sharing of information among different types of computers is a *network*: computers linked directly by cable to each other and to printers and other devices.

Files are shared on a network by making them available to some or all computers through the use of a *file server* — a computer with a hard disk containing the files that are shared. Some networks have one computer dedicated for operating the file server software; others allow any computer on the network to run the file server software.

The most popular network for linking Macintosh computers to PCs is the AppleTalk Personal Network from Apple. (3Com, described later, offers a PC network that can link to the AppleTalk Personal Network). AppleTalk networks are described in detail in Chapter 4, but we describe in this chapter how simple it is to transfer files from PCs to Macintosh computers and back again, and how users of both computers can share files.

The capability to connect Macintosh computers in an AppleTalk Personal Network comes with every Macintosh, and AppleTalk Personal Network cable is used to connect a LaserWriter to the network. You can easily share one or more LaserWriters among several Macintosh computers by adding more AppleTalk Personal Network cable. Eventually you can build a large network that combines PCs and Macintosh computers simply by adding more cable and connector cards to the PCs. You can then use a file server such as AppleShare (Apple Computer) or TOPS (TOPS Inc., formerly Centram Inc.), both of which offer PC file service.

To connect a PC to the AppleTalk Personal Network, you add an AppleTalk Personal Network adaptor card to the PC. The AppleTalk PC Card (Apple Computer, $399 for each PC), the PC MacBridge card (Tangent Technologies, $650 for each PC), and TOPS for the PC (TOPS Inc., $349 for each PC, $149 for each Macintosh) are the most widely used AppleTalk

Personal Network adaptor cards for PCs. The PC MacBridge and TOPS cards are supplied with software to share Laser-Writer printers among PCs, and to perform file transfers between the PC and at least one Macintosh. For example, the PC MacBridge software lets you transfer files by choosing that function from a menu (Figure 3-5). The AppleTalk PC Card is supplied only with software for sharing LaserWriters among PCs, but you can add the optional AppleShare PC software for file transfer.

All three AppleTalk adaptor cards are installed in a PC in the same manner — they are half-sized PC cards that fit into slots in the PC. Figure 3-6 shows how you would insert the TOPS AppleTalk card into an IBM PC AT-compatible computer. A connector on the card lets you attach the AppleTalk Personal Network cable, which links the PC to any other devices and computers on the AppleTalk network, including any Macintosh computers and LaserWriter printers.

Software supplied with the different cards offer basically the same features: the ability to transfer files to and from Macin-

```
*** SEND MAIL Menu ***

        A.  SENDER Name      :    Cheryl Rhodes
        B.  DESTINATION Name:    Tony Bove
        C.  MESSAGE          :    ***   See Below   *
        D.  FILE TO SEND     :    c:\screens\pm1a.pub
        E.  WHO Is ON-LINE
        F.  SEND

        Enter Selection:   F




    Current Message:
    Hi, Tony, here's a PC file
```

Figure
3-5

Tangent Technologies' PC MacBridge software initiating a file transfer to a Macintosh from the PC over the AppleTalk Personal Network.

125

tosh computers on the network and the PC, and the ability to send PC files to one or more LaserWriter printers over the network. PC MacBridge also offers the ability to use a PC to spool multiple files to a printer on the network (such as the LaserWriter), including files from WordStar (MicroPro), MultiMate (Ashton-Tate), 1-2-3 (Lotus), Word (Microsoft), and other PC application programs.

The benefits involved in using different methods of file sharing in a network are described more fully in Chapter 5, but for the purpose of providing a complete picture of communications with IBM personal computers, we present a brief introduction to file sharing with the file servers that support transfers to IBM PCs and IBM PS/2 computers. The two packages that offer network file sharing are AppleShare PC (Apple Computer) and TOPS (TOPS, Inc.). In addition, PC MacBridge (Tangent Technologies) offers file transfer to one Macintosh along with its AppleTalk adaptor card. Finally,

*Figure
3-6*

Adding an AppleTalk Personal Network adaptor card (this one is from TOPS) into an AST Premium 286 computer (compatible with an IBM PC AT).

InBox PC (Think Technologies) offers file transfer in addition to its electronic mail functions across an AppleTalk Personal Network of PCs and Macintosh computers. InBox works along with either the AppleTalk PC Card or the PC MacBridge card, and the company plans to make InBox work with the TOPS adaptor card.

Sharing Files With AppleShare PC

Many AppleTalk networks are set up with one or more AppleShare file servers, which are described in detail in Chapter 5. You can connect a PC or PS/2 computer to such a network using the AppleTalk PC Card and an AppleTalk Personal Network Connector Kit. The AppleShare PC is a pop-up memory resident program that can be activated by a function key while running a PC application. You can activate the program whenever you need to gain access to the files on network file servers.

AppleShare PC lets an MS-DOS user have full access to the folders and files stored on any AppleShare file server on the network. For convenient and secure AppleShare service, you would dedicate one or more Macintosh computers as AppleShare servers (you can also dedicate the same computers for other services, such as spooling and electronic mail, which are described in Chapter 5). MS-DOS users on the network can gain access to files and transfer files to and from the server. Folders on the AppleShare server appear to MS-DOS users as logical DOS disk drives (D:, E:, F:, and so on). Users need to remember a password, and the software automatically checks it to determine access privileges. (Access privileges in AppleShare are described in detail in Chapter 5).

With AppleShare PC version 1, the shared files must reside on the Macintosh server — to share PC files with other Macintosh users, first the files are copied to the server, then both PCs and Macintosh computers on the network can gain access to them.

Sharing Files with TOPS for the PC

TOPS for the PC, which has been available for over a year, lets you share PC files and Macintosh files over an AppleTalk network using its own AppleTalk adaptor card for the PC.

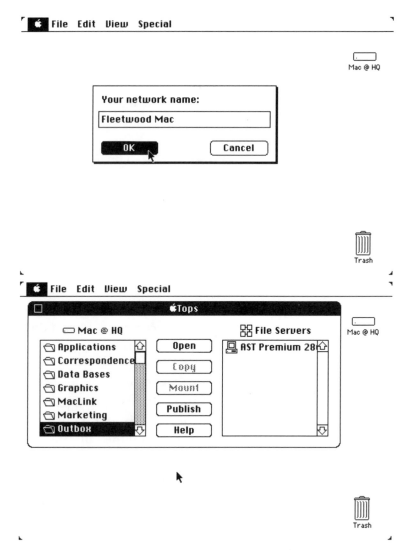

Figure 3-7   Publishing a Macintosh folder with TOPS to make it available to one or more PCs on an AppleTalk Personal Network.

```
┌──────────────────────────────────────────────────────────────────────┐
│  AST Premium Z86        Welcome to TOPS                      Main       │
├──────────────────────────────────────────────────────────────────────┤
│  Main Menu                                               Client         │
│    List directories and make them accessible             Server        │
│    to other users on the network.  Shows                 Remember       │
│    Clients and Volumes in use.                           Quit           │
│                                                                        │
└──────────────────────────────────────────────────────────────────────┘
```

```
┌──────────────────────────────────────────────────────────────────────┐
│  MENU INSTRUCTIONS                                                      │
│    Select a command using the space bar, up arrow, down arrow          │
│      or first letter of the command.                                   │
│    <ENTER>- Invoke a selected command.                                 │
│                                                                        │
│    <ESCAPE>- Return to the previous window.      <CNTRL-Q>- Exit to DOS.│
│                                                                        │
└──────────────────────────────────────────────────────────────────────┘
```

```
┌──────────────────────────────────────────────────────────────────────┐
│  AST Premium Z86        TOPS : Server Utilities            Server       │
├──────────────────────────────────────────────────────────────────────┤
│  Server Utilities Menu                                  Publish        │
│    Publish a Volume to allow network access.            Vols Published  │
│    You will be prompted for the full                    My Clients      │
│    pathname.  You must choose an                        Show Name       │
│    alias, mode and password.                                           │
└──────────────────────────────────────────────────────────────────────┘
```

```
┌──────────────────────────────────────────────────────────────────────┐
│  MENU INSTRUCTIONS                                                      │
│    Select a command using the space bar, up arrow, down arrow          │
│      or first letter of the command.                                   │
│    <ENTER>- Invoke a selected command.                                 │
│                                                                        │
│    <ESCAPE>- Return to the previous window.      <CNTRL-Q>- Exit to DOS.│
│                                                                        │
└──────────────────────────────────────────────────────────────────────┘
```

Figure 3-8   TOPS on the PC has a Client menu for mounting a volume from another computer (not shown), and a Server Utilities menu for selecting directories to publish (shown below main menu).

```
 ┌──────────────────────────────────────────────────────────────────────┐
 │ AST Premium Z86        TOPS : Server Utilities              Publish    │
 ├──────────────────────────────────────────────────────────────────────┤
 │ Publish a Volume for Network Access                                    │
 │                                                                        │
 │     Path:      c:\transfer                                             │
 │                                                                        │
 │                                                                        │
 └──────────────────────────────────────────────────────────────────────┘
```

```
 ┌──────────────────────────────────────────────────────────────────────┐
 │ MENU INSTRUCTIONS                                                      │
 │   Type each item as requested and press <ENTER>:                       │
 │     Full path including drive specification.                           │
 │                                                                        │
 │   <F1>- List directories on a local drive.                            │
 │   <ESCAPE>- Return to the previous window.      <CNTRL-Q>- Exit to DOS.│
 │                                                                        │
 └──────────────────────────────────────────────────────────────────────┘
```

```
 ┌──────────────────────────────────────────────────────────────────────┐
 │ AST Premium Z86        TOPS : Server Utilities              Publish    │
 ├──────────────────────────────────────────────────────────────────────┤
 │ Publish a Volume for Network Access                                    │
 │                                                                        │
 │     Path:        c:\transfer                                           │
 │     Alias:       transfer                                              │
 │     Password:                                                          │
 │     Mode:        RW                                                    │
 └──────────────────────────────────────────────────────────────────────┘
```

```
 ┌──────────────────────────────────────────────────────────────────────┐
 │ MENU INSTRUCTIONS                                                      │
 │   Type each item as requested and press <ENTER>:                       │
 │     1-16 character alias by which you want this Volume known on the network.│
 │     0-8 character password with which you wish to secure access.       │
 │     1 or Z character mode: R- Read Only; RW- Read/Write.               │
 │   <ESCAPE>- Start over with pathname.           <CNTRL-Q>- Exit to DOS.│
 │                                                                        │
 └──────────────────────────────────────────────────────────────────────┘
```

*Figure
3-9*

Using TOPS to publish a PC directory to make it available to Macintosh computers and other PCs on an AppleTalk Personal Network.

With TOPS you can select a PC directory or disk drive, or a Macintosh folder, to be "published" on the network. Everyone on the network using TOPS in their computer can then

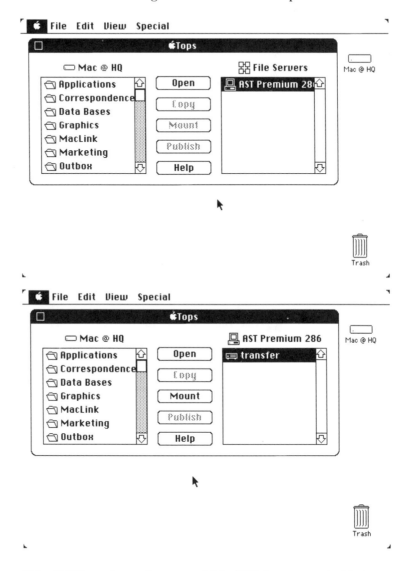

Figure
3-10

Using TOPS to select and open a published PC directory on the Macintosh.

"mount" the directory or drive so that it appears to be attached to their system.

For example, if you are primarily a PC user, you can use TOPS on a Macintosh to publish a disk or folder (Figure 3-7),

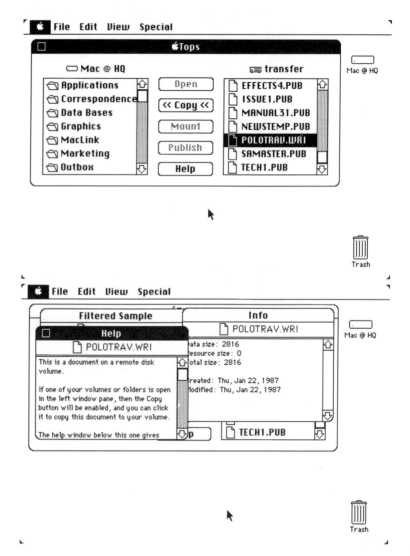

Figure 3-11   TOPS has a Help feature that displays three windows of information about any file on the network.

then use TOPS on a PC to mount the Macintosh disk or folder in the PC system, and treat the disk or folder as a separate disk drive on the PC (such as drive E). You can then use MS-DOS commands such as COPY to copy files back and forth, or you can access the drive from PC application programs.

If you are primarily a Macintosh user, you can make use of the PC's files without having to use PC commands (other than the initial commands to start the TOPS menu). For example, you can publish a PC disk or directory in the "RW" (read-write) mode, and treat the PC directory as a separate disk on the Macintosh (Figures 3-8 and 3-9).

Using TOPS on the Macintosh (even while using another application program), you can select and open the published directory (Figure 3-10), and use the Copy button to copy files to a Macintosh folder or to any other published volume on the network.

TOPS has a Help button that displays help windows containing information about that file, including a window showing its size and creation date (Figure 3-11).

TOPS also displays a window that shows a sample of the text in the file (if the file contains simple text) or a "filtered sample" of the printable text characters in the file (if the file is more than just simple text, such as formatted text or spread sheets).

You can mount the published directory or disk (Figure 3-12) so that it appears as a disk on the Macintosh desktop (Figure 3-13). You can then drag a file from that disk to another Macintosh disk or folder, or drag a file to that disk, just as if the disk was a normal Macintosh disk (Figure 3-14). You can also open and close files in the directory using an application program, just as if they were on a Macintosh disk.

Keep in mind, however, that the file names of Macintosh files transferred to the PC disk will appear with truncated names in the PC system as described earlier in this chapter. You can see the entire Macintosh name by pressing the F3 function key.

133

Compared to AppleShare, which provides high-performance file sharing and protection features suitable for departmental networks, TOPS is more for casual file sharing.

The inherent problem with this type of casual file sharing is

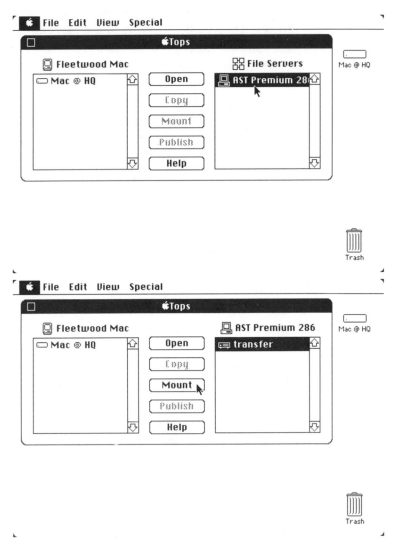

Figure
3-12

Using TOPS to mount a PC directory as a disk in the Macintosh system,
for use with the System, Finder, and any Macintosh application program.

134

that you could forget you have published folders that others are using when you switch off the computer and go home for the night.

Even so, TOPS provides an economical solution for sharing

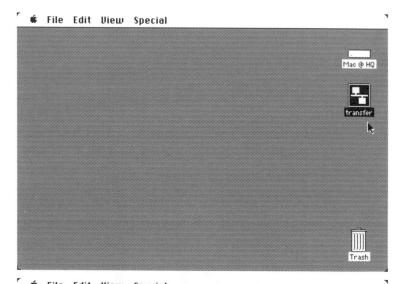

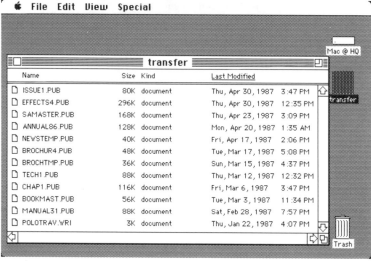

Figure
3-13

TOPS makes a mounted PC directory appear as a disk (with a special icon) on the Macintosh desktop.

files and printers among a network of Macintosh and PC computers.

The features and methods of file sharing over AppleTalk networks are explained in Chapter 5.

However, one feature of TOPS to mention in this chapter is the quick file conversion feature and the extensive file translation utility offered with TOPS. The quick conversion feature copies only ASCII text when transferring a file from one TOPS volume to another, leaving out any unrecognized characters (such as formatting and control characters). You can see what characters TOPS will recognize by first clicking the Help button for the selected file and looking at the "sample" or "filtered sample" window.

For file translations between formats such as MultiMate to MacWrite, or MacWrite to WordStar, or Lotus 1-2-3 to Excel, TOPS provides a version of the MacLink Plus program with settings documents (files you can use to launch an application program with appropriate settings already set), called TOPS

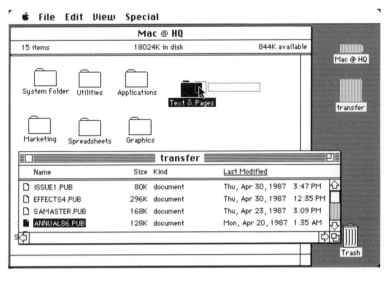

Figure
3-14

Once a PC directory is mounted on the Macintosh desktop using TOPS, you can drag files to and from it as if it were a Macintosh disk (using the Finder).

Translator. We describe MacLink Plus from Dataviz later in this chapter, and since TOPS Translator (written by Dataviz) uses the same menus and displays, the description applies to both packages.

Transferring Files With InBox/PC

Another program that offers file transfer over an AppleTalk network is the InBox/Mac electronic mail package from Think Technologies ($350 for up to 3 users, $125 each additional user), and InBox/PC ($195 per PC, requiring InBox/Mac). We describe how to set up and use the InBox electronic mail system in Chapter 5, with a brief description in this chapter of how InBox/PC and InBox/Mac can work together.

With InBox/Mac, you use one Macintosh on the network as the Message Center. This Macintosh should have a hard disk to be able to handle a lot of message traffic. Every user on the network can have an electronic mailbox in the Message Center. When you send a message to someone, the message is stored in this mailbox at the Message Center. The receiver can read the message and save it on his/her disk.

The benefit of this arrangement is that a Macintosh user can send or receive messages and transfer files with a PC user at any time, even when the PC user has turned off the machine. The PC user, of course, has the same benefit. Neither party has to leave their machine on in order to keep a published directory or folder available, as with TOPS file transfer. Nor do the people have to be actively involved at both ends of the transfer, as with MacLink Plus and other communication programs. However, either MacLink Plus or TOPS is useful for file translation, and either one can be used in addition to InBox as described in Chapter 5.

InBox was first developed for AppleTalk Personal Networks. You need an AppleTalk adaptor card to connect each PC to an AppleTalk network to run the version described in this chapter. You can use InBox with the AppleTalk PC Card and PC MacBridge, and a version will soon be working with the TOPS card. Any type of PC or Macintosh file can be sent clipped to an electronic mail message, and InBox can run simultaneously with TOPS and with both Apple's and Tangent's LaserWriter spooling programs for the PC, which are described later in this chapter.

On each Macintosh, InBox/Mac is installed as a desk accessory you can use from within an application or from the Finder. On the PC, InBox/PC is installed as a memory-resident pop-up program that you can activate from within an application or from the command line of the operating system.

The InBox/Mac display on the Macintosh (Figure 3-15) has function buttons for displaying current messages in your mailbox, displaying your address list, setting up a blank message pad for writing a new phone or memo message,

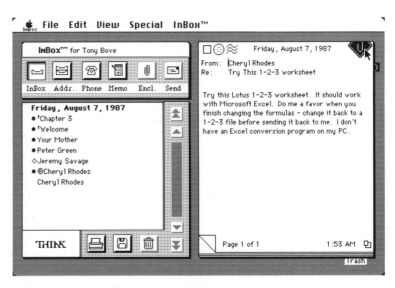

Figure 3-15

InBox/Mac on the Macintosh displays a list of messages and function buttons (see Chapter 5 for more details), and can send or receive any type of file while communicating with InBox/PC on a PC.

clipping a file to the message for transfer, and sending the message and clipped file.

InBox/PC runs on the PC as a memory-resident pop-up program. You activate it by typing a key sequence that is defined during installation. Once the InBox/PC program is running you can perform all the same functions available in

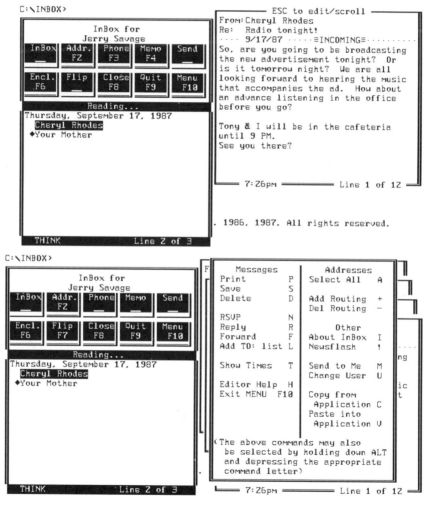

Figure 3-16 InBox/PC offers the same set of functions for sending and receiving messages and enclosing files.

the Macintosh version (Figure 3-16), including sending and receiving phone and memo messages, enclosing files for transfer, receiving files clipped to messages, and selecting messages for saving and printing.

InBox is a fully featured electronic mail system for business use, and the Message Center software can work in the background while you work in an application, even on that same Macintosh. One person usually acts as a network administrator, assigning mailboxes and taking care of backing up the hard disk that serves the Message Center. We describe how to set up and use electronic mail systems in Chapter 5.

Sharing Printers With PCs

Apple, Tangent Technologies, and TOPS offer AppleTalk adaptor cards for connecting a PC to an AppleTalk network, and all three offer an additional feature for the PC: the ability to share any LaserWriters and other printers on an AppleTalk network.

For example, the AppleTalk PC Card from Apple is supplied with a program called LW for sending output to any LaserWriter on an AppleTalk network. You can also rename a LaserWriter, and pick a LaserWriter in another zone of the network to receive the output (zones are described in Chapter 4). The program presents a series of menus for printing files from various word processing programs such as WordStar and MultiMate, and from applications such as Lotus 1-2-3. The program can also print PostScript files and ASCII files, and it can activate the LaserWriter's emulation of a Diablo 630 daisy-wheel printer. Application programs can use LaserWriter fonts by embedding codes in the files, and you can write PostScript code (if you were so inclined to spend the time programming) or download ready-made PostScript files for changing fonts and preparing the printer's memory.

Tangent provides the most comprehensive LaserWriter-PC sharing features as of this writing. PSPrint, supplied with

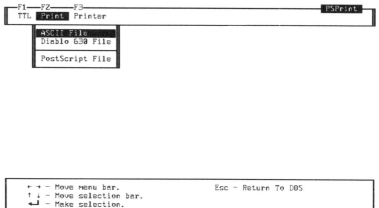

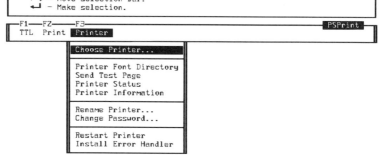

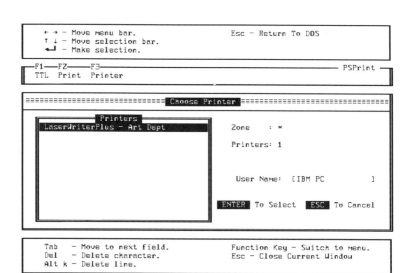

Figure 3-17 Tangent Technologies' PC MacBridge is supplied with a LaserWriter sharing program called PSPrint.

Tangent's PC MacBridge, lets a PC share one or more Post-Script devices (including LaserWriters) on the AppleTalk network of PCs and Macintosh computers (Figure 3-17). You can use PSPrint to print directly from any application programs that can prepare PostScript files (such as Microsoft Word, WordPerfect, and XyWrite), and from WordStar, NewWord, MultiMate, and Lotus 1-2-3. A version of PSPrint, called WinPrint, runs under Microsoft Windows.

PSPrint can also send PostScript and ASCII files to any PostScript device on the network, and activate the emulation of a Diablo 630 printer or a Hewlett-Packard Plotter. By embedding special codes in text files you can merge graphic images with text while sending the files to the printer. PSPrint has other special functions including the ability to capture a PC screen image for printing and for saving as an encapsulated PostScript file, and PostScript conversion capability for programs that do not output PostScript.

Tangent's TangentSpool package for PCs ($500) goes a step further to offer print spooling to up to four different printers (including PostScript devices such as a typesetter, and ImageWriter printers), using a PC as a spooling server. Requiring a dedicated PC XT or similar computer, Tangent-Spool can assign priority levels to print jobs, display printer status messages, print banner pages, and keep a log of all print jobs for accounting purposes.

PC Networks

The most common network for PCs and for UNIX-based workstations is Ethernet, which can be used with thick or thin coaxial cable, fiber optic cable, and twisted-pair wiring. Ethernet was developed jointly by several companies with leadership and official endorsement by Xerox, Hewlett-Packard, and Digital Equipment Corporation. Another popular network topology and wiring hardware is IBM's Token Ring which uses twisted-pair wiring.

Both types of networks can support Macintosh II and Macintosh SE computers as well as PCs, as long as you add an adaptor card for the Macintosh II or SE, or a *bridge* device that links one or more Macintosh computers to another type of network (other than the built-in AppleTalk Personal Network). For example, different Ethernet bridge devices and adaptor cards from Kinetics (described in Chapter 4) allow you to connect one Macintosh or an entire AppleTalk Personal Network to an Ethernet network. You can then transfer files to and from the file server on the Ethernet network.

3Com's Ethernet implementation is a popular network for PCs, and 3Com Corporation is one of the largest Ethernet suppliers. The 3+Share network from 3Com can link PCs and Macintosh SE and II computers using 3Com's Ethernet adaptor cards. Apple also offers EtherTalk, an adaptor card that connects a Macintosh II to an Ethernet network for running an AppleTalk network system on top of Ethernet.

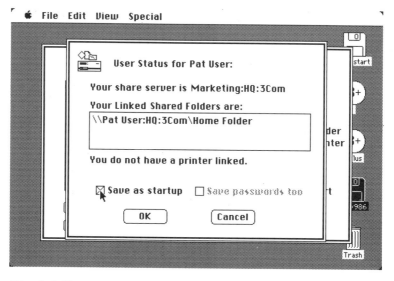

Figure 3-18

3Com's 3+Share PC-based network shows PC directories and disks as folders with special icons on the desktop.

With 3Com's 3+Share network you can share files and folders with PCs and Macintosh computers, control access with passwords and access rights, and share printers with printer spooling so that you can continue working without waiting for the printing to finish. PC directories and files appear as Macintosh folders and files on the Macintosh desktop (Figure 3-18). However, the 3+Share network does not offer folder-level access privileges as does AppleShare (both are described in more detail in Chapter 5).

The chief difference of a PC-based network (compared to an AppleTalk network) is that network management and file service is controlled from PC-based or PS/2-based workstations or, as in the case of the 3+Share network, by a dedicated server device (the 3Server3). The Macintosh computers can act independently and access the PC-based or PS/2-based servers when they need information from them. However, such networks do not presently offer the range of services and flexibility of an AppleShare file server on an AppleTalk network.

Bridge products and adaptor cards that let you attach an AppleTalk Personal Network or a single Macintosh to a PC-based or mainframe-based network are described along with gateways, bridges, and other network topology concepts in Chapter 4.

File Translation

After transferring a file from the PC to the Macintosh, you may also have to convert its format to the format used by a Macintosh application. The information in files is usually formatted according to the rules of a particular application, and that format may not be recognized by other applications. In addition, the file's system stores the file in a certain way. To *translate* a file is to both convert the file to another system storage method, and to convert its format to one used by another application.

Some programs have the ability to translate files that were created by their PC counterparts or by similar PC programs. Microsoft Word, for example, can recognize and convert several PC file formats including its own Microsoft Word for the PC and the standard Document Content Architecture (DCA) format from IBM that is often provided as an alternate format for text files on the PC. Another Macintosh program, Microsoft Excel, can translate Lotus 1-2-3 and Symphony files to Excel files, and vice-versa.

If you use other applications, you will probably need a file translation program, unless you only need to transfer unformatted ASCII text. However, even with ASCII text there are differences between Macintosh and PC files that you may have to deal with. For example, each line of text in a PC file may have "hard Returns," so when it is transferred to a Macintosh, each "hard Return" forces each line to act as a paragraph in programs such as MacWrite or Microsoft Word. With unformatted ASCII text files, if you don't use one of the conversion programs described in this section, you still have to delete the Returns at the end of each line of text in order to format paragraphs properly, or use one of the techniques described at the end of this chapter.

Apple File Exchange

The Apple File Exchange utility is a new Macintosh program that is included with every Macintosh and every Apple PC 5.25-inch drive package. In addition, owners of Macintosh computers can get the Apple File Exchange as part of the System version 5.0 update.

Apple File Exchange can copy files and entire folders (or PC directories) from one system to another, and also convert files from one format to another, including translating character sets when necessary. It can also convert a batch of files at once, even if the files are in different formats. The current version of the Apple File Exchange (AFE) can copy and convert files between Macintosh disks, 5.25-inch MS-DOS disks, and 800K ProDOS disks for the Apple //family (but not 5.25-inch ProDOS disks). The program requires a Macintosh with a built-in 800K drive.

The AFE is supplied in a folder that also contains translator files, which are used by the AFE. You need a translator file for each type of file conversion you do. The AFE is supplied with at least one translator file—DCA-RFT/MacWrite, which lets the AFE translate files in IBM's Document Content Architecture (DCA) Revisable Format for Text (RFT) to the MacWrite file format, and vice-versa. Other translators are available from your Apple dealer.

When you double-click the AFE icon, the utility program displays two directory listings and buttons for translating or removing files and folders, creating new folders, opening folders, and switching (or ejecting) disk drives. It also has a pull-down menu for selecting translators (Figure 3-19). The

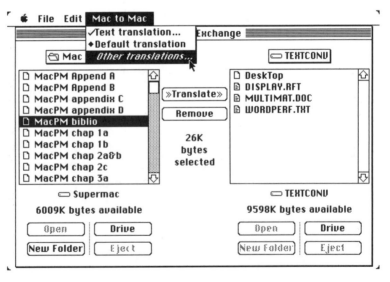

Figure 3-19

The Apple File Exchange utility program, which is free with every Macintosh (supplied with System 5.0), translates files between a PC or Apple// system and a Macintosh, and converts files from one format to another.

146

program automatically uses the Text translation for text files and the default translation (from one system to another) for all other files. It also lets you add translators to its menu and select an entire folder of files for batch translation, or a set of files by holding down the Shift key and selecting the first and last file in the list, or holding down the Command key while selecting individual files. Start the translation by clicking the Translate button, which displays directional arrows showing which is the original (or source) and which is the newly translated copy (or destination). The AFE then displays a progress window (Figure 3-20) showing the number of files copied and the percentage of the entire operation that has completed.

The AFE displays the amount of disk space and the size of the file or files selected. With this information you can make room for the newly translated files by erasing files or changing disks. A newly translated file is frequently longer than the original, depending on the type of translation.

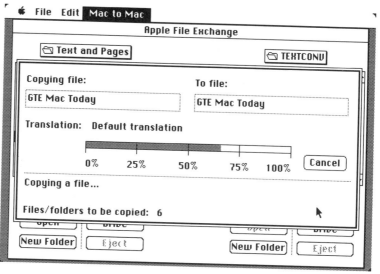

Figure
3-20

The Apple File Exchange's progress window during a translation and transfer operation.

The Well-Connected Macintosh

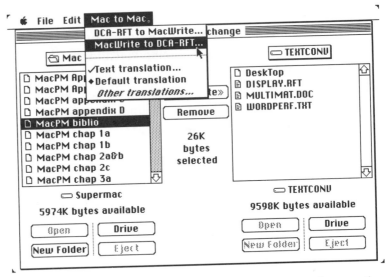

Figure
3-21

After adding translators to the Apple File Exchange program's menu, the program can translate a batch of files with different formats in one operation, choosing the appropriate translator for that file (as long as the translator is checked as shown).

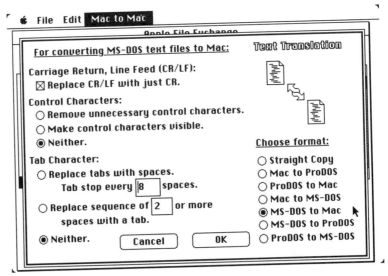

*Figure
3-22*

Options for the MS-DOS to Macintosh translation of text files, which you can change.

When you select a folder of files that are in different formats, the AFE automatically chooses the appropriate translator for the file as long as the translator appears checked in the translation menu (Figure 3-21) to show that it is active. If the AFE finds two or more active translators that would work for a given file (other than Text and Default), it displays a dialog box listing the appropriate translators and asking you to choose one.

You can also set options for the Text translator by selecting it to make the check reappear in the menu. The MS-DOS to Macintosh translation (Figure 3-22) can be customized to allow the replacement of a Carriage Return and Line Feed combination (which is usually at the end of every line in a PC text file) to simply a Carriage Return without the Line Feed (which is usually at the end of every line in a Macintosh text file). The Macintosh to MS-DOS translation (Figure 3-23) offers the reverse of this option. Both types of translations offer the options of replacing tab characters with a number of

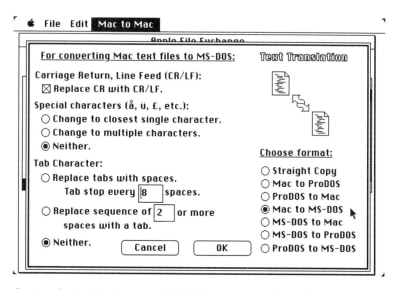

Figure 3-23

Options for the Macintosh to MS-DOS translation of text files, which you can change.

spaces or vice-versa, and dealing with control characters or special characters.

Although text format translators typically have no trouble translating text with paragraph breaks and some formatting instructions, they do not always translate all of the formatting instructions. For example, the DCA and MacWrite translator does not translate text fonts, sizes, and styles from the MacWrite format to the DCA format, nor does it translate footnotes in DCA files to MacWrite files. When the AFE is aware of this loss of information, it leaves a message in the User Log, which you can display with the Show User Log option in the File menu.

The Apple File Exchange is very useful for customized text file translations, but requires more translators to be effective at translation a variety of text files. It is the only utility that offers file translation to Apple // computers.

MacLink Plus (TOPS Translators)

MacLink Plus from Dataviz (also called TOPS Translator in the Centram TOPS package) is a widely used translation program for the Macintosh that has been available for a long time. The program is excellent for PC file transfers because it provides a table of file formats for the PC and a matching table of Macintosh formats, so that you can transfer MultiMate files to MacWrite or vice-versa. You can translate nearly every popular PC word processing file format into the formats used by the Macintosh version of Microsoft Word, or MacWrite. You can also translate data base information from dBASE III and other structures to Macintosh data base structures.

MacLink Plus is supplied with several preset startup files you can use to start MacLink Plus with the appropriate settings (Figure 3-24). You can use MacLink Plus with a serial cable connected to the PC, or with a modem connection. You can also use it to translate files that have already been transferred to a Macintosh disk, or files that are on a PC file server in a

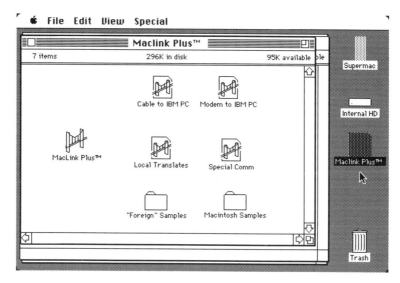

Figure
3-24

MacLink Plus is supplied with several startup files already set for communication and file transfer, plus folders with sample files for testing translations and a text file containing a record (log) of the session.

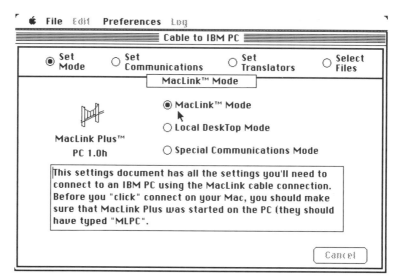

Figure
3-25

Starting off in MacLink mode, connected directly to a PC.

network. MacLink Plus also has a special communications mode for turning your Macintosh into a terminal on another computer system, as described in Chapter 6.

When you start a MacLink Plus settings document, such as Cable to IBM PC, you are automatically placed in MacLink mode (Figure 3-25). To communicate with the PC, you must first be running the MacLink Plus PC version — type **MLPC** from the command line to start the PC version. Alternatively, if you have already transferred files to the PC, you don't have to run a program on the PC. Start MacLink Plus with the Local Translates settings document (Figure 3-26).

To see what translators are available in the program, click the Set Translators button, which displays a window for Macintosh and PC file formats (Figure 3-27). The direction is first set to translate from a PC format to a Macintosh format. You would select a PC format, such as MultiMate (Ashton-Tate),

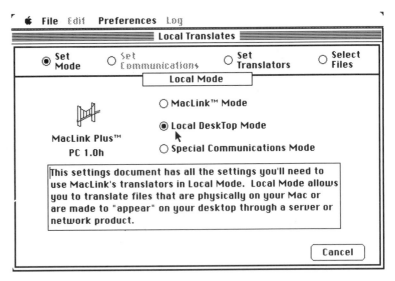

Figure 3-26

Starting MacLink Plus with the Local Translates settings document to translate files that are already on a Macintosh disk or on a server connected by network to the Macintosh.

and MacLink Plus displays a list of Macintosh formats that you can convert the MultiMate file into. You then select the format you want as a result, such as MacWrite, and move on to the next dialog box by clicking the Select Files button.

The translators change depending on which format you choose and in which direction you are translating. Figures 3-28 and 3-29 show examples of some translations between PC and Macintosh formats. After selecting the translators, click the Select Files button to move on and select the actual files for the translation (Figure 3-30).

For transferring files, start with a settings document that is preset for your communication session, or click the Set Mode button to change the mode to MacLink, and click the Set Communications button, which displays the MacLink Mode communications dialog box (Figure 3-31). You can change some of the settings in this dialog box by clicking the setting and dragging down the menu (as shown in Figure 3-32, where

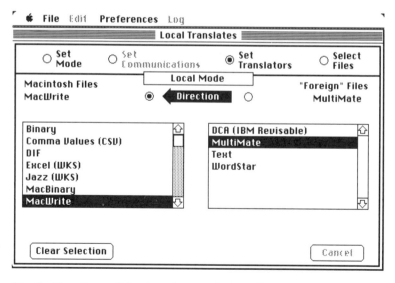

Figure 3-27

The Set Translators dialog box shows a window of Macintosh file formats (MacWrite is selected) that match a PC file format (MultiMate is selected).

The Well-Connected Macintosh

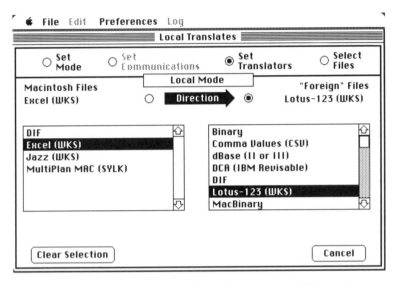

*Figure
3-28*

Translating a Microsoft Excel spread sheet into a Lotus 1-2-3 spread sheet.

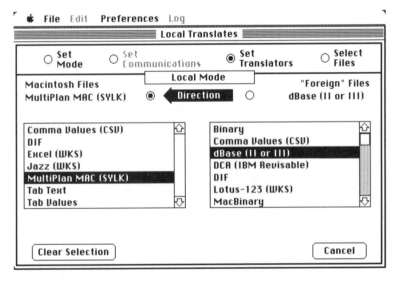

*Figure
3-29*

Translating a dBASE II or III data base into a Macintosh MultiPlan SYLK file.

the modem speed is changed to 2400). When starting up the Special Comm settings document, you can also set other file

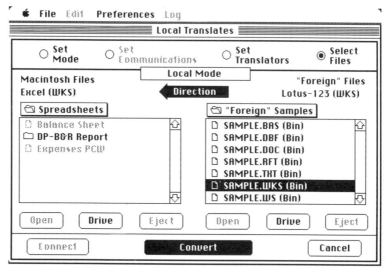

Figure
3-30

Selecting actual files for the transfer and translation.

Figure
3-31

The communication settings dialog box in MacLink Plus.

transfer protocols as well as communication and terminal settings (Figure 3-33 shows the Special Mode communication

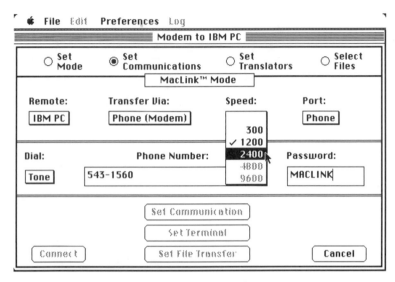

Figure 3-32

Changing the modem speed setting in the communication settings dialog box.

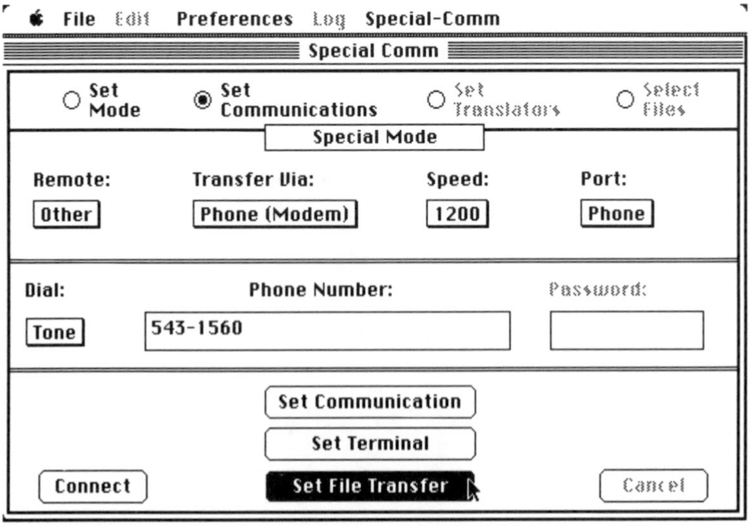

Figure 3-33

Using the Special Mode in MacLink Plus to set special communication and terminal settings, and using a different file transfer protocol.

settings dialog box, and Figure 3-34 shows the Special Mode file transfer settings).

In summary, you can use MacLink Plus in the following ways:

1. MacLink Plus running on both the Macintosh and the PC, with the computers connected directly by cable or over the phone line by modem. This is called MacLink Mode, and you use the MacLink Plus protocol for file transfer as well as MacLink Plus for file translation. Both transfer and translation happen simultaneously.

2. MacLink Plus running on the Macintosh without the need for a connection to the PC; files from the PC can be translated after they are transferred through some other method (communication program or network) to a Macintosh disk. This is called Local Mode.

3. MacLink Plus running on the Macintosh, connected via modem or cable to a PC or other computer running some

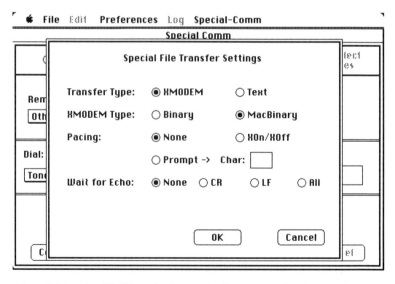

Figure 3-34

After clicking the File Transfer button in the communication settings dialog box, you can choose a different file transfer protocol, such as Xmodem.

other communication program. This is called Special Mode. You can use another file transfer protocol such as Xmodem.

New translators are continually being added to MacLink Plus, so by the time you read this, there may be translators already available in the latest version of the program that will handle special PC and Macintosh formats. We have been describing version 1.0h of the program.

Do-It-Yourself Translation

You can transfer files with ASCII text and use them without translating them, or by using a manual method of substituting control characters with the word processor's search and replace function.

The most important difference is that PC text files have two control characters, Carriage Return and Line Feed, at the end of each line. These control characters cause printers to move their printing heads back to the first column position (Carriage Return) and drop down one line (Line Feed). Macintosh text files usually have only Carriage Returns at the end of each line.

Text files on PC-compatible computers, CP/M computers, and even Radio Shack laptop computers can be transferred to a Macintosh and read into MacWrite. However, it is best to first edit the file on the computer it originated on, creating a copy that has only a Carriage Return at the end of each line and more closely matches the standard ASCII format for the Macintosh.

One easy way to translate text files is to use the PC MacTxt desk accessory for the Macintosh from Tangent Technologies, which can convert straight ASCII, WordStar, or DCA-formatted text to the MacWrite format.

Most word processors on the PC can create a pure unformatted ASCII file as well as a highly formatted file. Some applications, such as WordStar, do not create a pure ASCII file unless you use "non-document mode" or a similar feature. If you use WordStar on a PC or CP/M system, you should edit the file in WordStar's non-document mode, or use a utility program such as UNWS, available in the public domain, which will strip out control characters to make a pure ASCII file. On CP/M systems, you can use the PIP command with the Z option. You should also perform the search and replace function in non-document mode.

For most text file transfers, first use the search and replace function on the PC's word processor (such as WordStar) to substitute dummy markers for all the places where one actually wants to have Carriage Return/Line Feed combinations, such as single lines, titles, subtitles, and the ends of paragraphs. Then do a substitution to replace each remaining Carriage Return/Line Feed combination with one space, so that words at the ends of lines do not merge with words at the beginnings of subsequent lines. Finally substitute a Carriage Return for every dummy marker.

After transferring the file to a Macintosh, if you open it using MacWrite, which asks if you want Carriage Returns in the file to signify ends of lines or paragraphs, click the Paragraph button (Figure 3-35); otherwise, MacWrite strips out all Carriage Returns and you have to put them back in by hand. Microsoft Word opens a text file prepared in this manner without asking this question.

Graphics files, such as Encapsulated PostScript files and files formatted in TIFF (Tag Image File Format), can be

Should a Carriage Return signify a new paragraph or a line break?

[**Paragraphs**]   [**Line Breaks**]   [Cancel]

Figure 3-35

MacWrite displays this dialog box for foreign text files; the Lines button strips all Carriage Returns out of the file, and the Paragraph button leaves them in.

transferred without any problems and without any need for translating them, as long as you use an error-checking protocol with the communication software, or transfer them by network software. PostScript files are simple ASCII text anyway, so it is usually no problem to send it over a modem, cable, or network. However, these files can be huge, and network traffic could slow down considerably when you transfer a large, complex image that occupies over 200K. Do such transfers when everyone else on the network is at lunch or on break.

Although PostScript is very efficient for transferring line art and business graphics (vectors, geometric shapes, and other graphic objects with text), it does not compress a bit-mapped or scanned image. The TIFF (Tag Image File Format), now being accepted by most scanner manufacturers, provides ways to compress graphic files so that they can be easily transferred across a network.

Complete PageMaker publication files can be transferred to and from PCs and Macintosh computers, but object-oriented graphics and large images placed in those files cannot cross the Mac/PC border unless they are expressed in Post-Script and transferred separately. TIFF files should also be transferred separately.

4 The AppleTalk Network System

And the world will be as one. — John Lennon

Every Macintosh and LaserWriter has the built-in potential to be used in an AppleTalk network using the AppleTalk Personal Network cable. An AppleTalk network can grow to almost any size because it is not limited by the hardware or the method of cabling.

The term "AppleTalk" is an adjective describing a complete system of communications among computers and devices. It is not only possible to extend a single AppleTalk network beyond the physical limitations of the cable (using modems to connect to other computers anywhere in the world), it is also possible to replace your current AppleTalk cable with a different cable and still use the same AppleTalk-compatible network software. Within the AppleTalk system framework you have many choices of cabling methods and software that provides network services.

The significance of the AppleTalk system approach to networking is that any computer in a branch of a very large AppleTalk network can communicate with any other computer in any other branch, and that your Macintosh has the ability to communicate with all computers and use all devices on the entire network, no matter which cabling methods are used in other places in the network.

Since all models of Macintosh computers and LaserWriters are supplied with standard ports for the AppleTalk Personal Network cable connectors, you automatically have a simple AppleTalk network whenever you connect a LaserWriter to a Macintosh — all you need are more connectors, more cable, and software to manage file transfers and electronic mail to complete the picture.

AppleTalk networks can start with a simple structure (Figure 4-1) and expand with more Macintoshes and LaserWriters simply by adding cable and connectors, without any changes to existing hardware. A Macintosh can be designated as a message center for electronic mail software (Figure 4-2). Each

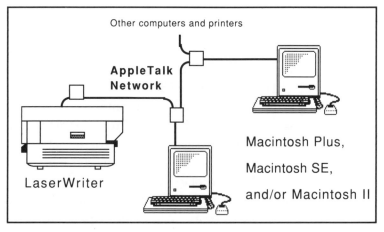

Figure
4-1
The simplest AppleTalk network consists of a Macintosh and a Laser-Writer.

Macintosh can then send and receive messages to and from anyone on the network.

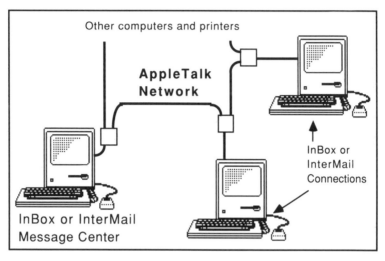

Figure 4-2

With more Macintosh computers it is feasible to add electronic mail software and a message center.

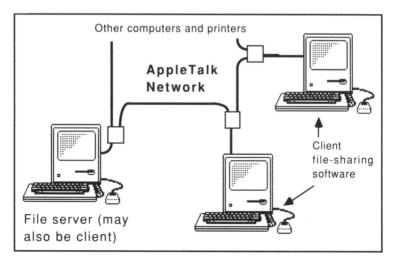

Figure 4-3

When you need file sharing on a regular basis, you can select one or more Macintosh computers to provide file-sharing service for the "client" computers on the network.

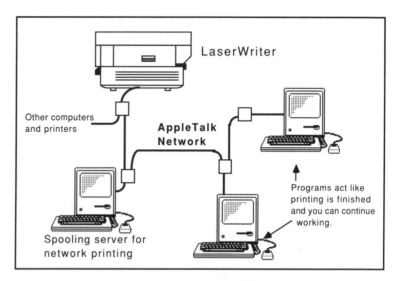

*Figure
4-4*

One benefit of dedicating a Macintosh to file service is the concurrent ability for it to control one or more printers and provide network spooling service.

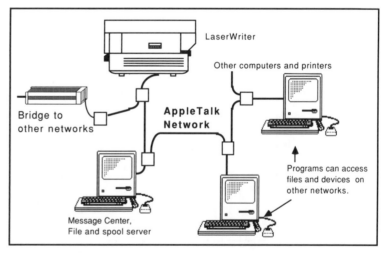

*Figure
4-5*

Within an AppleTalk internet, a bridge device links one network to another so that users of one network can share resources of the others.

When you have enough computers and need to share files more than just occasionally, you can dedicate a Macintosh to providing a file-sharing service (Figure 4-3). This dedicated Macintosh could also serve as the electronic mail message center, and as a server for spooling print jobs from the network (Figure 4-4) so that client computers can go back to work without waiting for print jobs to finish.

AppleTalk networks can also be linked so that users of one network can share resources, such as laser printers and file servers, on the other network. A link between two AppleTalk

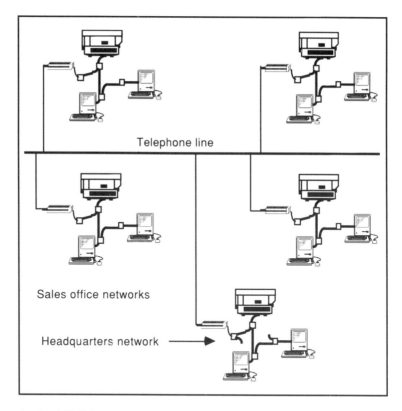

Figure
4-6

An AppleTalk internet: sales offices can use a different type of cable and bridge device, and still communicate effectively with the AppleTalk network at headquarters.

networks is called a *bridge* (Figure 4-5), and a set of linked networks is called an *internet*.

For example, you might have the sales offices of a corporation linked via bridges to headquarters in one large AppleTalk internet. Each sales office might have its own AppleTalk Personal Network with a bridge device and modem to connect with the network at headquarters. One sales office may be so large that it has an AppleTalk network from DuPont that uses fiber-optic cable. Headquarters may be using an AppleTalk network from Northern Telecom that uses private branch exchange (PBX) phone network cabling (Figure 4-6). Finally, a research and development wing may be using AppleTalk network software and servers over a high-speed network cabling system called Ethernet, with a bridge device to communicate with headquarters.

The significant factor is that AppleTalk networks can use a variety of cabling options and bridge devices to link different types of networks into one internet, and yet, each user of each

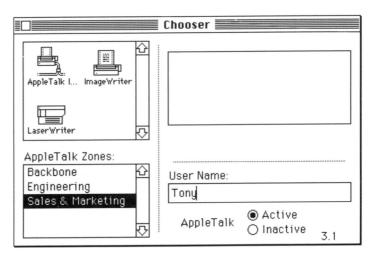

Figure 4-7

Using the Chooser to select another zone (a named group of one or more networks) within an internet in order to use resources, such as printers and servers, in that zone.

network can choose printers and file servers on other networks in the internet just as easily as they can choose printers and servers on their own network. Users on all networks can exchange electronic mail between message centers or use one message center for the entire internet.

When networks are linked, you can assign the same *zone* name to one or more networks, and they act as one. The Chooser desk accessory (Figure 4-7) lets you choose any device in a zone, and you can access linked networks outside of a zone by typing the zone name. A zone is a logical group of networks — each network belongs to a zone, which can contain many networks or only one.

One of the more important uses of zones is to manage high-volume networks and distribute the load and share devices in different zones. By segmenting an internet into zones, you can establish controls to ensure proper management of the servers and resources.

Levels of Networking

When we refer to an AppleTalk network, we are not describing the cable, nor are we describing the software that provides network services. To understand where AppleTalk fits into your system, refer to the chart in Figure 4-8.

At the top of the chart is the program that performs operations on the network, such as file sharing or electronic mail. At the bottom is the physical cable that carries the information. The AppleTalk system defines communication protocols that handle all levels between the top (application) and bottom (physical).

At the bottom level (the physical cable), Apple offers the AppleTalk Personal Network cable that can transfer data at the rate of about 234 kilobits per second. You can substitute DuPont's fiber optic cable, Northern Telecom's PBX cable, or other cabling methods at this level to extend the network beyond the limitations of the Personal Network cable.

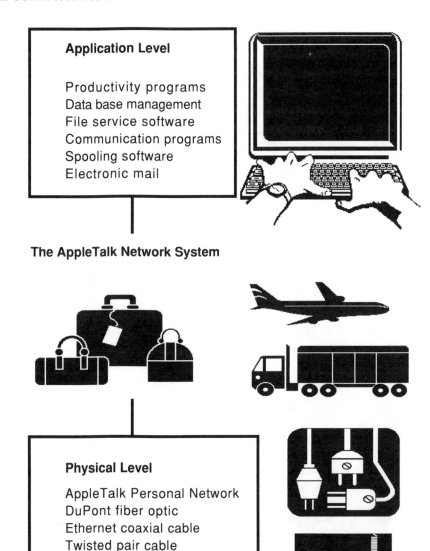

Application Level

Productivity programs
Data base management
File service software
Communication programs
Spooling software
Electronic mail

The AppleTalk Network System

Physical Level

AppleTalk Personal Network
DuPont fiber optic
Ethernet coaxial cable
Twisted pair cable
Telephone cable

Figure
4-8

The AppleTalk network system lies between your network operations and applications software and the cabling system.

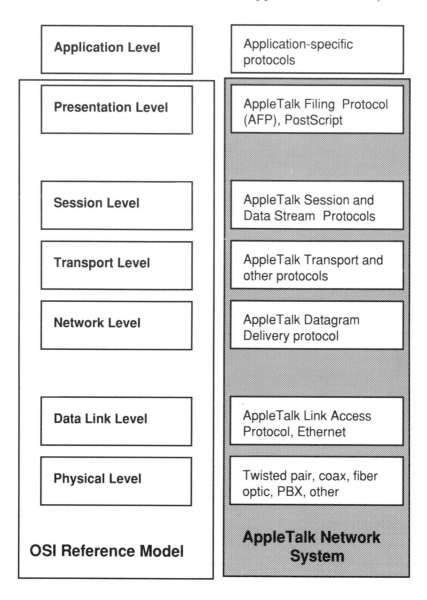

Figure 4-9   The Open Systems International Reference Model and AppleTalk .

At the next higher level, the *data link* level, the AppleTalk Link Access Protocol controls how the data is linked to the cabling medium for transmission and reception. At this level you can substitute other link-level networks, such as Ethernet (a widely-used network for PCs and UNIX systems) and IBM's Token Ring network. For example, the EtherTalk card lets you attach Ethernet cable directly to a Macintosh II and run AppleTalk network software using Ethernet as a backbone.

The middle levels are defined in the AppleTalk network system to coincide with a standard network diagram called the Open Systems International Reference Model (Figure 4-9), which is used as a framework to understand how different networks can establish communication and support the same higher-level software. The idea is that networks from one set of vendors (such as PC networks) will grow and become compatible with other networks (such as AppleTalk networks).

The OSI Reference Model can be compared to the network of transportation in the civilized world. At the very bottom level we have roads, highways, airports, terminals, and ports. At the middle level is the system (red lights, sea lanes, air traffic controllers) by which traffic is controlled. This middle level corresponds to the AppleTalk session, transport, and network levels. (You might say we have travel agents and ticket clerks at the top who steer us through the transportation system.)

As the analogy suggests, when data traffic increases, overall network activities tend to slow down. The slowest and shortest highway is the AppleTalk Personal Network cable, but faster and longer highways can be built to provide the same network services with better network performance.

AppleTalk Cabling and Extensions

The AppleTalk system defines a set of protocols for establishing two-way communications using packets of information. To communicate in the AppleTalk system, a computer or device sends information along with the address of the destination computer or device to the cable's connection box, where it is broadcast across the entire network. All devices are listening for messages addressed to them.

The AppleTalk protocols can be implemented on almost any type of physical cable and support almost any number of users, not just the physical cable supplied with Apple's AppleTalk Personal Network connector kits. For example, DuPont offers a fiber optic cable implementation, and Northern Telecom offers a PBX implementation. Farallon Computing offers conventional telephone cable with repeaters for long distances. Hayes offers the InterBridge device for linking AppleTalk Personal Networks or Farallon's PhoneNET networks in an internet.

AppleTalk Personal Network

No matter what your network plan is for the future, you can probably start with the inexpensive AppleTalk Personal Network and build up to an internet of different types of networks. The AppleTalk Personal Network cable costs $75 per Macintosh or LaserWriter connection, plus expansion cables.

The basic AppleTalk Personal Network can accommodate up to 32 devices, including computers, printers, file services, modems, and serial device connectors. There are many ways to extend it beyond 32 devices, but the stock AppleTalk Personal Network connector kits and cable from Apple support a network that is limited to 32 devices, although it can be extended in various ways.

The network topology for the AppleTalk Personal Network cabling is a straight line, not a circle (Figure 4-10). As shown in the topology diagram in Figure 4-11, an AppleTalk Personal Network can be set up so that expansion is painless. Just remember two rules: don't leave a cable dangling from a network without a connection, and don't connect the Personal Network cable in a circle — always connect it in a straight

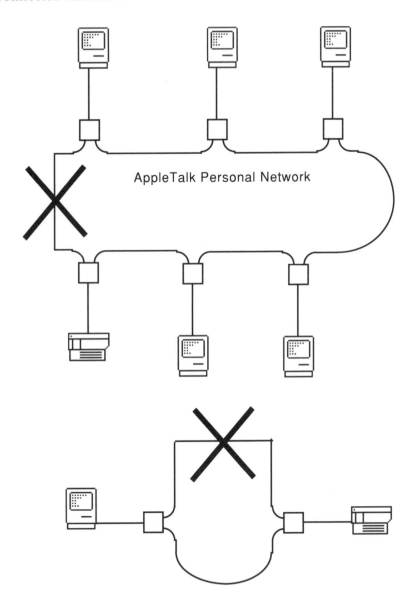

AppleTalk Personal Network

Figure
4-10

The AppleTalk Personal Network topology is a straight line, not a circle.

Proposed AppleTalk Personal Network

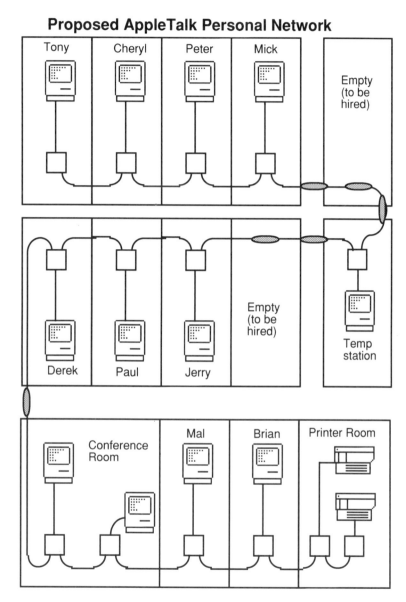

Figure 4-11

Topology for an extensive AppleTalk Personal Network (with Apple cabling) that can be expanded easily.

line, because the cable is designed for a linear *bus* network. The Personal Network cable can establish a network that is as long as 1000 feet (300 meters), which can be extended with bridges to other networks (such as the Hayes InterBridge, described later).

The AppleTalk Personal Network cable connects at one end to the computer or device, and has a connection box (Figure 4-12) at the other end for connecting extender cables to other connection boxes. You can connect the cable to either the printer or modem port of a Macintosh, then change the Chooser setting to show that the AppleTalk Personal Network port is activated (Figure 4-13).

Once this setting is established, AppleTalk's device icons (such as the LaserWriter) show up in the Chooser's window. You can add an AppleTalk Personal Network port to ImageWriter II printers by installing the ImageWriter II AppleTalk Option.

Figure
4-12

AppleTalk Personal Network connection box and cables; one connection box and cable is required for each computer and device.

The AppleTalk Personal Network cable has two limitations: only 32 devices (including printers and computers) can be connected to a single network, and the cable itself can't go beyond 1000 feet. Two products that circumvent these limitations are the Hayes InterBridge, which links two separate networks either directly or through the use of modems, and Farallon Computing's PhoneNET, which is a replacement for the AppleTalk cable that can extend up to 4000 feet. Farallon also offers network repeaters to extend a network even further and a network controller to connect 12 separate networks into one large network.

Hayes InterBridge

One of the more widely-used bridge devices for linking AppleTalk networks is the Hayes InterBridge (Hayes Microcomputer Products, $799). You can use the InterBridge either by itself or with a 2400 bps modem such as the Hayes Smart-

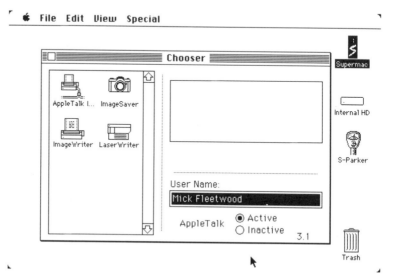

Figure
4-13

Activating AppleTalk with the Chooser.

modem 2400 (1200 bps is usually too slow for file sharing). The InterBridge works with any combination of Macintosh 512K, Plus, SE, and II computers and with all network service software and file servers described in Chapter 5.

You connect AppleTalk cable directly to the InterBridge device and run the Manager application to assign a network number and unique zone name to the network ports. Once installed, InterBridge bridges are transparent to users, who select zones in the Chooser window. The Chooser shows you the devices that are installed in a particular zone, and you can change the zone name to see devices in other zones.

InterBridge is most often used to connect two AppleTalk Personal Networks to form one internet with more than 32 stations. You can link as many as 15 networks using one bridge to connect each two networks. Another cabling system, Farallon's PhoneNET (described next), is compatible with the InterBridge and provides more than 32 network stations, or *nodes*.

By breaking up one network into several zones, you can restrict high-volume traffic to one or more zones and insulate other zones. To help identify traffic jams on a network, InterBridge can generate a diagnostic report that shows traffic problems and verifies that a network is working properly.

Farallon PhoneNET

Farallon Computing offers a range of AppleTalk-based network cabling products that let you extend the effective range of an AppleTalk network beyond 1000 feet and use inexpensive telephone wire for connections.

You can connect to the PhoneNET network at any location where you have a telephone — most telephone cables have four wires, but only two are used for telephone traffic, so you can use the other two for AppleTalk traffic. One PhoneNET

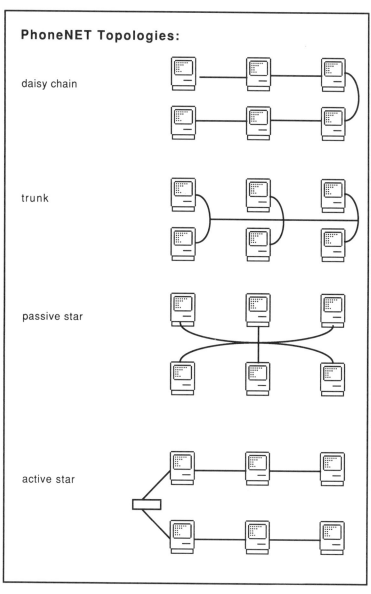

PhoneNET Topologies:

daisy chain

trunk

passive star

active star

Figure
4-14

Farallon Computing's PhoneNET cabling products can extend an
AppleTalk network beyond the limits of Apple's AppleTalk cable, using
standard telephone wire in various topologies.

connector is required for each device (printer, computer, etc.) connected to the network; you can mix AppleTalk Personal Network connectors and cable with PhoneNET connectors and telephone cable.

A PhoneNET network can be structured with four basic network topologies — daisy chain, trunk, passive star, and active star — and combinations of them (Figure 4-14). The rule about AppleTalk cabling still applies: no circular or loop connections.

The daisy topology is common for small installations where all devices are in the same room — It can be quickly constructed using modular telephone extension cables and RJ11-mounted terminating resistors supplied with each PhoneNET connector. You can use 26-gauge wire for daisy-type networks, with no more than 20 connectors (use trunk or star for more devices), and have a total network length of up to 2000 feet. You can remove a connector and split a daisy-type network into two separate networks.

If you want a longer network, and don't mind the expense of installing new cable rather than using existing telephone wire, you can still use inexpensive cable by using a trunk topology. Trunk topology consists of a single cable linking RJ11 modular wall boxes installed at each device location (up to 4000 feet using 22-gauge solid copper unshielded "telephone station" wall cable for the trunk). You attach a Phone-NET connector to each device and an extension cable to connect the device to the nearest wall box. You can disconnect from a trunk-type network without disturbing other users, and small daisy-chain networks can be connected as branches to a trunk.

To take further advantage of existing telephone wiring, you can use a passive star topology, in which six branches, or spokes, are connected at a central location, or hub. A branch can be a trunk with daisy chains connected to it. The sum of all branches equals the total network length, which can be up to 4000 feet.

For longer networks with more branches, you can use an active star topology that can have a network length (the sum of all branches) of 36,000 feet. An active star topology requires the use of Farallon's StarController, which has ports for 12 branches that can each be 3000 feet. The StarController operates by itself and can be controlled from a Macintosh running StarCommand software, which can monitor, test, and reconfigure the network.

Buildings have telephone cables that usually run from each telephone extension to a central location in the building (either a "terminal block" or a "punch down block") where they connect to service lines from the phone company. The wiring is similar to a star topology, which is why PhoneNET is set up to be configured in active or passive star topologies.

Farallon also supplies adaptors for using older computer wire such as RS-232 cabling, DEC Connect Cabling, and various IBM cabling systems. Farallon's Repeater, installed every 3000 feet, boosts signals to extend any part of a network beyond 4000 feet. You can also use a Repeater to separate a network into two networks (forming an internet).

Farallon also offers the CheckNET desk accessory for use with any AppleTalk network regardless of cabling schemes and topologies. CheckNET lets you see which devices are attached to the network and lets you search for specific devices or device types (Figure 4-15). CheckNET can also be configured to check other zones. If there is a problem in the connection, CheckNET will not find the name of the device. You can use CheckNET when you first set up an AppleTalk network, and periodically check the status of a network and test connections to devices.

Northern Telecom Meridian PBX

Another cabling option for an AppleTalk network is to use a private branch exchange (PBX) which may also have mainframes and minicomputers attached to it. Northern Telecom has already installed approximately 17,000 Meridian PBX integrated services (voice and data) networks, which can manage phone systems as well as data exchange.

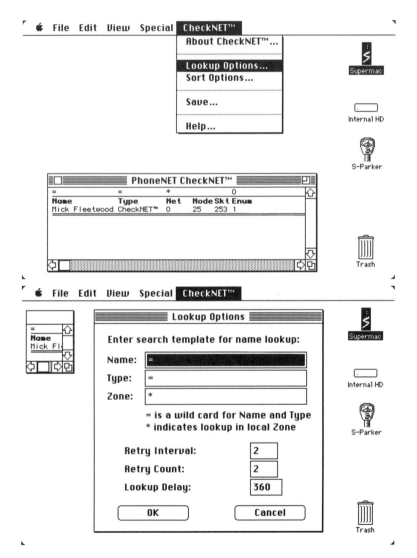

Figure
4-15

Farallon's CheckNET desk accessory lets you track down problems in any AppleTalk network.

Each Macintosh can connect to the phone system through the LANSTAR connection and a standard RJ11 phone jack. In addition, you can link separate AppleTalk networks with the Meridian PBX, use LaserWriter printers anywhere on the network, and perform file transfers and file conversion with a version of MacLink Plus (described in Chapter 3).

When used in conjunction with the Hayes InterBridge, the Meridian SL-1 can join separate AppleTalk networks into a common network sharing file servers, printers, and other devices even if they are in different buildings. The PBX is perhaps the best way to extend a Macintosh network over great distances. Individual AppleTalk networks can be located up to 4,000 feet from the Meridian SL-1 for a total of 8,000 feet, and a data speed of 9600 bps. You can access up to four networks directly and "dial up" other networks on the PBX. All Macintosh users connected to the Meridian SL-1 can remotely access any LaserWriter printer (up to 8,000 feet) as if it were connected directly to their AppleTalk network. To access the LaserWriter, a user selects a special printer driver icon in the Chooser, which displays a list of available LaserWriters. Also, a user with a modem can call into the PBX from home and gain access to a LaserWriter.

The Meridian PBX system will seem extravagant to those who have not yet needed an integrated voice and data network. However, voice and data networks are going to be important in the future, as IBM continues its development efforts to implement its Integrated Systems Digital Network for voice and data traffic. You can expect that such a network will offer, on a larger scale, the same kinds of features offered by Northern Telecom with its Meridian PBX.

DuPont Fiber Optics

DuPont Connector Systems offers an AppleTalk network based on fiber optic cable. Compared to copper wire, fiber optic cable has a higher signal bandwidth, greater transmission range, improved data security, and immunity to radio-frequency interference (RFI) or electromagnetic interference (EMI). As a result, signals can travel a greater distance without degradation, with fewer errors from noise.

Over 100 computers almost a mile apart can be connected into a network, and the hardy fiber optic cable is suitable for industrial use. Each computer and device is linked to a signal converter by a cable connected directly to an AppleTalk Personal Network port. The signal converter converts electrical signals from the computer and devices into optical signals which are transmitted across the network. Users never know the difference, because there is no difference in what the user does — AppleTalk file servers and multi-user software work just as if they were running on an AppleTalk Personal Network.

The fiber optic cable's ability to work over a great distance is convenient for routing cable underneath floors and throughout a building, and its light weight makes it easy to install. You can employ fiber optic wall outlets so that you can move computers and devices and still connect them to the building's network. From wall outlets cable can be routed in either a daisy chain topology (as with PhoneNET) or to a concentrator in a star topology, which is usually stored in a wiring closet; to reconfigure the network, you only need to switch cables on the concentrator panel.

DuPont's fiber optic network is the best choice for setting up an entire building with a network. All Macintosh users on the network (and PC users who are connected with AppleTalk PC adaptor cards) can share resources of the entire building, including printers, file servers, and modems.

AppleTalk on a Backbone Network

The AppleTalk Network System can be implemented as a network protocol using another network as a backbone at the Data Link Level, as long as the other network conforms to the

OSI reference model for open systems (a framework for an international standard network architecture).

Networks that can be used as a backbone include the popular Ethernet network and IBM's Token Ring network. In both cases, the AppleTalk suite of protocols run unobtrusively on top of the existing network without changing the network or its protocols. Users gain the benefit of the AppleTalk Network System services without losing whatever network services they already use.

This compatibility is achieved because the AppleTalk Network System was designed to be independent of the hardware and cabling methods used. The nuts and bolts of a network can change while the system of communicating remains the same, requiring no retraining.

Ethernet is a network architecture endorsed by Xerox, DEC, Intel, and now Apple, and it is the most popular network for office automation with largest installed base. It is also the first network to be targeted by Apple for acting as a backbone for AppleTalk, and connection devices are available from Apple, 3Com Corporation, and Kinetics.

The AppleTalk Network System provides a framework for a multiplicity of connection methods. For example, you have at least three connection choices in order to use Ethernet as a backbone for an AppleTalk network:

1. Connect an AppleTalk Personal Network of up to 32 devices to an Ethernet network using a bridge device such as the FastPath from Kinetics. This choice is less expensive per user, but slower since it is limited by the speed of the Personal Network (about 234 kilobits per second).

2. Connect individual Macintosh computers to Ethernet using a SCSI-based gateway device such as the Kinetics Ether-SC. Although it is more expensive per user, throughput is faster and Macintosh Plus computers can be connected directly to Ethernet.

3. Use an Ethernet network adaptor card in a Macintosh II, such as Apple's EtherTalk, or a card for the Macintosh SE such

as the Kinetics EtherPort SE, to directly connect those computers to Ethernet.

If you are planning to share a large data base, the direct connection choice is usually the best bet because it performs more quickly. However, if you use different models of Macintosh computers throughout a building that is wired for Ethernet, you may be better off with a mixed-vendor solution, employing Apple's EtherTalk for Macintosh II computers and the Kinetics FastPath bridge to link Personal Networks to the Ethernet network.

3Com Corporation's 3+ network, based on Ethernet and controlled by the 3+Share file server, is also a good choice for linking either Macintosh II computers or AppleTalk Personal Networks to Ethernet. 3Com's 3+Route is a bridge device that can link an AppleTalk Personal Network to Ethernet and Token Ring networks. Also, 3Com offers inexpensive twisted-pair cables as well as the usual thin and thick coaxial cables for its Ethernet network. The 3+Share server is described in Chapter 5.

EtherTalk: AppleTalk on Ethernet

The EtherTalk adaptor card lets you connect a Macintosh II directly to Ethernet cabling. Ethernet offers high-speed (up to 10 megabits per second) data transfer, although many Ethernet implementations for PC networks obtain approximately 1 megabit per second throughput. The advantage of Ethernet is that many more devices and computers can be added without degrading performance. EtherTalk, an implementation of the AppleTalk Network System using Ethernet as a backbone, can achieve speeds up to 2.4 megabits per second with normal network traffic.

The EtherTalk Interface Card ($699) includes software that provides transparent networking so that the Ethernet network appears the same as a Personal Network. AppleShare,

LaserShare, and other AppleTalk network service products are one hundred percent compatible. The software places a device icon in the Control Panel associated with the NET-WORK icon that lets you choose either the built-in AppleTalk Personal Network or EtherTalk (Figure 4-16).

As with the AppleTalk Personal Network, services are located and selected by using the Chooser. You can connect a LaserWriter directly to the Ethernet network using an an EtherTalk-compatible bridge such as the Kinetics FastPath 3, which connects to an AppleTalk Personal Network port.

The increase in performance of an EtherTalk network over the AppleTalk Personal Network is ten-fold — this by itself is the major reason why users requiring fast throughput are switching to Macintosh II computers and EtherTalk. Before, network cable was a limiting factor in performance; with EtherTalk-based Ethernet networks, disks and operating systems on servers are limiting factors.

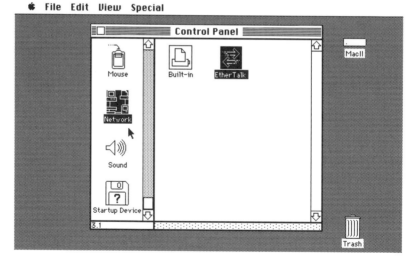

Figure
4-16

EtherTalk on the Macintosh II appears as an icon in the Control Panel, where you can choose between AppleTalk on Ethernet and the built-in AppleTalk Personal Network.

Connections to Ethernet: Kinetics and 3Com

Kinetics offers three methods for connecting Macintosh computers to the Ethernet network:

FastPath 3 — a bridge device ($2750) that connects an AppleTalk network to the Ethernet network, which provides both AppleTalk and TCP/IP (Transmission Control Protocol/Internet Protocol) which is widely used for communication between UNIX systems. A version of FastPath called FastPath 3 ($2750) includes an internal transceiver for connecting to Thin Ethernet (a full Ethernet implemented on inexpensive twisted-pair cable).

EtherSC — a device ($1250) that connects individual Macintosh computers to Ethernet using the Macintosh SCSI port (you can still use the port for additional hard disks and other SCSI devices).

EtherPortSE — a card ($850) for the Macintosh SE that connects it to Ethernet.

You can use any combination of these devices to connect computers to Ethernet (Figures 5-17). Since Ethernet connections are available with various mainframes and minicomputers, third-party vendors such as Kinetics, Alisa Systems, and Pacer Software offer mainframe-based and minicomputer-based software systems for connecting to AppleTalk networks using Ethernet as a backbone. Some of these offerings are described in Chapter 6.

3Com offers the Ethernet-based 3+ network of PCs and Macintosh computers managed by a file server ($495 for unlimited Macintosh users on an existing server and 3+ network). You can attach an AppleTalk Personal Network to the 3Com 3Server3 hardware device, which is a dedicated file server with hard disks and printers. Any computer on the Ethernet network running 3+ network software can access files on the server or use the server's printers. Macintosh users can use PC files and PC users can use Macintosh files on the same server, running on the 3+ network.

The internet feature of 3Com's 3+ network is very powerful.

The 3+Route bridge device can link diverse networks of PCs and Macintosh into one internet for sharing files and devices. AppleTalk Personal Networks, Ethernet networks, and Token

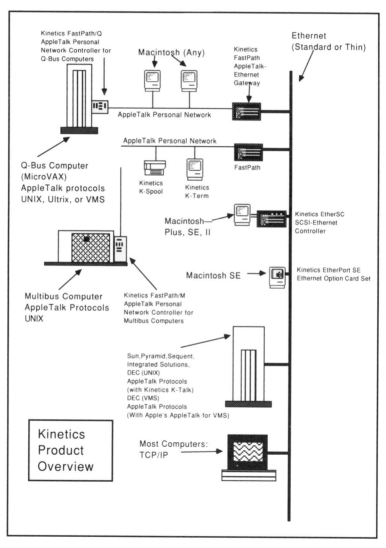

Figure
4-17

Kinetics' FastPath 3 connects an AppleTalk Personal Network to Ethernet, and its EtherSC and EtherPort SE connect Macintosh Plus and SE computers directly to Ethernet, which can also support mainframes and minicomputers.

187

Ring networks can be linked in a 3+ internet using 3+Route. Despite the fact that the networks are fundamentally different, users see no difference in network software operation. 3Com's network products can use either thick or thin coaxial cable or inexpensive twisted-pair cable.

The 3+Share file server software is the key to compatibility across 3Com's networks. 3+Share can run on a 3Com server on the same network at the same time as AppleShare on a dedicated Macintosh, and is described in detail in Chapter 5.

Other Networks as Backbones

By the time you read this, several products linking the AppleTalk Personal Network to Token Ring networks will be available, using Token Ring as a backbone in the same way that Ethernet is used. There will also be several products for connecting a Macintosh II or SE directly to a Token Ring network.

The AppleTalk Network System will be used by some of the largest network vendors, such as 3Com, Novell, and Ungermann-Bass. Some of these companies will implement AppleTalk on top of an existing network configuration (such as 3Com's 3+ network), and others will implement AppleTalk on top of Token Ring. Still others will implement the AppleTalk Personal Network on high-performance cable.

Since the AppleTalk Personal Network cable has proliferated with the spread of Macintosh computers and LaserWriters, you can expect that future network solutions will incorporate *gateways* (devices to link separate types of networks, such as Ethernet to Token Ring) to existing AppleTalk Personal Networks, just as there are gateways between IBM and Digital Equipment Corporation networks.

Incorporating a mainframe or minicomputer network with a personal computer network can be simple or complex, depending on your applications. The desire to link to larger systems may influence your decision on what to use for an

AppleTalk network. You can base a network on mainframes and minicomputers and run the AppleTalk Network System on top of it, using it as a backbone; or you can use gateways to connect an AppleTalk network to another type of network. Sometimes an application is better served by connecting a Macintosh directly to a mainframe or minicomputer. Since there are so many alternatives, you should read Chapter 5 for information about AppleTalk Network Services, then Chapter 6 for information about mainframe and minicomputer connection alternatives, to get the full picture of your future network needs.

5   AppleTalk Network Services

As we live a life of ease,
Ev'ry one of us has all we need...
—John Lennon/Paul McCartney

The reason for connecting computers in a network is to share devices and files so that every user has access to them. The products that provide methods for sharing these resources are called *network services.*

The three main types of services are file sharing (or disk sharing), electronic mail routing, and print spooling. Some services can be combined on a single, dedicated computer or piece of hardware acting as a server; for example, AppleShare can provide file service for an entire network, and InBox can provide electronic mail for the same network while running simultaneously on the same computer with the AppleShare file server.

There are basically two types of file servers: dedicated file servers, such as Apple's AppleShare and 3Com's 3+Share, and background file servers, such as TOPS and General Computer's HyperNet. They represent two paradigms for sharing files on a network — the centralized model, in which a dedicated server managed by a network administrator holds all files to be shared on the network, and the distributed model, in which each user's computer on the network can also act as a server, and each user has the responsibility to maintain the files shared on his/her server computer.

Dedicated file servers require dedicated hardware, but you can usually add other services to run on this hardware. For example, you can dedicate a Macintosh Plus for file service using Apple's AppleShare, and add LaserShare, Apple's dedicated print server, thus offering both file and print service to the entire network (and to other networks over bridges). The expense of dedicating a computer and hard disk to this type of service is outweighed by the need for management and control features. You can also put the InBox electronic mail center on the same AppleShare server.

Background servers do not require a dedicated computer or piece of hardware — they let you share folders stored on almost any disk drive connected to any Macintosh on the network. While it is possible for all users of a network to actively share folders on drives connected to different computers, the distributed model as offered by TOPS and HyperNet does not offer as many security features as the centralized model offered by AppleShare and 3+Share.

For casual file sharing, the distributed model using background servers is preferred; for intense file sharing, the centralized model using a dedicated server is preferred. If your needs are somewhere between casual and intense file sharing, and you choose the distributed model to save the expense of dedicating hardware to services, you will have to institute volunteer management controls to maintain shared files. You wouldn't want a user on the network whose folders are currently being shared to suddenly turn off his/her system, disrupting file sharing operations. Dedicated servers by their nature are usually managed by someone, so there is less likelihood of disruption. Both types of file servers can operate with electronic mail message centers and with printer spoolers.

An alternative to file sharing is disk sharing with a product such as MacServe (Infosphere). MacServe is a *disk server* that let users share parts of a hard disk. MacServe lets you partition a hard disk into *volumes* (separate areas) that can be shared with other users, under certain access restrictions. Sharing a disk drive is fundamentally simpler and less expensive than sharing folders and files, but does not provide the flexibility of file sharing.

Electronic mail increases the productivity of users on a network by reducing the interruptions that would normally occur when people need to get messages to each other, and it can be preferable to face-to-face conversation for any number of reasons. Most importantly, electronic mail is a must for networks that are bridged over a long distance. Inside Apple Computer's headquarters, for example, there are many networks linked by bridges to other networks, and the company uses electronic mail packages such as InBox and Internet to link everyone in the company into an internal mail service.

Even a single user with a LaserWriter can derive benefit by using network products such as a print spooler, as it greatly reduces the waiting time involved in printing operations by letting you go back to work on your computer while the printing takes place. There are two types of spoolers for a network: a *client spooler,* which spools print jobs from that computer only (other users need their own copies of the client spooler to spool jobs), and a *network spooler,* which runs on a dedicated server and provides a spooling service for everyone on the network.

We have already covered the sharing of modems in Chapter 2, and you share printers simply by connecting them to the network and, when you are ready to print, choosing which printer you want with the Chooser (as shown in Chapter 1). Print spooling is the next logical type of service to add to a network, even if you don't perform file sharing and do not use electronic mail. We cover print spooling first because on some networks, users can become more productive simply by adding this service, without adding other services.

Print Spooling

The most popular activity on small AppleTalk networks is sharing laser printers and typesetters. You can automatically share these devices by simply linking them to an AppleTalk Personal Network (they have built-in ports for connecting the cable). The LaserWriter uses the network to send messages back to users to inform them of the status of the print jobs, so that users on a network know if the printer, which may be at another location, is out of paper or if a paper jam occurred.

Print spoolers let you continue to work on your Macintosh while your documents are being printed. The spooler receives messages from the printer, and whoever's Macintosh is running the spooler can control the spooling operation, promoting some jobs in the priority list above others, terminating other jobs, and reacting to paper-out messages, while other users go on working without any delay.

When you are sharing a printer with other users who are also trying to print, you sometimes get the Printer Busy message and the status of the other print job; during that time you usually have to wait. With a print spooler, you don't have to wait. Your print job is placed in a queue of jobs, and you go back to work. Eventually your print job is handled by the spooler without bothering you. The spooler does not make the printer run faster; it just allows each Macintosh user to be more productive.

Spoolers are programs that intercept data on its way to the printer and store the data in a disk file called a *spool file*. The disk accepts the data faster than the printer, so the Macintosh issuing the print command thinks that printing has finished and returns control to you. The spooler then initiates printing (*despooling*) and queues other print requests.

Print spooling can be complicated on the Macintosh, especially if you are using downloadable fonts, or a special printer preparation file such as PageMaker's Aldus Prep rather than Apple's Laser Prep. This is because the Macintosh System uses the QuickDraw language to describe a page to the Image-Writer, and translates QuickDraw to the PostScript description language for printing on PostScript devices such as the LaserWriter and Linotronic 100 typesetter. The use of two description languages and the appropriate fonts can make spooling a complicated operation.

Most spoolers work by intercepting the data bound for the printer in either of two places: right after the Macintosh constructs QuickDraw commands to describe the page to be printed, or right after the Macintosh translates the Quick-Draw commands to PostScript. Usually a spooler that intercepts at the QuickDraw stage is faster at freeing up the Macintosh than a spooler that waits until after PostScript conversion.

Other differences between spoolers, besides speed, is how much disk space and memory space is taken up by the spooler and spool files, whether the spooler can handle downloadable fonts and programs such as PageMaker, and how the spooler lets you manage the queue. Spool files created at the Quick-Draw stage are usually smaller than spool files created at the PostScript stage.

The basic difference between a client spooler and a network spooler is that a network spooler offers spooling for all users on the network from a dedicated server, and a client spooler offers spooling from any individual Macintosh on the net-work. Both types of spoolers can manage the sharing of a PostScript printer with multiple users on a network.

The most popular spoolers for the Macintosh are Laser-Speed (Think Technologies, $99 per user), LaserServe (Infosphere, $95 per user), and SuperLaserSpool (SuperMac Software, $150 per user). Apple has just introduced another spooler, PrintMaster, supplied with the MultiFinder as a background application. All these are client spoolers that run on individual Macintosh computers. SuperLaserSpool comes in a multiuser package for five users, but essentially offers client spooling from each Macintosh. The popular network spooler, LaserShare, is described by itself after the descriptions of the client spoolers.

SuperLaserSpool for Client Spooling

Of the client spoolers, SuperLaserSpool offers the most features and the best overall performance. The spooler works with the ImageWriter as well as LaserWriter and other PostScript devices (such as the Linotronic typesetters), and intercepts data at the QuickDraw level, saving compact QuickDraw code in the spool file. SuperLaserSpool uses less disk space than other spoolers that store PostScript (which takes up more space), and offers a Preview function that lets you display pages while they are in the print queue.

Another great feature of SuperLaserSpool is the ability to take spool files and despool them on another Macintosh running SuperLaserSpool. For example, you could take spool files to your typesetting service and despool them without running the application program; however, you may need the downloadable font files and prep files associated with the application. You can also designate a folder on a published TOPS volume that resides on another Macintosh, then ship spool files to that volume for spooling from that Macintosh. This is a casual form of network spooling for those who are already casually sharing files with a background file server like TOPS or HyperNet, or a disk server like MacServe.

The only drawback of this feature-laden program is that it takes up more RAM than other spoolers. However, you can specify small, medium, or large amounts of memory to be occupied, and SuperLaserSpool lets you suspend its operation and regain memory for other uses.

SuperLaserSpool

You install SuperLaserSpool by double-clicking its icon. The spooler displays a dialog box for changing the memory settings (Figure 5-1). To leave this box on the screen, click anywhere quickly, otherwise it disappears and the spooler installs itself with its normal memory setting. You can have SuperLaserSpool automatically install itself every time you start your Macintosh with the same System Folder — first select the spooler's icon, then use the Set Startup command in the Finder's Special menu. You can also direct SuperLaser-Spool to automatically "chain" to another program — that is, launch another program after installing itself. Use this feature if you already have a Startup program set and you want to make SuperLaserSpool the Startup program.

To print with SuperLaserSpool, follow the usual printing procedures, specifying settings in the printing dialog box as usual and choosing your printer on the network with Chooser. SuperLaserSpool remembers the printer you've chosen and uses it for all spooled print jobs. The spooler also creates a file

SuperLaserSpool

Click mouse button to change Spooler Settings.   [Continue...]

Select spool buffer allocation size:

○ Small
● Medium
○ Large

Application to chain to following this launch:

None

[Set Chain...]

SuperLaserSpool Copyright, ©1987 Nick Gault and Andy Nuss

Figure 5-1

SuperMac's SuperLaserSpool installation dialog box lets you change the amount of memory (RAM) used by the spooler.

197

in your system folder called SLS Queue to keep track of print jobs, and a folder called SLS Spool Files (on whatever volume you set for spooling) to hold the spool files. You can copy this folder to another system for despooling from that system.

You don't need the Laser Queue desk accessory to print with SuperLaserSpool, but it is useful. Install Laser Queue in your system with Apple's Font/DA Mover utility; selecting it brings up a dialog box with a window showing the print jobs (Figure 5-2). You can drag to change the order if you check the box for this feature, and select a different disk or volume for the "magic folder" for storing spooled files (this could be a published TOPS volume somewhere out on the network). You can delete print jobs from the queue, and pause the printer for changing paper. When the accessory is on, you can see the usual LaserWriter status messages in its window.

Network priority can be set for each user. Normally AppleTalk handles print requests on a first-come first-served basis, but you can change your priority to high (your print

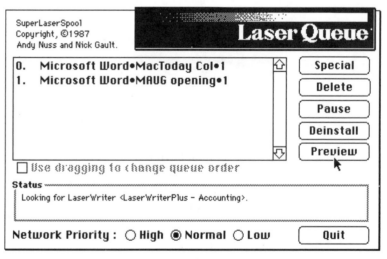

Figure
5-2

SuperLaserSpool's Laser Queue desk accessory presents a window of print jobs, priority buttons, and functions for pausing and deleting jobs and de-installing the spooler.

requests are processed before any others), or low (your requests are handled after all others). Users can defeat this feature by always setting themselves to high priority; in such cases, everyone is still on equal footing. The best situation is to leave everyone at normal, and only switch to high when printing special jobs.

LaserSpeed for Client Spooling

LaserSpeed, from Think Technologies (version 1.5, $99), is a client spooler that spools PostScript files, downloads Prep files, and offers a printer reset function. LaserSpeed uses a desk accessory to manage the print queue and an invisible desk accessory (called a *driver*) to handle despooling. LaserSpeed can spool PageMaker files, send entire PostScript files directly to the printer, and spool with downloadable fonts. Most importantly, LaserSpeed can operate in conjunction with the company's InBox electronic mail service (described later in this chapter).

Installing LaserSpeed is as easy as dragging the installer and spooler files to your System Folder and double-clicking the installer. After restarting the Macintosh, run the desk accessory, LaserSpeed, to display a dialog box with a window of print jobs and another window of LaserWriter messages (Figure 5-3).

LaserSpeed's control buttons are gray when they are turned on and white when off. One button controls printing: turn on the "Print spooled output while I work" button to print, and turn it off to pause printing. Either way, spooling continues as usual, with print jobs collecting in the queue.

You start spooling files by printing as you normally would (using the application's Print command or other printing function), and LaserSpeed intercepts the print job after the computer has translated QuickDraw into PostScript. The spool files (containing PostScript code) are stored on disk, and they are printed by the spooler if you turn on the "Print spooled output while I work" button. During the spooling,

LaserSpeed flashes the LaserWriter icon in place of the Apple logo in the menu bar and displays messages from the printer in the LaserSpeed window (which you can view at any time by using the LaserSpeed accessory).

In the LaserSpeed window containing the names of spooled jobs (output), you can drag a job to be a lower or higher priority to other jobs in the queue. You can also remove jobs.

A unique feature of LaserSpeed is its ability to send laser printer Prep files directly, speeding up all printing operations. Apple supplies a Laser Prep file that most applications can use. The other popular Prep file in use is Aldus Prep for PageMaker. With LaserSpeed you can download either Prep file before spooling; this is a necessary procedure every time you turn on the LaserWriter. If you use an application that does not use Apple's Laser Prep but supplies its own Prep utility, it may not work with LaserSpeed.

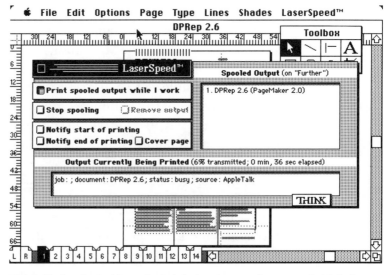

Figure 5-3

Think Technologies' LaserSpeed desk accessory shows spooled jobs in a window in which you can drag jobs to be a lower or higher priority in the queue, or remove jobs.

For PostScript applications that do not use a prep file such as JustText, which prepares complete PostScript files, you can spool the files using the Spool PostScript File command. LaserSpeed also offers a command to reset the printer.

One drawback with LaserSpeed is that it occupies 28K of RAM whether or not you use it. Another problem, common to many spoolers except SuperLaserSpool, is that spool files stored on disk are invisible to the Finder, so you can't move or delete them; after a system crash, if LaserSpeed can't rebuild its queue, the files continue to take up space on disk until you use a disk utility such as Fedit Plus (MacMaster Systems, $40). The workaround for this problem is to use floppy disks for spool files, which can be reformatted quickly and reused.

Other Client Spoolers and Alternatives

Several other spoolers on the market offer different features but are categorized in the same manner: either intercepting at the QuickDraw stage, such as SuperLaserSpool, or intercepting at the PostScript stage, such as LaserSpeed. Most spoolers are client spoolers, although some (like SuperLaserSpool) let you store spool files on a published TOPS folder elsewhere on the network, so that several users can share the spooling features.

Another spooler with similar capabilities is Infosphere's LaserServe, which also offers the ability to spool to an ImageWriter connected to an AppleTalk Personal Network. LaserServe saves font data in the spooled files, which can take up a lot of disk space and remain invisible to the Finder; however, LaserServe does keep track of the files. When an error occurs, LaserServe offers the ability to cancel a job, restart from the beginning, or continue from where the error occurred.

LaserSpool (MacAmerica) was one of the first spoolers available for the Macintosh, and is mentioned here because it may cause trouble to users on a network. It uses a customized

LaserWriter driver based on an early version (3.1) of Apple's driver, which can cause the printer to be reset or simply fail when other users are trying to use upgraded drivers. When a network of users want to share a LaserWriter, the best policy is for every user to use the same version of the LaserWriter driver from Apple, and if possible, use the most recently upgraded version (4.0 as of this writing).

An alternative to using client spoolers is to use a hardware print server, also called a *buffer*, that handles the print jobs for a network. Although a buffer is more expensive than a spooler package, one buffer serves an entire network. The spooled files are stored in the buffer's memory, alleviating storage problems for individual users. Examples of buffers are the MacBuffer LW (Ergotron Corporation, $2295 for one mega-byte of memory, $2695 for two megabytes) and the Laser-Server (DataSpace Corporation, $2295 for two megabytes and five expansion slots).

LaserShare for Network Spooling

Apple offers a network spooler called LaserShare (Apple, $299) that works simultaneously with the AppleShare file server (described later). LaserShare runs on a Macintosh (512KE, Plus, SE, or II) dedicated to file serving and spooling. The program requires a dedicated computer but it does not require AppleShare.

LaserShare manages a LaserWriter or any other printing device on an AppleTalk network that uses the Apple Laser-Writer driver. All print jobs sent to that printer are sent instead to the server computer that is running LaserShare. Spooled jobs are stored on the server's hard disk, and users on the network go back to work immediately without waiting for printing. Besides the time saved, users don't have to store spooled files on their disks.

Following the same strategy as the AppleShare file server, LaserShare is designed to be managed by an administrator who determines the priority of spooled jobs. As administrator you can stop the spooling from network users, stop the despooling to the printer, remove print jobs from the spool queue, move any job to the front of the queue, and print an ID banner page with each job.

LaserShare works with all existing Macintosh applications using normal print commands or functions. LaserShare can be used by anyone on the network — it appears as a Laser-Writer in each user's Chooser window (Figure 5-4), where it can be chosen as a LaserWriter. You can also bypass the spooler and print directly from your computer by choosing the actual printer rather than the LaserShare spooler.

Apple supplies an Installer utility for installing LaserShare with the appropriate Macintosh System. You can install Laser-Share by itself on any Macintosh with a single 800K floppy drive, and dedicate that Macintosh for network spooling. It is recommended, however, that you install LaserShare on a computer that has a hard disk, and use it in conjunction with AppleShare to derive more benefit from dedicating a computer to network services.

LaserShare can be installed so that it displays on the screen (in the *foreground*) while AppleShare runs behind it (in the *background*). You can't monitor AppleShare's activities without first quitting LaserShare's print queue window.

When you quit LaserShare, you can either complete the spooling or printing operations or quit abruptly without completing them. When LaserShare's window is closed, spooled jobs remain on disk ready to be printed. To reopen Laser-Share's print queue window, use the Open LaserShare command in AppleShare's File menu (shown later this chapter).

As users spool jobs for the printer, the print queue window (Figure 5-5) shows the document status, name, user name, date and time of spooling, and number of pages spooled. You can make any print job print next by choosing the Print Next command in the Queue menu. You can remove jobs, and you can maintain and print a log of spooling activity.

The options icons in the status bar (upper right corner of the display) reflect the options you can set when you control a printer using LaserShare (Figure 5-6). You can control

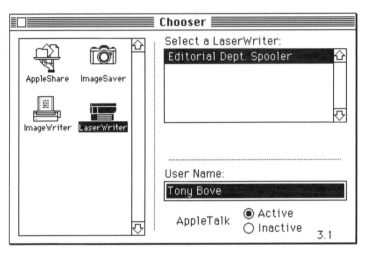

Figure
5-4

Apple's LaserShare server-based network spooler runs on a dedicated computer that could also be a file server; the spooler appears to each user as a LaserWriter in the Chooser window.

Figure
5-5

The LaserShare print queue window with spooled print jobs from the network.

spooling and printing as well as allow users to bypass the spooler and print directly. When you allow bypassing, both the name of the spooler and the name of the printer appear in each user's Chooser window; without the bypass option, the spooler-controlled printer's name does not appear, and network users can choose only the spooler and any released printers.

When a document leaves the print queue, either by despooling or removal, information is added to the print log, which you can display (Figure 5-7). The status tells you if a

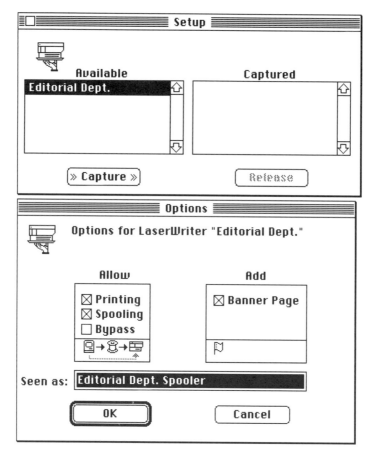

Figure
5-6
LaserShare options when you set up the program; the bypass option lets users bypass the spooler and print directly.

print job was completed or deleted, or if there was an error. The pages column show the number of pages in the spooled document and the number of pages printed. The print log can hold up to 250 print jobs before deleting old jobs to add new ones. You can save the print log on disk (for printing later) with the Save Print Log command in the File menu, and clear it with the Clear Print Log command.

You can leave the server unattended, and if the printer runs out of paper, LaserShare beeps and a message appears not just on the server, but on any computer that is currently trying to print files to the spooler.

Automatic font downloading is supported by LaserShare, but you can also manually download fonts if you allow the bypass option to download the fonts, then use the Print Next command with the document that needs those fonts.

LaserShare handles a power failure with grace and recovers any documents left in the queue when the power went off. LaserShare will print those documents in the order assigned in the queue.

⌘ File Edit Spooler Queue				
Print Queue for Editorial Dept. Spooler				
Status: LaserShare is printing on LaserWriter "Editorial Dept."...				
Status	**Document**	**User**	**Date/Time**	**Pages**
	biographical-latest t&c	Tony Bove	9/25/87 11:58:01 PM	2
	FutureEditions (Aug)	Tony Bove	9/26/87 12:00:04 AM	3

Print Log for Editorial Dept. Spooler				
Status	**Document**	**User**	**Date/Time**	**Pages**
Completed	Ch5 scr2	Tony Bove	9/25/87 11:54:37 PM	1
			9/25/87 11:56:48 PM	1
Completed	Folio NY Great Debate	Tony Bove	9/25/87 11:56:04 PM	2
			9/26/87 12:01:00 AM	2
Deleted	Expert Tips (Sept. spec s...	Tony Bove	9/25/87 11:59:04 PM	15
			9/26/87 12:01:45 AM	0

Figure 5-7

LaserShare's print log showing the date and time of each job's start in the spool queue and its finish (either by printing, deleting, or error).

Although a dedicated print server seems extravagant, many network applications have a need for file service from a dedicated server such as AppleShare, and LaserShare offers network spooling from the same computer. In addition, there is often a need to control access to printers, and to designate someone as a network administrator who can determine print job priorities. LaserShare offers the ability to maintain an accounting of printer usage. It also can help multiple users on a network manage the use of downloadable fonts — most fonts can be stored on the LaserShare computer and not clutter up each individual user's disks.

LaserShare with AppleShare is an effective combination to set up large networks with multiple printers. However, if you are going to use a mainframe or minicomputer as a file server, read this chapter and Chapter 6 about network spooling from a mainframe.

Private Electronic Mail

The ability to send someone a message, perhaps with a file attached, is an important business tool. But people should not have to be interrupted for messages — they need to be notified in a way that does not interfere with work.

With electronic mail, you can send a message with an attached file to a message center computer. The recipient gets a message flash that does not interrupt their work, and can react by ignoring it and waiting until later to pick up the mail, or by checking the mail immediately. As the sender, you perform the transfer once and go back to work. You could have addressed the message and file to many network users, and although many users can make copies, only one copy occupies space at the message center.

Users can check their mail when they first start up their computers, or if they see a message flash by telling them they have mail — and then only if they feel like checking it. At the same time, emergency messages can reach a computer user faster than running down the hall.

In Chapter 2 we described electronic mail using worldwide services that link people around the globe. Private, or in-house, electronic mail links people who share work files and who work together in a small business or a department of a large company.

With the AppleTalk Network System you can create networks that are linked by modems and bridge devices. The networks themselves can use different cabling schemes and be located anywhere in the world. With electronic mail packages you can set up a private electronic mail system that spans all of these networks.

The benefits are enormous when you consider how much time is wasted trying to set up conferences with people who are in different time zones. An electronic meeting, where every-one types messages, allows the meeting's minutes to be edited without retyping.

For example, you could have your entire sales force in France using an internet of AppleTalk Personal Networks defined as one zone (perhaps called "Paris Office"), and your department in San Francisco using an AppleTalk Personal Network or Ethernet-based AppleTalk network, and send and receive messages to and from the message centers located in each network. You could transfer large documents, spread sheets, data bases, software, graphics, publication files, and any other type of Macintosh file along with electronic memos and telephone-style message notes.

We introduced an electronic mail and messaging program called InBox/Mac and InBox/PC (Think Technologies) in Chapter 3. InBox/PC lets PCs that are connected to an AppleTalk network send and receive messages and files with Macintosh computers on the same network running InBox/Mac. InBox/Mac is described in detail in this chapter.

InterMail (Internet) offers electronic mail and messaging over an AppleTalk network and can perform the function of a gateway to larger X.400 networks, sharing electronic mail.

Both programs provide the ability to send and receive messages and files and maintain electronic addresses. Both use a Macintosh as a central message center, but without having to dedicate the computer to this single task — they run in the background so that you can run a program in the foreground. Both can work with AppleShare to put their central message center on the dedicated server computer. However, you can't use the programs together — you must choose InBox or InterMail for your network, and if you want to extend the mail system beyond to other networks, you must use the same software on those networks.

InBox is currently more popular because you can use a version of the program with regular PCs. However, if PC compatibility is not an issue, the programs are relatively similar in features.

InBox, however, has several advantages over InterMail. One is that you can check someone else's mailbox with InBox and read their mail if you know the password. As an InBox network administrator, you can log into a message center from any Macintosh to manage message files.

Another advantage of InBox is that you can have more than one message center on a network, thus dividing a network into work groups, each with its own message center. Users of each message center can send and receive mail from other centers.

For both programs you must choose a Macintosh for each message center to run in the background (you can still run programs in the foreground). Your choice should be a Macintosh that has at least one hard disk and is in a location where it can be left on all the time, even over weekends.

InBox

The InBox packages let you establish electronic mail across an entire AppleTalk network, including PCs connected with AppleTalk adaptor cards and running InBox/PC. InBox/Mac (Think Technologies) is priced according to the number of users: $295 for up to three users, and $75 for each additional user. InBox/PC, introduced earlier (Chapter 3), is $195 for each PC user and requires both an AppleTalk adaptor card for the PC and InBox/Mac running on at least one Macintosh acting as a message center.

Unlike InterMail, InBox can use more than one Macintosh on the network as message centers (each center should have a hard disk), although you must buy additional copies of the Administrator program for each center. The message center software runs in the background on the server Macintosh so that you can run programs in the foreground. However, InBox handles message requests faster if you use a dedicated Macintosh, and if you dedicate a Macintosh to AppleShare, you can also establish an InBox message center on it. You need to set aside at least 100K of disk space per mailbox, and at least 512K of RAM to run the message center software.

Every user on the network has an electronic mailbox in one of the message centers; InBox can support up to 100 mailboxes on each address list per message center. You can send and receive messages, with files attached to them, and save messages on your disk.

InBox's Personal Connection software (to send and receive messages) is a desk accessory you can activate from within an application or while using the Finder. InBox lets you display current messages in your mailbox, your address list, or a blank message pad for writing a new phone or memo message. To see a list of messages sent to you, click the InBox button (Figure 5-8). The bullet symbols indicate messages not yet read (they disappear after you read the messages), and the diamond symbols indicate that the messages were sent with an RSVP (please respond) request.

To save one or more messages, select them by clicking the names, or click a date to select all messages for that day, then click the Disk button. When you click the disk button to save messages, the dialog box (Figure 5-9) lets you save messages in

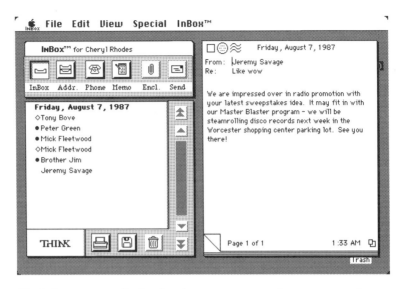

Figure
5-8

The InBox message display showing a message sent from a user on the network and a list of other messages.

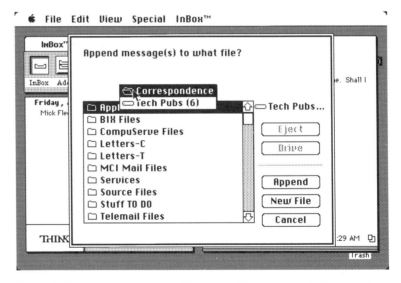

Figure
5-9

Saving InBox messages on your disk in new files or appended to a single file.

a new file or append them to an existing file. The Print button prints the message on your printer, and the trash can is for removing messages from your mailbox. The names or dates in the list remain selected so that you can continue with functions that treat them as a group (such as saving them on disk and then removing them from the mailbox).

To write a memo, click the Memo button to display a blank page with "From:" at the top, and type your message (Figure 5-10). Click the folded corner of the page to turn the page, and click the RSVP button to get confirmation when the recipient reads the message. You can also write a message in the style of a conventional phone message, by first clicking the Phone button to display the form (Figure 5-11).

To enclose a file to transfer with the memo or phone message, click the Encl. button to display the Enclose dialog box (Figure 5-12), and select a file. The Addr. button displays your address list (Figure 5-13), and you select recipients by clicking their names (a check mark appears next to selected names). Your own name appears in bold in the list. Finally,

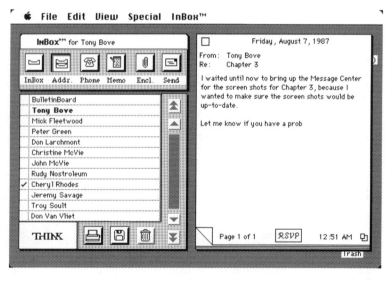

Figure 5-10

Writing an InBox memo to be sent to a user that has a mailbox at the message center.

click the Send button to send to each recipient's mailbox the message and file, which are stored at the Message Center until they are retrieved.

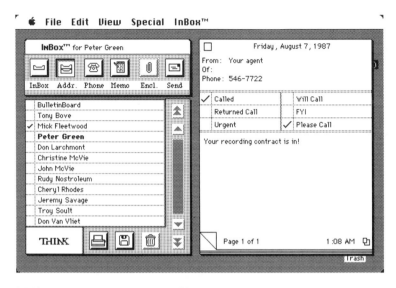

Figure 5-11 Writing an InBox message resembling a conventional phone message.

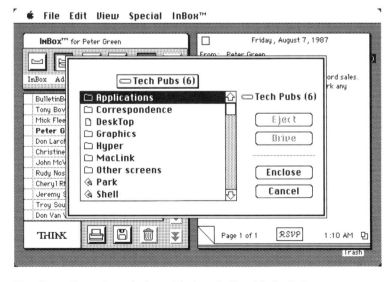

Figure 5-12 User Peter Green is enclosing a Macintosh file with the InBox message.

InBox uses a paper clip icon to show you that a file is clipped to a message. To receive a file clipped to a message, click the paper clip icon at the upper right corner of the displayed

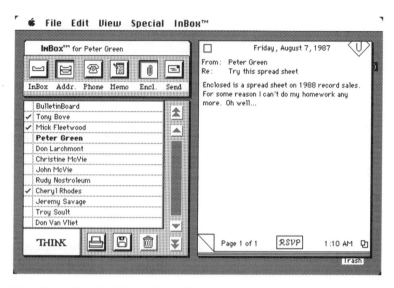

Figure
5-13

User Peter Green's InBox address list, with recipients checked.

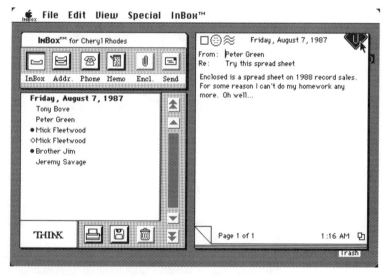

Figure
5-14

A recipient uses InBox to receive the file that was clipped to a message sent by Peter Green.

message (Figure 5-14) to display the Transfer dialog box (Figure 5-15). First you change folders and change the name

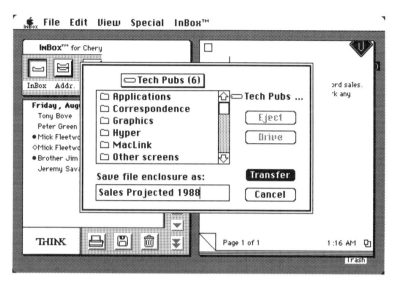

Figure 5-15

After clicking the paper clip icon, InBox displays the Transfer dialog box to save the enclosed file on disk.

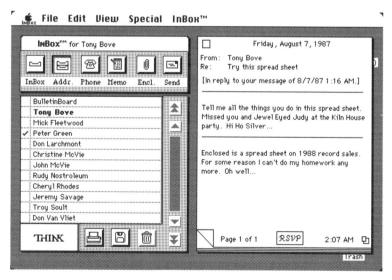

Figure 5-16

When you reply to an InBox message, the program displays the original message and lets you type the reply above it.

of the received file you will store on your disk (if necessary), then you can click the Transfer button.

InBox's menu lets you automatically reply to a message; forward a message; add more names to the list of recipients for a message; send a copy of your outgoing message to yourself; select all names in the mailbox quickly; and create or delete routing lists.

To reply while reading the original message, select Reply from the InBox menu, and then type your reply on the standard message form that appears (Figure 5-16); InBox automatically puts a From: and To: heading and a note stating that the message is in reply to another message. The Forward command performs a similar function.

A *routing list* can be set up to address a group of people. To create a routing list, check all the names in the address list that should be in the list, and choose the Add Routing List command in the InBox menu (Figure 5-17) which lets you type a name for the routing list. Routing lists always appear in italics at the top of your address list, so that they are easy to find (Figure 5-18). You can also send messages to addresses at another message center by using the Inter Office Send command.

In addition to changing the window positions for the mailbox icons, the address list, and the memo/telephone pad, you can tell InBox to remember these positions with the Remember Positions command in the InBox menu.

You can also set preference options when you first log into InBox. After typing your password, you can click the Options button (Figure 5-19) and InBox displays the Personal Connection Options window (Figure 5-20). For example, you can have InBox remember your name and password so that you don't have to type it every time you log in. You can change the new mail alert to be audible (a tone), visual (a banner across the screen), or both; this alert can be repeated or performed only once. You can also set InBox to print a log of every outgoing phone message (as long as a printer is attached to your modem port), which is useful for a receptionist.

The option to keep the desk accessory resident is provided to let you run InBox more quickly in Macintosh computers with at least a megabyte of RAM. Without this option, the desk accessory operates slower on startup and adds a little extra

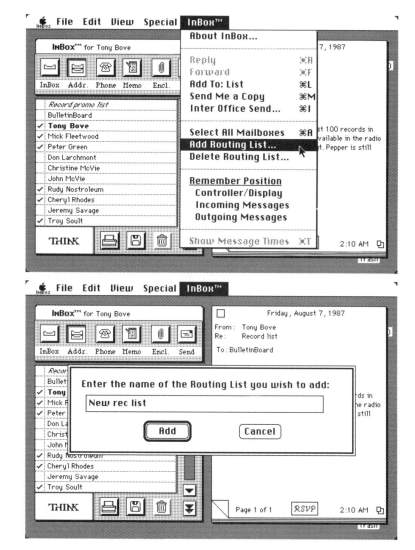

Figure
5-17

Adding a routing list to InBox's list of addresses.

overhead to network traffic, but you are then able to run InBox on Macintosh computers with less than a megabyte of RAM.

InBox is compatible with applications that provide very little memory space for desk accessories (such as Microsoft Excel and Word 3.0). You can usually copy or cut and paste text from any word processor or application program into a memo, and vice-versa.

You can install the InBox Personal Connection desk accessory in each computer after attaching the computer to an AppleTalk network and installing and bringing up a message center. The Administrator program installs the message center software, and a special AppleShare Installer installs the message center on an AppleShare file server (you don't need any special installation procedures to run InBox with TOPS). The designated administrator can log into a message center from any Macintosh and perform message management functions, such as adding and deleting users, performing

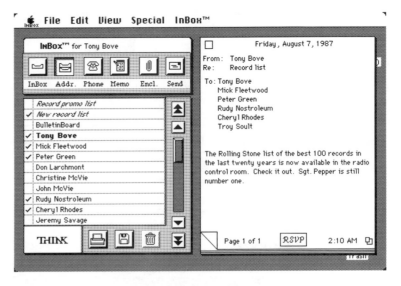

Figure
5-18

Routing list names appear at the top of your address list in italics; selecting a routing list automatically selects the names in the list.

backups, and compressing the message data file to reclaim disk space at the message center.

You can set up 100 mailboxes at a message center — one for each user, plus public mailboxes (with well-known or blank passwords) that anyone can access (Figure 5-21). InBox is supplied with one public mailbox called the BulletinBoard. You can use the Cut Mailbox and Paste Mailbox buttons to

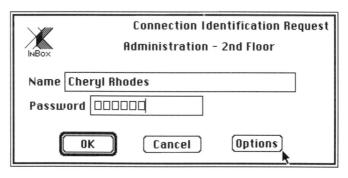

Figure 5-19

After typing your password to log into an InBox message center, you can change your preferences with the Options button.

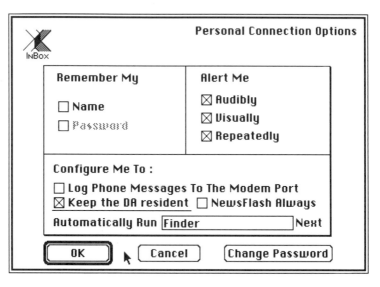

Figure 5-20

InBox's Personal Connection Options window for changing preferences.

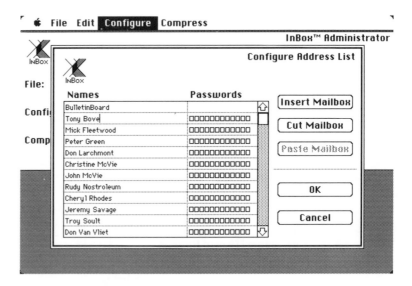

Figure 5-21

The InBox address list for a message center, set up by a designated network administrator.

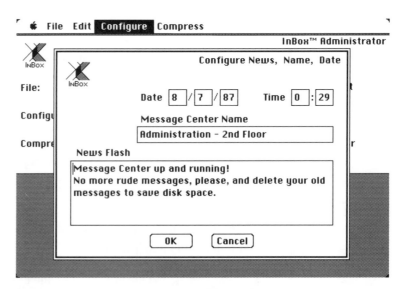

Figure 5-22

The InBox news flash that appears to each user logging on to check the mail.

move names on the list. After setting up mailboxes, you can set up a news flash message (Figure 5-22) that will appear on each user's Macintosh when first logging into InBox/Mac (or PC, when running InBox/PC). The administrator can change the news flash periodically to inform all users of news or events.

InBox has built-in security precautions to prevent electronic eavesdropping, and password control over mailboxes so that even the administrator doesn't know the passwords (although the administrator can assign new passwords, users can change them immediately). In addition, the Installer prevents two connections with the same serial number from running at the same time, which would indicate an unauthorized user. Finally, InBox provides a password-protected administrator's disk.

The administrator can monitor activities at a message center by using the Administrator program to open the center. InBox displays a status window (Figure 5-23) that shows the total number of messages written and read since the message

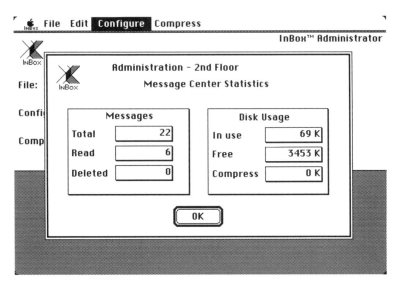

Figure 5-23   The InBox message center status window for the network administrator.

center was created, and the total number deleted since the last data compression, along with a message telling you how much disk space would be reclaimed if you compressed the center's data file at this time. You can see how much disk space is currently in use and how much is available for more files, and the program counts all transactions and displays the total activity since the message center was created.

The status window also shows the total number of files enclosed with messages that are currently stored at the center. Since files can take up the most space, InBox will automatically delete files clipped to messages when all the recipients of the messages delete them from their mailboxes.

Mailboxes can hold up to 500 messages before they are full; if any one mailbox is 80 percent full, a message appears in the status window and you can do two important operations: tell users to read and delete messages from their mailboxes, and compress the data file to reclaim space. As administrator, you can set up an automatic compression timer (Figure 5-24).

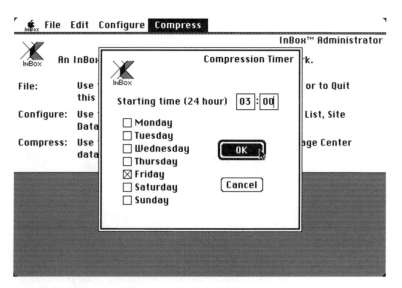

Figure
5-24

InBox lets the administrator set up an automatic timer to compress the data file to reclaim disk space at the message center.

InBox/Mac and InBox/PC provide a complete electronic mail system for Macintosh computers and PCs on an Apple-Talk network. InBox is compatible with TOPS and Apple-Share, which are described later in this chapter.

InterMail

InterMail (Internet) is also priced according to the number of users: $300 for up to 4 users, $450 for up to 10, $750 for up to 20, and $950 for over 21. Multiple-zone support is an extra $200.

InterMail provides electronic mail service among all the Macintosh users of an AppleTalk network, plus other AppleTalk networks linked via bridge devices (as does InBox). Unlike InBox, InterMail can connect to mailboxes on X.400 networks involving mainframe or minicomputer systems.

You can send messages to one or more names, or to groups of names, and receive messages whenever you log into the mail system — your mailbox in the message center (a Macintosh with a hard disk is recommended for the message center) keeps your messages until you delete them. You can send and receive files, forward messages, request a return receipt to confirm that messages were received, and generate automatic replies. You can save messages on disk, print them, and then delete them from your mailbox. You can also buy custom message forms for InterMail. Besides standard messages and telephone-style messages, you can pay extra for network reminders ($80) and graphic messages ($60).

Installation of an InterMail system consists of two steps: setting up the *server station* for the message center (a Macintosh with a hard disk is recommended), and setting up *user stations* — individual users with mailboxes. The server station installs itself after you drag the Server icon into the System Folder for the station and use Font/DA Mover to install the InterMail desk accessory. InterMail asks for your server's name, which is the name your message center will be known by across the networks. Choose this name carefully because you are not given an opportunity to change it unless you reinstall the server station software.

The next step is to add user mailboxes to the message center. First activate the InterMail desk accessory and sign in as Network Manager (Figure 5-25) with the appropriate password as described in the manual (the password is displayed as asterisks). The program displays the Network Manager message center (Figure 5-26) and then displays the network manager's window when you double-click the Management icon. From this window you can add new user mailboxes, modify user's mailboxes, create groups of users, and delete user mailboxes.

If you add a user's mailbox without adding a password for the user, and the user's name in his/her system file (as entered when you set up the user station) is the same as the

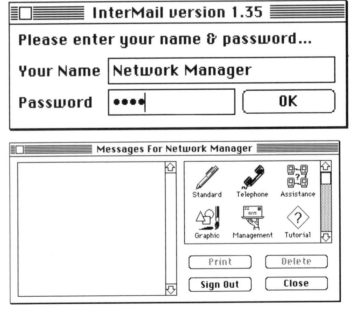

Figure 5-25

Signing into InterMail as Network Manager to add or delete user mailboxes and manage the mail system.

name for the mailbox, then that user's Macintosh will automatically log into the message center when it is started; otherwise, the user activates the InterMail accessory to log into the center. Only by logging into the center can users pick up and drop off their mail.

To create user stations, install the InterMail desk accessory into each System file of each Macintosh, and use the Chooser on each Macintosh to type the name of the user exactly as it appears on the mailbox. Finally, drag the InterMail user file into the System Folder for that Macintosh.

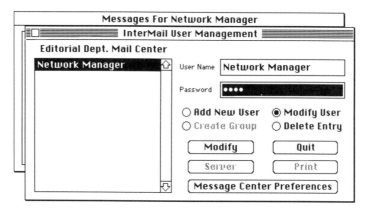

Figure 5-26

InterMail's Network Manager message center; pressing the Management icon presents the network manager's window.

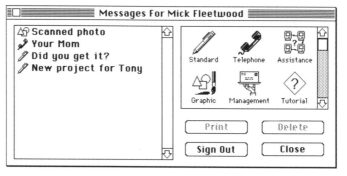

Figure 5-27

InterMail appears to each user as a message center with mail management functions and a message window. When a message is received, InterMail beeps your Macintosh and displays an alert message.

225

Although InterMail assumes the same name for your user name as you typed in the Chooser dialog box, any user can log into the message center from any Macintosh by supplying the appropriate name and password in the sign-in window when you activate the InterMail accessory.

The message center (Figure 5-27) appears when you log in and lets you send and receive messages. To the left of each message displayed in the message center window is an icon that identifies the type of message. The message types include the standard message (up to 32,000 characters, or 32K), telephone-style with boxes to check, optional reminders to pop-up on a user's desktop at an appointed time, and graphic messages you can paste into applications that accept graphics. You can attach a file of any length to a standard message.

When your computer receives a message, it immediately displays a new message alert box (Figure 5-28). You can choose to read the message at that time, or click OK to hold the message in your mailbox at the message center.

You can select one or more messages as a batch to be read, printed, or deleted, by holding down Shift as you click each

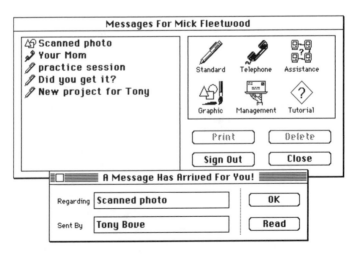

Figure 5-28

When a new InterMail message arrives, your system immediately displays an alert box so that you can choose to read the message, or save it in your mailbox by clicking OK.

message, or dragging over the messages. Double-click any message and the program displays the message window (Figure 5-29 shows a standard message), which lets you prepare a reply to the sender, forward the message, print the message, save it on your disk by any name you choose, and delete it from your mailbox.

Standard

To send a message, double-click the icon for the message type (the pen icon for a standard message), and the program displays the message form (Figure 5-30). The address list in

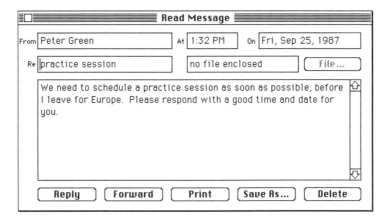

Figure 5-29   Reading a standard InterMail message.

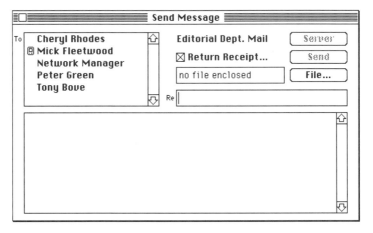

Figure 5-30   The standard message form in InterMail.

227

the upper left corner includes all message center mailboxes (alphabetically listed by first name if you list full names as in our example; you could use last names only). You can scroll through the list and select a recipient by clicking the name. A check mark appears next to a name you select, and you can click the name again to de-select it. You can click as many names as you want (or drag across names to select them). Those names that have a system icon next to them are active on the network and will receive the message immediately.

You can pick another message center by clicking the Server button until its name appears. The address list is automatically updated for the new InterMail server station. You can enclose a file with a standard message by clicking the File button, which displays a standard Open dialog box and file name window. You can also request a return receipt (Figure 5-31) with the date and time that your message was read, by clicking that option in the send message window.

When you send the message to another server that is not available at that moment, your InterMail server station holds the message and sends it when the other server is available.

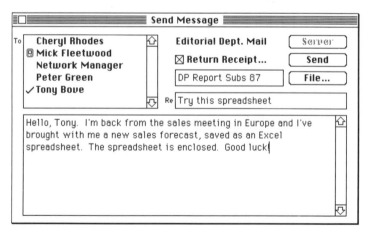

		Send Message	
To	Cheryl Rhodes	Editorial Dept. Mail	Server
	Mick Fleetwood	☒ Return Receipt...	Send
	Network Manager		
	Peter Green	DP Report Subs 87	File...
	✓ Tony Bove	Re Try this spreadsheet	

Hello, Tony. I'm back from the sales meeting in Europe and I've brought with me a new sales forecast, saved as an Excel spreadsheet. The spreadsheet is enclosed. Good luck

*Figure
5-31*

With InterMail you can request a return receipt with a standard message, as well as enclose a file with a message.

Management

The Management icon lets you change your mailbox name and password (or delete your password), create personal mailing lists called *groups*, print the names of all possible recipients on a server, and set preference options. Messages sent to a group are sent to all members simultaneously.

To set preferences, click the Message Center Preferences button (Figure 5-32). To make changes, click the preference boxes to activate or deactivate them, then click the Update button to keep the changes, or the Cancel button to cancel them. You can change the fonts in messages to laser printer fonts (Helvetica and Times) so that they print with these fonts on laser printers. You can change the order of your address list display from alphabetical to "last sent" (so that frequent recipients are at the top of your list). Return receipts can be a default setting (so that you would have to check Return Receipts to turn *off* receipts), and you can have the text of received messages automatically copied to reply forms to help in making replies. You can also set messages to be deleted as soon as you answer them.

Preferences

Always:
- ☐ Remember window positions
- ☒ Print messages with laser fonts

[Update]
[Cancel]

When sending messages:
- ☐ Display the address list in "last sent" order
- ☒ Request a return receipt as default

When reading messages:
- ☒ Copy message text to reply as default
- ☒ Delete original message after sending reply

When new mail is delivered:
- ☒ Display alert dialog
- ☒ Display menu bar icon   ◉ Flash ○ Don't flash
- ☒ Sound chime   ○ Once ◉ Twice ○ Three times
- ☒ Always display urgent telephone messages

---

*Figure
5-32*

Setting preferences for your InterMail message displays.

You can experiment with these preferences without tampering with anyone's mail or mailbox, because you can only change your mailbox and message center display — you have no control over other mailboxes (only the network manager has control).

The Zone Support Driver, which costs extra with InterMail, lets you gain access to your message server from any other zone. It replaces the InterMail user icon in your System Folder. If, for example, you were using a Macintosh in another zone, you could use Chooser to select a different zone, then select an InterMail server in the newly selected zone.

Dedicated File Sharing: AppleShare

AppleShare provides the richest file-sharing environment for networks that require password-controlled file access. Users in corporate departments usually want the combination of security and transparent file access so that beginners can be trained easily. AppleShare makes file sharing as easy as dragging icons across your Macintosh desktop, and fits into the Macintosh System as an integral part of it.

We have described the difference between a distributed file-sharing environment, in which every computer has the potential to provide file-sharing services to other computers on the network, and a dedicated file-sharing environment, which uses one or more dedicated computers or hardware devices to provide file service to everyone on the network and to other networks.

Dedicated file servers can make use of the resources and full memory of a dedicated computer; as a result they can be faster, handling more tasks efficiently. As network services expand, there are benefits in having a larger, dedicated piece of equipment that is performing all network services including file service, electronic mail, and print spooling. There is also a greater measure of protection and access control in servers like AppleShare, because it is designed to be maintained by a designated network manager who can also double as the message center manager for InBox or InterMail, and the print manager for LaserShare (all of which can run on the same dedicated Macintosh with AppleShare).

AppleShare (Apple, $795) requires a dedicated Macintosh Plus, SE, or II and one or more hard disks. It is a good example of how a dedicated file server should work on an AppleTalk network. Programs designed to be run with AppleShare include InBox and InterMail electronic mail message centers, and Apple's LaserShare network spooler. In addition, you can access an AppleShare server from a PC that has an AppleTalk PC adaptor card using the AppleShare PC software as described in Chapter 3.

AppleShare lets all users on an AppleTalk network, or in other zones of an internet (up to 50 users simultaneously), read and write documents and data files and use applications that are stored on the server's hard disks.

AppleShare's hard disks appear to clients as disks on their systems, and anyone with the appropriate access privileges can access any folder or file on the disk. All users on the network receive updated information in their Finder windows whenever a file or folder on the server changes, as when someone creates, deletes, or moves a file or folder. You gain access to the file server by using the Chooser to select the AppleShare icon; Chooser also lets you change zones to choose an AppleShare server on another network.

When you create a folder on a server disk, you can control whether the contents of that folder will be shared or private, and if shared, whether the contents will be shared with everyone on the network, or with only a select work group. You can also control several access privileges — the ability to see other folders and files inside the folder, and make changes to the folder (such as adding new folders and files or changing folders and files inside it). You only need one password to use a server, and once you've identified yourself, AppleShare remembers your name and password to control future access.

Most applications are compatible with AppleShare, and some applications take full advantage of multiuser capabilities for multilaunching applications by several users, and having multiple access to the same data base file.

AppleShare lets you organize users into *work groups* with names to identify them. Folder owners (anyone who creates a folder) can then grant access privileges to a group without having to name group members individually. You are allowed to have an unlimited number of registered group names. This means that you can define work groups in different ways to manage file access; for example, a sales department's network may have several project teams that need to share sensitive documents that other sales project teams should not see.

Installation and Setup

There is no limit to the number of AppleShare servers you can have in an AppleTalk network or internet. There is also no limit to the number of servers per zone. Each AppleShare server can handle as many disk drives as the current Finder can handle, which as of this writing is seven SCSI disk drives and two Apple Hard Disk 20 drives connected to the floppy drive port, using Finder 5.5.

The requirements for an AppleShare server are one dedicated Macintosh Plus, SE, or II (with at least one megabyte of RAM), and at least one hard disk that uses the Hierarchical File System (HFS). A SCSI disk such as Apple's HD SCSI or the SuperMac DataFrame (Figure 5-33) provides much better performance than a disk interfaced to the floppy port (such as the Apple HD 20). You also need one or more computers to act as clients on the network. They can be a mixture of Macintosh 512K, 512KE, Plus, SE, and II computers.

A designated network administrator installs the server software on the dedicated Macintosh Plus, SE, or II, and each user runs the Workstation Installer to update their System and Finder files and to add AppleShare software.

AppleShare lets you set up a Macintosh II, with more than one megabyte of RAM, to allow up to 50 users to simultaneously access the server. With one megabyte, you are limited (as with a Macintosh Plus and SE) to 25 users sharing files simultaneously. You can have an unlimited number of registered users.

A special folder, called Server Folder, is created by AppleShare on each server volume to contain information about the volume. When you run the AppleShare Admin program to install the server software, you designate one volume as the server start-up volume, which sets up the other volumes for service (Figure 5-34). You also supply a name for the server that will be recognized by users on this and other networks (Figure 5-35). If you've attached several hard disks to the server, each one can be prepared by AppleShare, or skipped.

In addition to the Administrator key (which is a password for managing the server itself), you define a custodian name

Figure
5-33

An AppleShare file server running on a Macintosh Plus using a DataFrame hard disk.

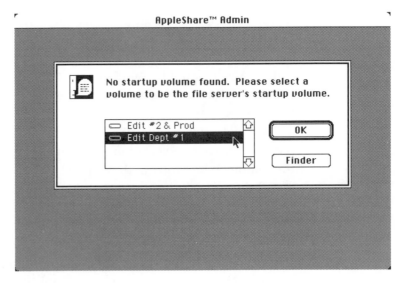

Figure
5-34

Designating a start-up volume for AppleShare during the installation process.

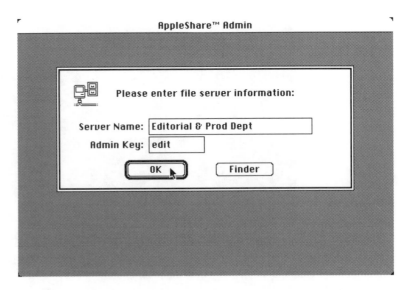

Figure
5-35

Naming the AppleShare server and typing a key for managing the network.

and password. The custodian is a user who will control access (be the *owner*) of all existing files and folders on the disks before installing the server. The custodian also becomes the owner of any file or folder with incomplete ownership information.

After checking that AppleTalk is connected (using Chooser), and making necessary corrections to the time and date in the Alarm Clock desk accessory, use the Restart command to shut down and restart your Macintosh. AppleShare prepares your disks for file service and starts up, displaying its server status window (Figure 5-36). This window shows a list of all active volumes on the server, and the number of users currently using the server. The activity meter shows how much the server is being used.

Before users can access the server, they have to install the AppleShare workstation software, and update the System and Finder files if necessary to System version 4.1 and Finder

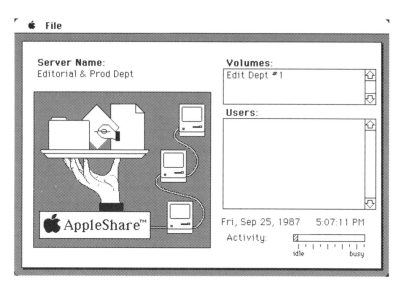

Figure 5-36

The AppleShare server status window appears on the server's display when it is active.

version 5.5 or newer versions. The administrator must register each user's name and add any group names; new names can always be added and old ones deleted. To add users, the administrator runs the AppleShare Admin program and types the key, then chooses the Create User command from the Users menu. AppleShare displays a user list and group list window, and an individual user information window on top (Figure 5-37), and lets you type the user's name and password.

To register groups, an administrator first decides which is the *primary group* for any users that are in more than one group. AppleShare lets a user assign one group to any folder that he/she owns; to start, AppleShare picks the user's primary group. The owner can set access privileges for that folder so that members of the group have access, or allow another group to have access. Since folder access can be restricted to one or more groups, the grouping assignments are powerful tools for managing access.

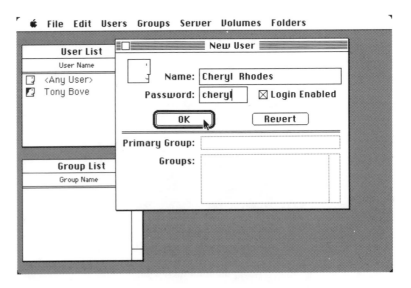

Figure 5-37

AppleShare's user information window for each user registered for the server.

To create a group, the administrator chooses the Create Group command from the Group menu to display the group list window, then selects and drags user names from the user list window (Figure 5-38) to the membership list. The administrator (or the person using the administrator key) is the only person who can assign users to a group or remove users from a group.

As administrator you can create as many groups as you need for that server. Users can be members of many groups, but as administrator you can assign a primary group name to each user. First select the user from the user list window, then drag

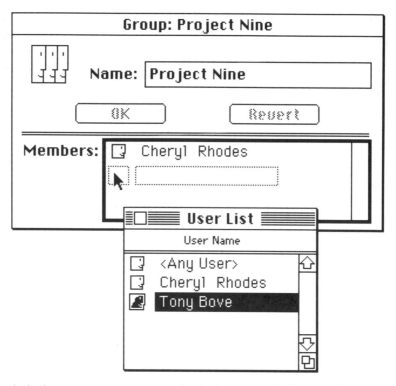

Figure 5-38

Assigning users to a group on an AppleShare server by dragging their names into the membership list of the group information window.

the group name up to the primary group slot (Figure 5-39).

When you are finished administering the server, you can copy the users and groups in a special file in case AppleShare crashes and you want to rebuild the server. Use the Save Users & Groups command in the File menu.

Any registered user for the server can create and own folders on the server; the folder is automatically set up to be

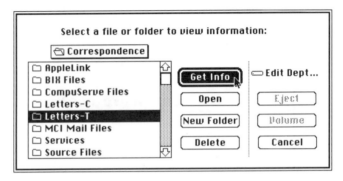

Figure
5-40

The AppleShare administrator's Get Info dialog box.

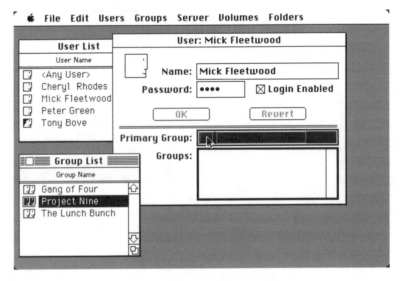

Figure
5-39

Assigning a primary group to a user.

private — only that user can access the folder until he/she changes the access privileges to allow others access. As administrator you can also set up folders and access privileges, by choosing File & Folder Info from the Folders menu and clicking the New Folder button in the Get Info dialog box (Figure 5-40), which displays the folder information window (Figure 5-41). As administrator you can drag any user from the user list and any group name from the group list to the folder information window.

Using the Server

To gain access to a server, any user on the network who has installed the workstation software can select Chooser and then select an AppleShare server by clicking the server icon (Figure 5-42). If your network has a bridge to other zones, you can access servers on those zones by first selecting the zone, and then select the server.

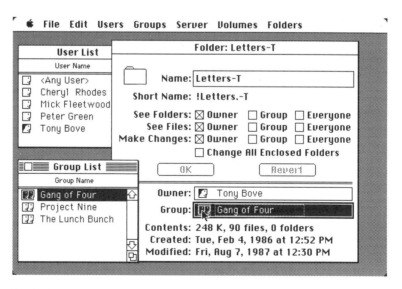

Figure
5-41

AppleShare lets the administrator create folders and manage folder access.

After selecting the server, AppleShare asks you to identify yourself as a registered user or as a guest (Figure 5-43). Any users on the network or in another zone can log into a server as guests (as long as they have installed the workstation software). Guests can create folders but can't own them — anyone can access them.

You can then select the volumes on the server you want to mount on your desktop (Figure 5-44). You can set up automatic access for your start-up disk by first selecting the boxes next to volumes you want to access automatically upon start-up; you can also select whether the start-up disk should remember your password (in case someone else uses your start-up disk).

Edit Dept #1

The mounted volumes appear on your desktop with a special icon. Also, two arrows appear in the upper left corner of your screen near the Apple logo that shows when you are transferring information to and from an AppleShare server. You can open the mounted volumes just like any other

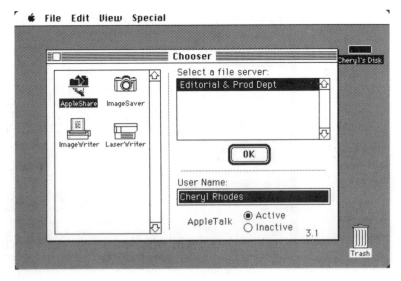

Figure
5-42

Using Chooser to select an AppleShare server.

Figure
5-43

Identifying yourself to the AppleShare server as a registered user.

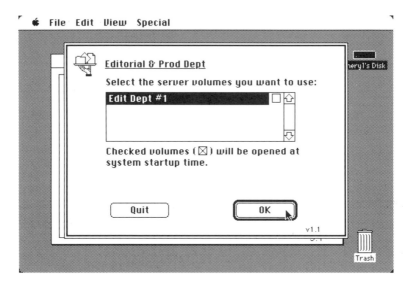

Figure
5-44

Selecting one or more volumes on the server to mount.

volumes or disks attached to your system. The folders in these volumes have different icons depending on your access privileges.

To log off the server, simply drag the icons for the volumes into your trash can. You should log off the server if you are not using it, since you are occupying a slot (only 25 users can log on simultaneously, or 50 if your server has more than one megabyte of memory) and possibly slowing down others who are using the server.

Access Privileges

Although you can see folders not owned by you, they appear gray (Figure 5-45) if you do not have access privileges to them, and you can't gain access without privileges set by the owner or administrator. Access can be controlled so that you can see folders within a restricted folder, but not files. You can also set up folders that can be copied to by everyone on the network,

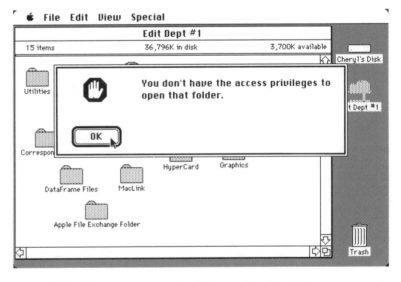

Figure
5-45

Inaccessible folders are gray on the desktop of an AppleShare server, and you can't gain access without having access privileges.

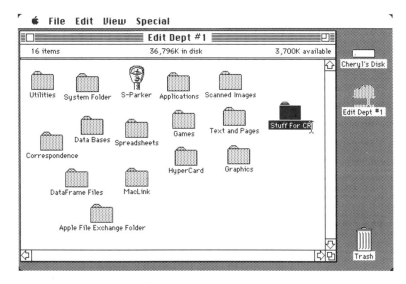

Figure
5-46

After creating a folder on the server (which appears with a darkened tab), you can change the access privileges for it.

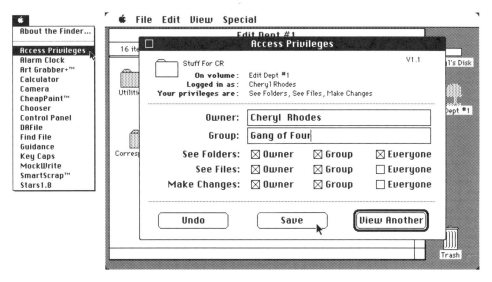

Figure
5-47

The Access Privileges desk accessory lets you set access privileges for your folders on the AppleShare server.

but not opened. Access privileges can be defined for individuals and groups.

You can create new folders on the server's disks by using the New Folder command in your File menu, just as you would normally do with folders on your disks (Figure 5-46). When you first create a folder, you are the owner and no one else can open or use the folder. Only you, the owner, can grant access privileges, although your folder can be taken over by the administrator.

Stuff For CR

The folders you own have a darkened tab. After creating folders on the server, change the access privileges for them using the Access Privileges desk accessory (Figure 5-47). You can grant three types of access:

See folders. Others can see the folders inside the folder, but not necessarily the files.

See files. Others can see the files inside the folder, open the files, and copy them (or save them with new names on their disks), but not change them or add new files to the folder.

Make changes. Others can make changes to the contents of the folder, including moving or deleting any files, adding files and folders, and changing files. However, folders within a folder may restrict your access to those folders.

You can assign a set of privileges to yourself (the owner), to a specific group, or to everyone. When you assign an access privilege to everyone, it is automatically assigned to yourself (the owner) and to all groups. The matrix of possibilities virtually guarantees controlled access and privacy.

For example, if you can see files in a folder, you can copy the file, open it from an application, and save it under a new name on your disk. You may also be able to change the file on the server, or delete it, if you have the privilege to make changes. If, however, you can't see the file, you can't copy it or open it to save it under a new name.

If you can't change the contents of a folder, you can't add files to it. If you can't see the files or folders in the folder, but

can make changes, then the folder is acting like a drop box —
you can drop things in, but you can't pull things out (Figure
5-48). You can also create a bulletin board: a folder where
everyone can see the contents but nothing can be changed
(Figure 5-49).

Travel Exp Drop

Folders that have drop-box access privileges are gray but
have a down-arrow attached to them to indicate that you can
drag files or folders to drop into them. Folders to which you
have the privilege to see their contents are shown as normal
folders. The folders you own and control access to are shown
with a darkened tab.

You can see the access privileges you have to folders that do
not belong to you by choosing the Access Privileges desk
accessory, selecting the name of the folder, and clicking the
Folder Info button to display the access privileges window, just
as you did with folders you own. The only information displayed is the name of any group that also has access to the
folder, as well as your name.

```
 ⌘  File  Edit  View  Special

┌────────────────────────────────────────────┐
│ □              Access Privileges            │   ┌──────────┐
│                                             │   Cheryl's Disk
│   ┌──┐  Travel Exp Drop           V1.1      │
│   │  │     On volume:  Edit Dept #1         │
│   └──┘  Logged in as:  Cheryl Rhodes        │
│      Your privileges are:  See Folders, See Files, Make Changes │   ┌──────────┐
│                                             │   Edit Dept #1
│         Owner:  │Cheryl Rhodes          │   │
│                                             │
│         Group:  │                      │   │
│                                             │
│   See Folders:  ⊠ Owner  □ Group  □ Everyone│
│     See Files:  ⊠ Owner  □ Group  □ Everyone│
│  Make Changes:  ⊠ Owner  ⊠ Group  ⊠ Everyone│
│                                             │
│   ┌─────────┐  ┌─────────┐  ┌─────────────┐ │   ┌──┐
│   │  Undo   │  │  Save   │  │ View Another│ │   │  │ Trash
│   └─────────┘  └─────────┘  └─────────────┘ │   └──┘
│                            Travel Exp Drop  │
└────────────────────────────────────────────┘
```

*Figure
5-48*

Access privileges set for a drop box folder on the AppleShare server.

245

Managing the Server

AppleShare Admin

The primary function of the Admin program is to let the administrator add new users, delete old users, and create or delete groups. The administrator can warn users that the server is about to be shut down, and then perform the shut down, back up the server's disks, and restart the server. The administrator can also generate two reports:

The server report. A listing of all registered users and groups, how many files and folders each user has in a volume, and how much space they occupy.

The volume report. A listing with information about each volume including the names of files and folders inside each folder, and each folder's owner, associated group, and access privileges.

The AppleShare server status window remains on the server's display unless you run another program concurrent with AppleShare, such as the InBox message center or Laser-Share print server display. The server status window monitors

```
 ⌐   ⧉  File  Edit  View  Special                         ¬
┌─────────────────────────────────────────────────────────┐
│ □               Access Privileges                    │le │──────│
│  ┌──────┐                                      V1.1       │Cheryl's Disk│
│  │      │ Bulletins                                       │
│  └──────┘    On volume:  Edit Dept #1                     │
│         Logged in as:  Cheryl Rhodes                      │
│     Your privileges are:  See Folders, See Files, Make Changes │
│  ......................................................   │   🌲   │
│              Owner:  │ Cheryl  Rhodes              │      │Edit Dept #1│
│              Group:  │                             │      │
│        See Folders:  ⊠ Owner    ⊠ Group    ⊠ Everyone     │
│          See Files:  ⊠ Owner    ⊠ Group    ⊠ Everyone     │
│       Make Changes:  ⊠ Owner    ☐ Group    ☐ Everyone     │
│  ......................................................   │
│   ┌──────────┐     ┌──────────┐     ┌────────────────┐   │
│   │   Undo   │     │   Save   │▖    │ ▌View Another▐ │   │
│   └──────────┘     └──────────┘     └────────────────┘   │
│                                          ▐Bulletins▌     │  🗑  │
│                                                          │ Trash│
└─────────────────────────────────────────────────────────┘
```

Figure 5-49

The access privileges set for a bulletin board folder on the AppleShare server.

activity on the server — the user list changes according to who is logged on or off, and the volumes list shows which volumes the server found ready for use when it started up.

AppleShare does not have a backup function, but backup is perhaps the most important operation for a network administrator. Network DiskFit (SuperMac Software, $395) keeps folder attributes intact when it backs up a server's hard disks, and lets users on the network back up their personal disks. Multiple users can launch the program from a server to perform backups. Users can also limit backup operations to those folders owned by them.

AppleShare, LaserShare, InBox or InterMail, and Network DiskFit were designed to work together to provide a complete file sharing environment suitable for most corporate departments and work groups. In conjunction with the other services, AppleShare makes the dedication of a Macintosh a practical alternative that provides better performance over distributed file service.

Dedicated File Sharing: 3+

3Com offers the extensive 3+ network that links PCs and Macintosh computers and supports both PC and Macintosh file systems and the AppleTalk Network System protocols. The 3+ network uses Ethernet as a backbone network for AppleTalk, Ethernet, and Token Ring network services. As described in Chapter 4, 3Com's Ethernet network offers several cabling alternatives from thick and thin coaxial cable to twisted-pair wiring.

The 3+ network, which connects PCs using the standard NetBIOS protocols and the Microsoft Redirector, also supports IBM's Token Ring network protocols as well as standard Ethernet protocols. All of 3Com's network products work on a 3+ network mixed with PCs and Macintosh computers. In addition, AppleShare servers on an AppleTalk network can coexist with 3Com's 3Server3 server on a 3+ network.

3Com offers file sharing software called 3+Share ($1790) that manages network access, and an electronic mail system called 3+Mail ($495 for up to five users, or $990 for unlimited users) that lets you send or receive mail to and from all *netstations* (connected computers, whether they are PCs or Macintosh computers) on the network. To connect to the 3+ network, you attach an AppleTalk Personal Network to the 3Com 3Server3 hardware device ($5995), which is a dedicated file server with hard disks and printers. An alternative is to connect Macintosh II or SE computers directly to the Ethernet network with 3Com adaptor cards. Any computer on the Ethernet network running 3+ network software can access files on the server or use the server's printers.

3+Share file-sharing software is very similar to AppleShare in its security features and network management functions, and it includes network spooling, a backup utility, and the ability to extend its electronic mail package to mainframe and minicomputer networks. The hardware server (3Server3) is optimized for fast performance with many users and is supplied with one or more hard disks; however, if this device or its hard disks fail for any reason, you can't simply substitute another computer to use as a server, as you can with AppleShare (which runs on any Macintosh Plus, SE, or II).

With 3+ network software, your Macintosh desktop looks exactly the same, except that the 3+Share server appears as another volume you can open and copy files to and from with your mouse. You log into the 3+ network using the Chooser desk accessory — the 3+File and 3+Print icons appear in the Chooser window (Figure 5-50). The log-in procedure is one of the security features of this network (Figure 5-51).

The 3+ Network Window (Figure 5-52) gives you access to the tree-structured folder system, and displays the Home Folder, which is a personal storage area on the server. At the top level is the organization folder (for the entire company), followed by the domain folder (for departments), the user folder (for users in each department), and finally a Home

Folder (for each user). When you switch to a domain, the Network Window displays a list of users (Figure 5-53). You can link your computer to your Home Folder by clicking your

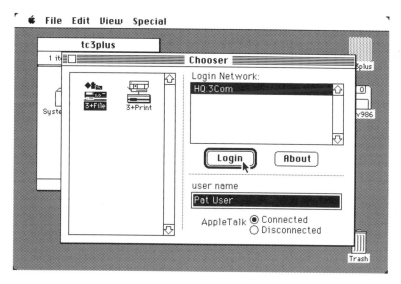

Figure 5-50   Using Chooser to select a 3Com 3+ network.

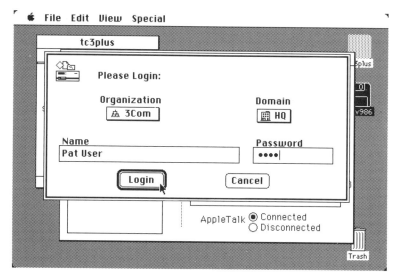

Figure 5-51   Logging into the 3Com 3+ network.

name in the list and clicking the Open button, then clicking the Link button for that folder.

When you click the Status button at the bottom of the Network Window, the software displays your status on the

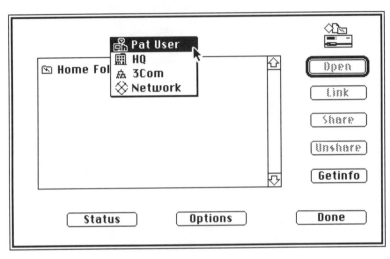

Figure
5-52
The 3+ Network Window lists your Home Folder and lets you change to a higher level in the network folder structure.

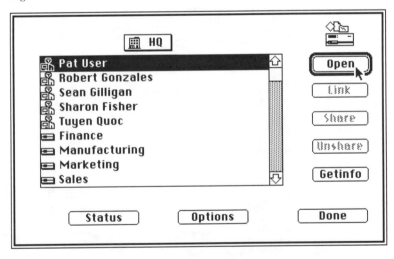

Figure
5-53
After moving up to the domain level, the Network Window displays a list of users.

network (Figure 5-54), including which server your Home Folder resides on, which shared folders you have linked to your desktop, and which printer you are linked to. You can save these settings by clicking the Save as start-up button, thereby customizing your start-up for every time you log into 3+Share. You can always link other folders by changing these settings to further customize your start-up actions.

You have the choice of saving your password as part of the automatic start-up, or not saving it (which means you have to type it each time). Your network connection is more secure if you do not save the password; otherwise anyone can use your Macintosh start-up disk to gain entry to the file server and your Home Folder.

After initial log-on, you can leave the network connection and return at any time without logging back on (Figure 5-55).

To use a printer on the Ethernet network, open the Chooser and select the 3+Print icon, then select a printer in the list (Figure 5-56). You can determine the printer's status

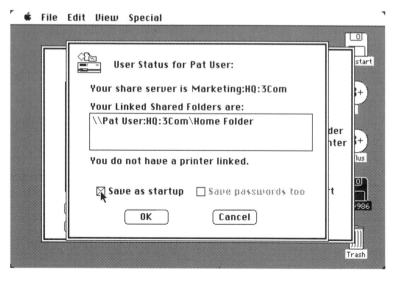

Figure 5-54

The status dialog box presented when you click the Status button in the Network Window (3+Share).

The Well-Connected Macintosh

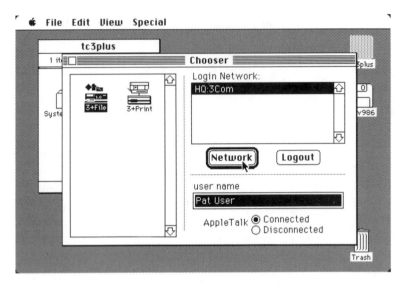

Figure
5-55
Chooser lets you log out of the network, and log back in, without going through the log-in procedure.

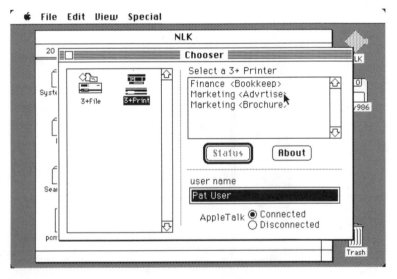

Figure
5-56
Selecting a PostScript printer on the 3+ Ethernet network.

by clicking the Status button. To send jobs to the printer, simply use your application's Print command or printing function; the software automatically looks for the PostScript device you've chosen in the Chooser.

The 3+Print software handles a spool queue and shows you the status of that queue in the display called up by the Chooser's Status button. You can remove print jobs from the queue, defer jobs to print after other jobs, and drag a priority level that looks like a volume control (Figure 5-57). You can also set options for print jobs by using the Options button in the Chooser dialog box — you can set the form number (1 for standard paper), leave subsequent print jobs on hold (retain them for the end of the queue), or defer printing to a future time.

Using *shared folders*, you can share applications as well as data files with other users. You can drag any file or folder from your personal folders to the designated shared folder (as can

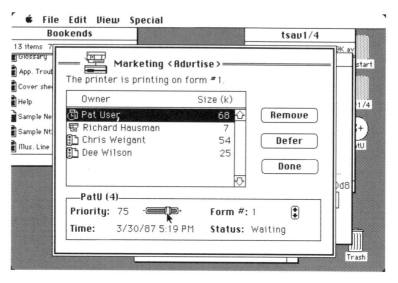

Figure 5-57   Changing priorities for print jobs for a PostScript printer on the 3+ Ethernet network.

other users), and share those files and folders by first using the Chooser desk accesory to link to the shared folder and then clicking the Share button, which displays the share dialog box (Figure 5-58). Private access guarantees that only one user (who knows the password) can access the shared folder at a time; if you don't supply a password, only you have access. Read-only means other users can read files in the folder and copy them out to another folder, but only you can change the files inside the folder or create new ones.

The 3+ network can grow to include a large number of users. To help you search through a very large network, you can set search options by clicking the Options button in the Network Window, which is displayed by the Chooser when you log in or link to folders (Figure 5-59). For example, you can remove several layers of folders from the Network Window to simplify searching, or expand to include layers that were formerly excluded.

The 3Com 3Server3 and 3+ network are designed for centralized management of a network by a network adminis-

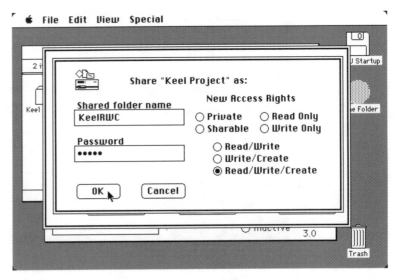

Figure
5-58

Setting up access privileges in a shared folder on the 3+ Ethernet network.

trator. Although 3+Share does not have the Finder-like flexibility of AppleShare — you still have to link to folders rather
than simply opening them, and the tree-structure with a
Home folder is more rigid — you can share files on the server
with multiple PCs connected to Ethernet or Token Ring
networks, and thereby set up corporate-wide networks with
Macintosh computers used as both stand-alone desktop
computers and as file-sharing computers.

Distributed File Sharing

We described earlier the difference between a *distributed*
server, which can offer file or disk sharing from any Macintosh
computer on the network (which is also being used for
running applications), and a *dedicated* server, which is a
computer or hardware device dedicated to the task of providing file service, print spooling, and perhaps electronic mail
service (as a message center).

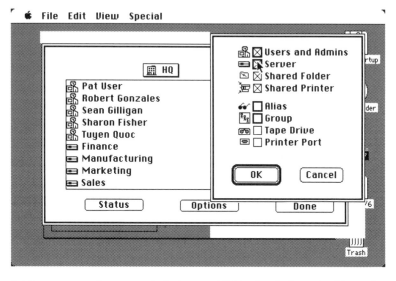

Figure
5-59

Adding or removing network devices and folder levels from the Network
Window to simplify or expand access on a large 3+ network.

Distributed servers are sometimes preferred especially if file sharing will be casual (only when necessary). In fact, network users can transfer files using electronic mail programs, but actual file or disk sharing cannot be accomplished with electronic mail.

A distributed file server running in the background means that you can use the computer to run applications in the foreground, and not have to dedicate it for file service. For example, TOPS (introduced in Chapter 3) lets users *publish* (make available) a folder of files on their disk so that other users on the network can share them without copying the folders to another storage device. With a dedicated server, users have to copy files and folders to the server to make them available for sharing.

Distributed servers tend to have less protection features and are more anarchistic. However, when you publish a folder with TOPS or HyperNet, you can set an access mode such as *write protected* (no one can change any file in the folder, or add to the folder). You can also open the folder with writing access for one or more users so that files can be added to or deleted from the folder.

Note that although a file can be opened by more than one user, the file can't be changed by more than one user at the same time unless the application program is designed to be *network-aware*. To be network-aware, applications must offer a secure environment for file sharing by providing at least record locking, which prevents another user from opening the same section of a file that you're editing and changing its contents without your knowing it. Without such precautions, changing a file by multiple users would be dangerous — files might be improperly updated or they might lose information.

There are two types of distributed servers: *disk servers* let users share parts of designated disks, and *file servers* let users share individual folders and files.

An example of a disk server is MacServe (InfoSphere), which lets you partition a hard disk into *volumes* (separate areas) that can be shared with other users, under certain access restrictions.

An example of a distributed file server is TOPS, which lets any user on the network publish one or more folders to share with other users.

The principal differences are in what is being shared — either a folder of files, or a volume on a hard disk — and how this is accomplished. MacServe lets more than one Macintosh dedicate a hard disk volume for sharing, but if more than one user wants access to the same volume, neither user can update the volume by copying files to it or changing files in it. This type of access is often called *read-only* access, because no writing is allowed.

TOPS, on the other hand, lets any number of users have access to the same folder, and if the folder is published for "many writers," everyone can update the folder by adding or changing files (although no two users can change the same file at the same time).

MacServe disk sharing is simpler to understand than distributed file sharing with TOPS and HyperNet. Both types of servers are designed as alternatives to having no file sharing at all, and these distributed server packages were available before AppleShare. MacServe was perhaps the first disk server for an AppleTalk network.

MacServe

MacServe (InfoSphere, $250) is software that works with a variety of hard disks to provide disk sharing in the background while you continue to work on the same Macintosh in the foreground.

MacServe requires a Macintosh 512K, Plus, SE, or II with at least 200K of disk space for the MacServe manager, and a hard disk. The users on the network do not need hard disks, but each user needs at least 80K of free disk space for the MacServe resources that are installed in each user's System file. With

MacServe you can have as many servers and users as you need on the network.

There is no typical configuration for MacServe because any number of users on the network can implement MacServe and create a shared disk drive. The MacServe installer adds the appropriate resources to the System File. Each copy of MacServe can create one disk server, which is called a *host*, and an unlimited number of users (Figure 5-60), and lets you specify your AppleTalk user name (which also appears in the Chooser window).

Disk volumes provide a convenient way to control access to areas of a disk. MacServe volumes appear on your desktop as separate disks, even though they are part of one disk.

To select a MacServe volume, you activate the MacServe desk accessory, which displays a volume selection dialog box (Figure 5-61). You can switch server disks by clicking the Volumes button, and the window to the left of the buttons shows a list of available volumes. Volume names with check marks are volumes you already have open — you can have up to six volumes open at the same time on multiple servers.

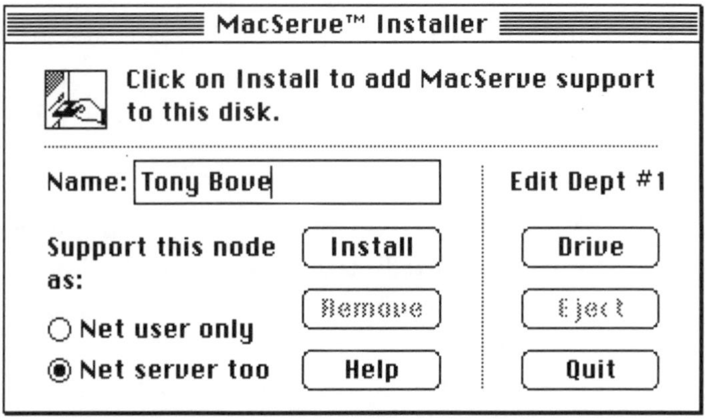
MacServe™ Installer
Click on Install to add MacServe support to this disk.
Name: Tony Bove
Edit Dept #1
Support this node as:
Net user only
Net server too
Install
Remove
Help
Drive
Eject
Quit

Figure 5-60 Installing MacServe as both a user and a server.

If you click a volume and click the Shared access button, you will have read-only access to the volume; if you click the Private button, you will have complete access to the volume, and everyone else will be locked out until you release the volume. MacServe can set up volumes to have password-controlled access.

After selecting a volume and clicking either Shared or Private, you can close the accessory, and the volume appears on your desktop as a disk. If you have Private access, you can treat the disk as any other disk on your desktop; if you have Shared access, you can only copy files from the disk or read files. To release a volume, you can drag its icon into the trash can or use the desk accessory's Release button.

MacServe also lets you share ImageWriters or special printers connected to individual Macintosh computers through their modem ports (AppleTalk must be connected to the printer ports). InfoSphere also provides a LaserWriter spooler, LaserServe, which was described earlier in this chapter.

Manager

MacServe's Manager software has menus for displaying the names of all users on the network, all the AppleTalk devices,

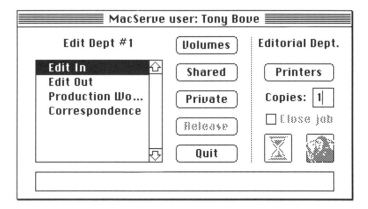

Figure 5-61

Using MacServe to select a volume and declare it to be shared or private.

all the available volumes, and all the print jobs currently spooled. Managers can also change the priority of print jobs in the queue number and the number of copies printed.

MacServe, which has been in use for a long time on AppleTalk networks, is one of the most reliable products for sharing information, but it is also one of the most limiting, especially when compared to TOPS and AppleShare. Nevertheless MacServe still has the cost-effective edge if you need to share hard disks without too much complexity.

TOPS

The TOPS file server (TOPS, $149 per user for the Mac version, $389 for the PC version including AppleTalk adaptor card) was introduced in Chapter 3. TOPS file service can extend across an AppleTalk internet and share files with users on PCs as well as with users of UNIX systems, a popular operating system for minicomputers.

TOPS is supplied with the TOPS Translators utility, a version of MacLink Plus, that converts files to and from Macintosh and PC formats (TOPS Translators and MacLink Plus are described in Chapter 3).

Any computer running TOPS and connected to an AppleTalk network can act as a file server as well as a server's client (a client is a user requesting file service). You can *publish* a folder (or a directory in a PC or UNIX system) to make it available to everyone on the network, and clients can *mount* the folder (link it to their desktops) so that it appears as a disk on their desktops.

TOPS can be installed on any computer in an AppleTalk network. There is no limit on the number of TOPS users on a network, and TOPS can offer file service to other AppleTalk networks and zones. There is no need for a designated network manager. The program is not copy protected, but TOPS will not allow two computers using the same TOPS serial number to work on the same network.

Once TOPS is installed (a very simple process), your Macintosh automatically starts TOPS every time you start the computer (you can bypass the starting of TOPS by holding down the Option key). You have the option of placing TOPS files on a separate disk and running TOPS by holding down the Option and Command keys while double-clicking the TOPS icon. A file called InterBase is provided if you are sharing files with PCs, but otherwise is unnecessary. You can also take out the TOPS desk accessory from start-up disks and put it only on working disks if you have limited disk space.

TOPS broadcasts your network name for everyone else to see when they are looking for servers. When you run the TOPS desk accessory, you see a window on the left showing your disks, volumes, and folders, and a window on the right showing TOPS servers (Figure 5-62).

You can publish any volume, disk, or folder in your system (as described in Chapter 3), and mount any volume, disk, or folder from a server. The dialog box is similar to the standard Open dialog box for Macintosh applications — to open a volume, disk, or folder, click its name and the Open button, or double-click its name. The open function follows the hierarchy of network, stations, volumes and disks, folders (or directories), and files and programs.

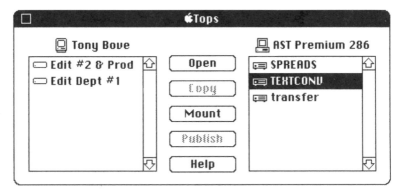

Figure 5-62

The TOPS desk accessory displays a dialog box for accessing and mounting folders from servers.

TOPS lets you copy directly from one published folder or volume to a folder on your disk, or vice-versa, without bothering to mount the published folder or volume. Or you can mount one or more published volumes and they will appear on your desktop as mounted volumes. If the published volume requires a password, you have to type it before TOPS will mount the volume. Unmounting volumes is as easy as dragging them to the trash can, or using the Unmount button.

You can control the access mode of a volume you publish, and of a volume you mount, by holding down the Option key while selecting either the Publish or Mount buttons. When you hold down Option while publishing, TOPS displays a dialog box for setting the access mode and optional password (Figure 5-63). The access modes are:

Write protected. Writing means the ability to change a file, add files, or delete files in the mounted volume. Write protected, or read-only access, lets you view or copy the file to your volume only, or save it with a new name on your system.

One writer only. Only one client can write to the volume (along with the server). Other clients will be able to read and copy files but the volume will be locked for them (a small lock appears in the upper left corner of the display).

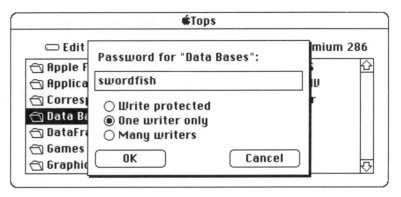

Figure 5-63

Using TOPS to set the access mode and optional password while publishing a folder or volume.

Many writers. Any client can write to the volume, and all clients see the mounted volume as unlocked. For example, two clients can save different files from the same volume at the same time.

Note that files themselves are not shared unless the application is network-aware and offers file sharing. Examples of applications that allow file sharing under TOPS are Blyth's Omnis 3 and 4th Dimension from Acius.

When you mount a volume, you can set the access mode by holding down the Option key to display the mounting access modes. Read-only access is the same as write protected — prohibiting any change in the folder or volume, including the number of files. You don't have to do this if the volume or folder is published as "write protected." Read/write access is simply the ability to write as well as read — full access — which is granted only if the published volume or folder is set to one or many writers.

If you don't hold down the Option key while publishing or mounting, you get the default access mode for both, which is many writers and read/write access. One client can launch an application that is stored in a mounted volume or folder, but the Macintosh does not usually allow two users to run the same program at the same time unless the application is designed for multiuser access. Other clients can launch the same application under TOPS only if the volume is write protected and mounted with read-only access.

You can list the clients who have mounted a published volume or folder by selecting the volume or folder and clicking the Help button. The extensive help feature of TOPS, and typical examples of using TOPS to transfer files, are shown in Chapter 3.

TEXTCONV

TOPS also offers quick text conversion in its copy function. When you copy a file from a published volume or folder to your folder, or vice-versa, the usual setting copies the entire file as is. However, if you hold down the Option key while clicking Copy, TOPS lets you choose whether or not to convert a text file to a Macintosh text file, stripping out any bytes that are not printable ASCII characters. This conversion function also takes out printer control characters and the "line feed" character. The conversion function does not work with spread sheets or data bases — you should use TOPS Translators or MacLink Plus to convert these types of files.

TOPS allows almost any program to run in the foreground as it is providing file service in the background. The exceptions are programs that do not usually allow desk accessories such as games, programming language compilers (while they're compiling), the MiniFinder, and the disk formatting program. You can tell clients to stop using the published folders or volumes on your Macintosh (InBox or InterMail could be used), then unpublish the folders or volumes before running a program that does not allow desk accessories.

TOPS is a freewheeling file server system, offering few security precautions and only the basic read/write level of protection. However, it makes up for these weaknesses by providing an easy mechanism for publishing and unpublishing folders or entire volumes that is as flexible as your needs. TOPS can be used without dedicating a computer, and yet you can set up a protected, dedicated server by first publishing the volumes of a Macintosh dedicated to running the TOPS desk accessory, and then unplugging its keyboard and mouse to prevent anyone from changing it.

HyperNet

HyperNet (General Computer, $299 per server) is a distributed file-serving software package that lets users share files on any hard disks designated as servers on an AppleTalk Network. You can use HyperNet with any combination of Macintosh 512KE, Plus, SE, and II computers.

With one copy of HyperNet you can install the server software in one Macintosh (to create one server) and designate one or more disk drives attached to the Macintosh as shared volumes that can be accessed by all other Macintosh users on the same network. After installing the server software you can use the same disk to install client software in each Macintosh. To be a server, a Macintosh must have a hard disk attached (it does not have to be a General Computer Hyper-Drive). You can buy as many copies of HyperNet as you need servers — each server is not dedicated, so you can still run applications on them; however, as with all distributed servers, you might notice performance degradation.

The HyperNet installer places resources in the system files of the server and client start-up disks. The program accepts the name for your Macintosh on the network, and identifies any servers and clients on the network. A client can then choose the HyperNet desk accessory to see the servers available on the network and select a server. HyperNet then displays volumes that are available for sharing (including volumes organized in the older flat Macintosh File System, or MFS, as well as the modern Hierarchical File System, or HFS). A client can mount any volume and type a password if the volume is protected.

Once mounted, the volume appears on your desktop with a special icon, and you can use the Open dialog box of all applications to open files in a mounted volume. Only one client can launch applications from the mounted volume and add or change a file; other clients mounting that volume get an "in use" message if they try to access the same file. These clients can still read and copy the file, or save it with a new name on their systems.

Some applications are designed for multiuser access, allowing simultaneous modification of a file by multiple users. As with TOPS and MacServe, HyperNet supports applications such as Blyth Software's Omnis 3, a package that provides simultaneous access to a data base. Most applications that are not designed for multiuser access (such as MacWrite or Microsoft Excel) will let the first person who uses a document have read/write access; HyperNet warns any subsequent users that the document is in use, but lets those users read the file and save it with a different name on their systems.

As with TOPS and MacServe, HyperNet lets a client use a System file in the System Folder of the start-up disk of a server. This is one way to share a large System file, including fonts and desk accessories, with clients on a network who don't have room for large System files. However, with copy-protected applications the user must insert key disks at the server. To avoid this inconvenience, many vendors offer a way to install a network version of the application.

HyperNet includes the HyperNet Installer program to manage a server, and the HyperNet accessory's Server menu to change priorities. One way to protect a volume on the server is to use the Installer to assign or change the volume's password.

Since up to 32 users of an AppleTalk network can access a server's disk (plus the server can be accessed from another zone), the server's performance may degrade considerably. To minimize performance degradation on servers, you can designate priorities to favor either server or client speed of access using the Server menu. You can use this feature to take control of a server computer to accomplish a high-priority task and then relinquish that control when the task is finished. The three settings of this feature are:

Client priority. This setting provides unlimited use of the server's volumes by anyone on the network.

Server priority. — This removes the server's name from the list of available servers so that no new clients can mount volumes. Existing clients with mounted volumes are not affected.

Moderated. — With the default setting, HyperNet constantly checks the server for signs of use (such as typing or program processing). When in use, the server is given more processing power, and client processing power is reduced. A client can be restricted to as low as 10 percent of the total processing power, depending on the application in use on the server.

With HyperNet, clients can use multiuser applications only if they unmount their volumes and then mount the volumes with the multiuser application. When using such an application, a client can access only one server at a time, and that server should not have any mounted volumes from other servers.

HyperNet has special controls over *semaphores*, which are controls that prevent more than one user from changing the same part of a document at the same time. The program also has the ability to create special files to be used as temporary files by applications. When more than one client uses the same application on the same server volume, the application may create temporary files that overwrite another client's temporary files. Using the Add Special Files command in the Installer's Special menu you can list the temporary files for HyperNet to manage as special files. HyperNet can then create uniquely named temporary files for any number of clients using the same application.

Overall, HyperNet is a good choice for applications requiring disk volume sharing and occasional access to the server, or for networks that can dedicate (at least temporarily) a server or to only run applications that are not going to be affected by performance (such as InBox or InterMail at a receptionist's desk).

HyperNet offers features for sharing application programs and System files, but often the performance degradation is so extensive that users are better off with their own System file and applications to share data files.

Network-aware Programs

Programs said to be *network-aware* are designed with networks in mind and typically offer the ability to share files without damaging them or failing to update them properly.

One example of a network-aware application that supports multiple users is the Omnis 3 Plus, a data base management system (Blyth Software, $495), that can take advantage of an AppleShare file server to provide data base sharing among individuals and work groups. Up to 25 users can simultaneously use an Omnis 3 data base on an AppleShare file server.

Omnis 3 Plus is a programmable data base program for creating customized data base management systems. Each of your data base files can be 160 megabytes. The multiuser version for use with the AppleShare file server lets each user on the network read and write data base records in the same file simultaneously. Any user can generate a data base report without disturbing other users who are also accessing the same data base.

AppleShare offers folder-level access protection, but Omnis 3 Plus goes a step further to offer nine levels of password-controlled access to further protect sensitive records in a data base. Automatic record locking ensures the integrity of data even while multiple users are changing records — no two users can change the same record at the same time, yet every user immediately sees the changes made to the records.

Omnis 3 Plus can be used first as a single-user data base management system, then upgraded to a multiuser system. You don't need special codes or commands to add users, since the record locking is automatic. Also, Omnis 3 Plus works on any AppleShare server, whether the server is accessed by AppleTalk or by another cabling scheme such as Ethernet or PhoneNET. It also provides remote access from other networks linked by bridges. Omnis 3 Plus can run concurrently with Apple's LaserShare print spooler on an AppleShare file server.

When you install Omnis 3 Plus in the AppleShare file server, be sure to set access privileges for the Omnis folder so that everyone can make changes to the folder. You can then use Omnis 3 Plus protection features, such as a password that controls access to the data base itself, or a lock on library formats that are used for designing a data base structure. You can also set access levels for types of users, which could be work groups (up to eight different types and associated passwords can be created). You can restrict users from accessing the entire Options menu and the Omnis Utilities program, or from options on the menus controlling the format of individual entry layouts, reports, searches, or individual entry sequences.

Without security precautions, file sharing can be dangerous, even with network-aware programs. Applications that are *not* network-aware or otherwise capable of locking the files they use can be a liability if shared by many people on a network. One person could update a shared file while others are trying to use it, causing data loss or even a system crash. Also, files that you think are updated correctly can turn out not to be.

Network-aware applications like PageMaker (version 2.0) provide minimal safeguards that usually work. One or more users can launch PageMaker from a file server, thereby saving disk space (only one copy of PageMaker is needed, which is stored on the server disk). However, performance may suffer because transfer over an AppleTalk Personal Network cable is slower than disk access, and PageMaker is slower during heavy use (you can get adequate performance with EtherTalk — an AppleTalk network using Ethernet cabling). You can easily copy the PageMaker program to your hard disk and run it, but you should have a network license agreement with Aldus (supplied by your PageMaker dealer).

A network file server makes it easier to have text and graphics available to a work group without making a lot of copies of the files. Only one person can have the original PageMaker publication file open for work, but any number of users can open a copy of the publication file (PageMaker's Open dialog box has an option for opening a copy rather than opening the original). The other users can then save their copies of the publication file under new names, or pick an existing name to overwrite another publication file. One word of caution, however: image files larger than 64K are linked to a PageMaker publication file when placed into the publication, so they should be moved into the same folder as the publication file, then placed in the publication.

As for word processing and spread sheet programs, the best policy is to copy the files from the server folder or disk to your disk, and use them on your disk. Word processing and spread sheet files usually require lengthy access while you work on them, and the word processing and spread sheet software works best on your disk rather than over the AppleTalk Personal Network. If you want to maintain a high level of performance, leave productivity software on your disk, not on a server (unless it is there simply to be copied). Use the server to share data files rather than sharing the application.

Network-aware programs are only beginning to appear, but there are many such programs in development and on the drawing boards at software companies. Eventually we will have programs that pass messages and data back and forth without user intervention, using protocols similar to IBM's Advanced Program-to-Program Communications (APPC), also known as the LU (Logical Unit) 6.2 protocols. These protocols allow programs to communicate as equals (called *peer-to-peer communications*), as well as slaves to a master program, which is the traditional relationship between mainframe programs and personal computer programs.

For example, transaction processing applications could transfer data directly to accounting programs and perform automatic updates. Stock market programs could automatically update charts and graphs. Computations could be performed on one or more computers on a network and results could be transferred to one computer for presentations. Apple has announced that it will support peer-to-peer communications between programs in future Macintosh operating systems. We expect that network services will be improved and that utility programs for monitoring and managing network usage will soon be available for AppleTalk networks.

6   Mainframes and Minicomputers

I get by with a little help from my friends.
—John Lennon/Paul McCartney

Large to medium-sized computer systems, called *mainframes* and *minicomputers*, operate in most corporations, educational institutions, and government. Traditionally the mainframe computer was the repository of all information, and each department of the corporation had a minicomputer and terminals to access the mainframe data as well as process large amounts of departmental data.

Data processing has changed now that local area network (LAN) architectures, such as the AppleTalk Network System, can link together powerful personal computers and workstations on a network to handle departmental tasks. Most corporate computer users still need to access data stored on mainframes and use minicomputers in productive ways. There are

271

two ways of doing this, and you can use either method or mix them according to your needs:

1. *Terminal connection.* Essentially your Macintosh emulates one or more of the older VDTs (video display terminals) you used to access the mainframe or minicomputer. First you connect individual Macintosh computers to mainframes or minicomputers using serial cable, with modems for remote connection. Then you use terminal emulation packages to act like a terminal on the mainframe or minicomputer, and transfer files to and from the mainframe or minicomputer. Some terminal emulation packages offer enough terminals to emulate that you can use the same program to switch between a mainframe and a minicomputer.

2. *Networking and file service.* You can connect an AppleTalk network by a gateway to another network, such as the IBM's 3274 cluster controllers or networks, Digital Equipment Corporation's DECNet networks, or standard Ethernet networks, which are typically managed by the mainframe or minicomputer providing file and print services. Another alternative is to connect the Macintosh computers directly to the mainframe-controlled or mini-controlled network (such as MAPS, a network for managing a manufacturing plant). Most of the innovative product development is occurring in this area of mini-mainframe communications.

The major difference between the first and second choices can be summarized by comparing the use of resources (hard disks, printers, modems) to the use of computational power (using several processors in a single task, setting up program-to-program communication). The first choice lets you use the resources of the mainframe or minicomputer. The second choice lets you share the resources of a network of mixed mainframes, minicomputers, and workstations, and opens the way toward future development in sharing computational power as well as resources.

The major benefit of the first choice (terminal emulation) is that in most cases, you don't have to change anything in the mainframe or minicomputer system, or even tell the system manager of the mainframe or minicomputer system that you are using a Macintosh as a terminal. It is also less expensive than most other solutions because you don't have to change any hardware or software on the mainframe or minicomputer side — just add asynchronous cable, software, and possibly modems.

The major benefits of the second choice (networking) are faster throughput, complete emulation of a cluster controller or other network traffic-controlling device, and more productive use of the mainframe or minicomputer by using it to perform file and print service. It may also be cheaper to use the second choice if you have not already bought the cluster controllers, terminals, and other networking hardware for the mainframe or minicomputer. This choice is cost-effective for connecting many personal computers to whatever network is already in place and controlled by the mainframe or minicomputer, such as an IBM 3274 cluster controller network of terminals, or an Ethernet network of UNIX workstations.

The two major choices — terminal connection or network transfer — are sometimes combined in a single package (such as Tri-Data's Netway 1000A, or Pacer's pcLINK software). In some cases the network approach is merely a different way to physically connect the hardware while you are using the same terminal emulation and file transfer software on the Macintosh.

What makes mainframe linking more confusing is that new products are constantly being introduced, and some will be addressing the inadequacies in existing products. In order to gain a perspective, it is helpful to look at mainframe connectivity from different viewpoints: the IBM world of mainframes and minicomputers, including all Systems Network Architecture (SNA) networks, and the *other* world. This other world includes industry giants like Digital Equipment Corporation (DEC) and Wang Laboratories, workstation manufacturers such as Sun Microsystems and Apollo Computer, other minicomputer manufacturers such as Data General Corporation and Prime Computer, and a variety of workstations and minicomputers that use the UNIX operating system and the Ethernet network.

The IBM Mainframe World

To communicate with the IBM 43XX, 370 or 308X mainframes, you need something similar to an IBM 3278 or a DEC VT100 terminal (a CRT and keyboard). The Macintosh has a built-in CRT and keyboard, so if you add the software to emulate either an IBM 3278 terminal (best choice) or a DEC VT100 terminal (adequate), you are most of the way toward establishing simple communications with the IBM mainframe, which is called the *host* computer.

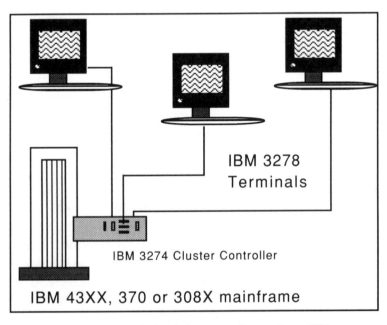

IBM 3278 Terminals

IBM 3274 Cluster Controller

IBM 43XX, 370 or 308X mainframe

*Figure
6-1*

Communicating with an IBM mainframe usually requires a 3278-type terminal connected to an expensive cluster controller, which allows several terminals to connect to the mainframe.

The next step is to establish a physical connection. You could use a modem, if the mainframe directly supports asynchronous modems. You could then use a number of communication programs that can emulate terminals, such as MacTerminal or MicroPhone (described in Chapter 2) and VersaTerm Pro (Peripherals Computers & Supplies, $295). However, these programs do not support file transfer to and from an IBM mainframe unless the mainframe is running a program that uses the Kermit, Xmodem or MacBinary protocols. To support file transfer, you need to use the same file transfer software protocols on both the host computer and the Macintosh.

Modem communication is slow at best. The most widely used physical communication facility for accessing IBM mainframes is the 3270 communications and a hardware protocol converter, such as a 3274/76 Cluster Controller. You would normally attach several IBM 3278-2 terminals to the cluster controller, which in turn communicates either directly or over a synchronous modem to the mainframe's front-end processor (Figure 6-1).

There are several ways to connect a Macintosh computer or network to an IBM mainframe that utilizes 3270-style communications and protocol conversion:

AppleLine. Apple's version of the popular IRMAline file transfer and emulation product for PCs from DCA (Digital Communications Associates) connects to the modem port of one Macintosh to let it communicate with an IBM 3274/76 Cluster Controller, and includes MacTerminal software that lets a Macintosh emulate an IBM 3278-2 terminal (Figure 6-2). Apple also offers the AppleLine 3270 File Transfer software for linking with DCA's file transfer software on the host computer.

MacMainFrame DX and SE. Avatar's DX protocol converter also connects to any Macintosh modem port, and the SE product installs inside a Macintosh SE and connects to coaxial cable. Either one lets one Macintosh communicate with an

IBM 3274/76 Cluster Controller. Avatar offers the MacMain-Frame desk accessory and Host File Transfer (HFT) software for the mainframe allowing complete file transfers.

Netway 1000A. Tri-Data's substitute device for a 3274 Cluster Controller lets any number of Macintosh computers on an AppleTalk Personal Network communicate with the mainframe — up to 16 Macintosh computers simultaneously (Figure 6-3). Tri-Data offers the Mac-Windows 3270 program that works with multiple Netways to access up to four different mainframes and show all four sessions on each Macintosh display. Tri-Data also offers MacMover, which is a version of Avatar's MacMainFrame software for file transfer to and from HFT on the host.

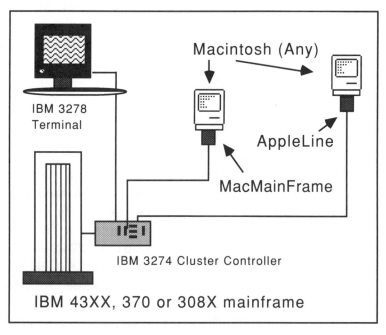

IBM 3278 Terminal

Macintosh (Any)

AppleLine

MacMainFrame

IBM 3274 Cluster Controller

IBM 43XX, 370 or 308X mainframe

Figure 6-2

A Macintosh can emulate an IBM 3278 terminal and connect to a 3274/76 Cluster Controller using AppleLine or Avatar's MacMainFrame DX.

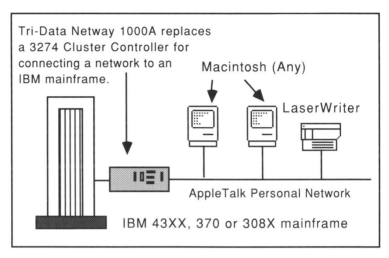

Tri-Data Netway 1000A replaces a 3274 Cluster Controller for connecting a network to an IBM mainframe.

Macintosh (Any)

LaserWriter

AppleTalk Personal Network

IBM 43XX, 370 or 308X mainframe

Figure
6-3

You can substitute the Tri-Data Netway 1000A for the IBM 3274 cluster controller and connect an entire AppleTalk Personal Network to the mainframe.

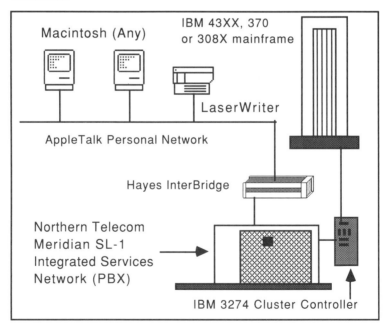

Macintosh (Any)

IBM 43XX, 370 or 308X mainframe

LaserWriter

AppleTalk Personal Network

Hayes InterBridge

Northern Telecom Meridian SL-1 Integrated Services Network (PBX)

IBM 3274 Cluster Controller

Figure
6-4

Another way to connect Macintosh computers and networks to mainframes is through Northern Telecom's Meridian Integrated Services Network and PBX.

277

PBX network. The Meridien SL-1 Integrated Services Network and PBX (private branch exchange), from Northern Telecom, lets you connect Macintosh computers and an AppleTalk Personal Networks to IBM mainframes (Figure 6-4).

There are a number of options and alternatives associated with these methods of communicating with IBM mainframes, so let's examine them in more detail.

AppleLine

AppleLine (Apple Computer, $1295) is a device that connects any Macintosh computer to an IBM 3274/76 Cluster Controller with coaxial cable. With MacTerminal or a similar program running on the Macintosh, you can emulate a 3278 Model 2 terminal. The AppleLine protocol converter attaches to the modem port of a Macintosh using a serial cable, and you can also use a modem between the modem port and the AppleLine device for remote connection.

With the AppleLine device you can use the AppleLine 3270 File Transfer software ($99), which lets you send and receive files to and from an IBM mainframe. The AppleLine 3270 File Transfer software is designed to be used in conjunction with MacTerminal, which provides basic interactive 3270 emulation. AppleLine 3270 File Transfer emulates a 3278 terminal and supports a 24-line display with a 25th status line. It supports all 3278 keys on screen and has a function key bar you can configure according to your needs.

The file transfer software works with DCA's IRMAlink host software and operates in both MVS/TSO and VM/CMS environments, allowing a Macintosh to exchange multiple file types (MacBinary, PC binary, text, assembly, COBOL, DATA, and so on) with a mainframe. It also lets you use a mainframe as an intermediary for transferring files to PCs as well as other Macintosh computers.

For example, you can use AppleLine 3270 File Transfer to transfer a Lotus 1-2-3 file, which was initially created on an

IBM PC and stored on an IBM mainframe, to a Macintosh using the PC binary format, then use the files with Microsoft Excel on the Macintosh. In order to use the file transfer software you must use IRMAlink FT/TSO or FT/CMS (from DCA) on the mainframe. (This is the same software that enables PCs with DCA IRMA boards to transfer files to IBM host computers.) You can order one free copy of the host software from DCA if you purchase the AppleLine 3270 File Transfer package.

MacMainFrame

MacMainFrame DX (Avatar Technologies, $1195) is a hardware and software package that lets you connect any Macintosh to a 3270 cluster controller device and provides 3278 terminal emulation. MacMainFrame is a desk accessory used with MacTerminal that provides file transfer. The package includes the PA100G micro-to-mainframe hardware link to connect the Macintosh to a cluster controller using coaxial cable. The PA100G contains an auxiliary asynchronous port that you can use to connect your Macintosh to a Digital Equipment Corporation (DEC) VAX minicomputer (which acts as another host), and the MacMainFrame software lets you switch back and forth between sessions running simultaneously with the two hosts. The device is also compatible with AppleLine 3270 File Transfer software.

Avatar Technologies also offers MacMainFrame SE ($795), a card designed specifically for the Macintosh SE that provides 3278 terminal emulation and file transfer. The card has a connector for coaxial cable to connect to an IBM control unit or Display Printer Adapter (type A coax). MacMainFrame SE software is a program that does not need MacTerminal to establish communication and emulate a terminal, nor does it need the PA100G to connect to the cluster controller.

The major benefit in using Avatar's MacMainFrame DX or SE is that the host computer does not need to know that a

Macintosh is connected rather than a terminal. The coaxial cable can transfer data at a rate of 2.35 megabits per second and is much faster than asynchronous cable (which has a top speed of 19.2 kilobits).

MacMainFrame SE lets you set terminal preferences (Figure 6-5) including the EBCDIC language set used in mainframes or the ASCII set used in microcomputers (including the Macintosh). Its emulation is as close as possible to the IBM 3278 Model 2 terminal, including the IBM icons in the bottom status line of the display (Figure 6-6). You can edit and delete text on the display, just as with an IBM 3278 when it is in page mode, using the keyboard equivalents (Figures 6-7 and 6-8). MacMainFrame transfers the entire screen to the mainframe.

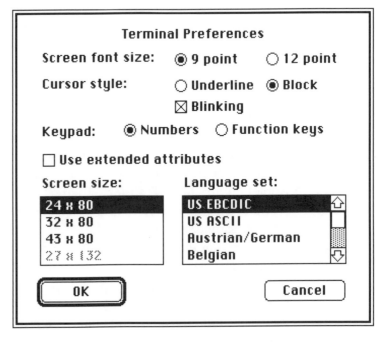

Figure
6-5

MacMainFrame SE software lets you tailor your terminal preferences.

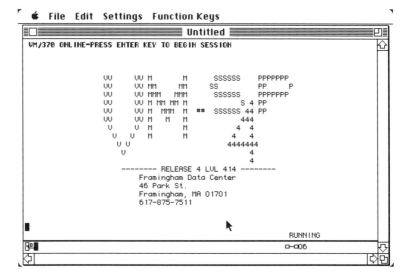

Figure
6-6

Logging onto a mainframe computer using MacMainFrame.

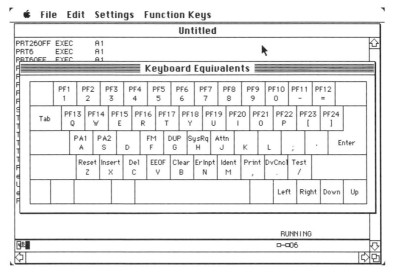

Figure
6-7

MacMainFrame SE provides keyboard equivalents for performing page
mode functions using a Macintosh as an IBM 3278 terminal.

You can specify the mainframe system and the name of the host file transfer software (Figure 6-9). You need to run

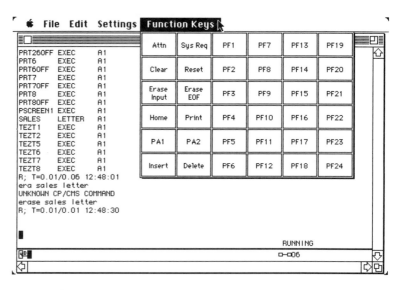

Figure
6-8

You can click a MacMainFrame function key with your mouse.

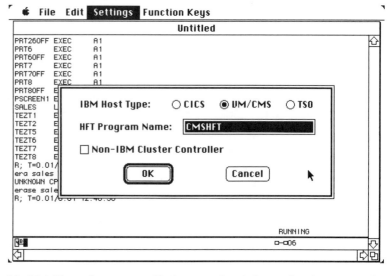

Figure
6-9

MacMainFrame lets you specify the type of mainframe (host) system and the name of the host file transfer program.

Avatar's Host File Transfer (HFT) software in CICS, TSO, or CMS mainframe operating systems in order to perform file transfer. MacMainFrame offers three modes of transfer: text, binary, and document (Figure 6-10), and lets you specify the name, file type, and file mode for the copy stored on the mainframe.

Document mode transfers an exact image of a Macintosh file so that the mainframe computer can store all types of Macintosh programs and files. Binary mode transfers non-Macintosh files such as Lotus 1-2-3 WKS files, Microsoft SYLK files, and IBM Document Content Architecture (DCA) documents.

During file transfer, MacMainFrame displays relevant information, including number of bytes transferred (Figure 6-11) and the status of the operation (the hand icon points to the status).

MacMainFrame can expand the tab settings of text files (Figure 6-12) to conform to the tab settings of data files

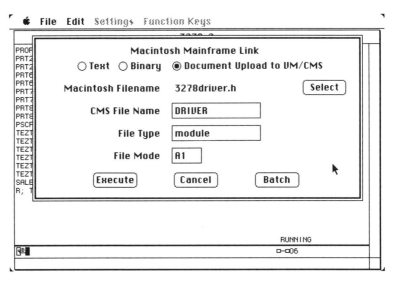

Figure 6-10

MacMainFrame offers three modes of file transfer: text, binary (for non-Macintosh files), and document (for Macintosh files).

associated with programs on the mainframe. You can use the mouse to click tab settings (Figure 6-13), then clear all settings, set standard tabs of eight spaces, or revert back to the tab settings in the file. You can also embed control characters in the text by preceding them with a backslash (\).

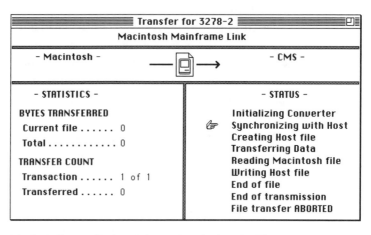

*Figure
6-11*

MacMainFrame displays information during the file transfer; you can also set up a "batch" of files to transfer in one session.

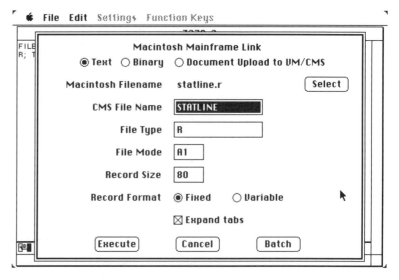

*Figure
6-12*

On text file transfers to the host, MacMainFrame can expand tab settings.

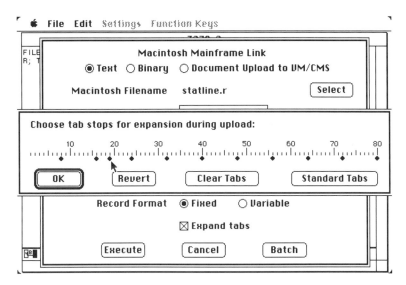

Figure
6-13

You can choose the tab settings for expansion during the text file transfer.

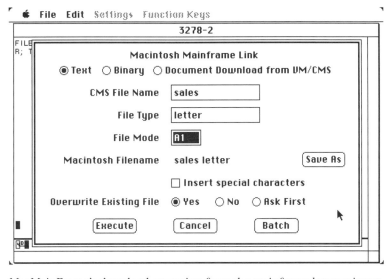

Figure
6-14

MacMainFrame's download operation from the mainframe lets you insert special characters, save the file by another name, or overwrite the existing file.

When receiving in document mode, MacMainFrame picks up the entire image including the file's icon and file name. With text files (Figure 6-14), MacMainFrame combines the file name and type to form the Macintosh file name; you can change its name with the Save As command or overwrite any existing file by the same name.

Avatar Technologies designed MacMainFrame using a custom 3270 Gate Array chip and an Applications Program Interface (API), which gives software developers the ability to write applications linked to mainframe applications, using 3270 emulation and file transfer. The MacMainFrame DX product has been in use since 1985 and is reliable.

Netway 1000A

Tri-Data offers an AppleTalk-to-mainframe connection box that can be substituted for an expensive 3274 Cluster Controller. The Netway 1000A ($3195) lets every Macintosh user on an AppleTalk Personal Network gain access to the mainframe's front-end processor, with up to 16 users accessing the mainframe simultaneously. With AppleTalk Personal Networks proliferating, Tri-Data's Netway device represents an economical alternative to providing mainframe access to a group of individual Macintosh users. Any user on an AppleTalk Personal Network or internet can gain access to the mainframe.

The Netway 1000A emulates an IBM 3274 Cluster Controller and lets an entire AppleTalk Personal Network of Macintosh computers connect to the mainframe and use the Tri-Data software to emulate IBM 3278 terminals. You can connect more than one Netway 1000A to an AppleTalk Personal Network so that you can communicate with several host mainframes and minicomputers. The Netway 1000A also includes a 3278 software emulation package (which is not copy protected) that provides session control between Macintosh computers and the Netway.

The Netway 1000A can connect to a mainframe by modem with a supplied modem cable (at up to 19,200 bps). It supports either the SNA/SDLC (Systems Network Architecture/Synchronous Data Link Control) protocol or the BSC (bisynchronous) protocol. The host mainframe system must be generated to define the Netway 1000A as an IBM 3274-51C or 61C controller. Otherwise, the installation of a Netway 1000A takes only a few minutes.

For file transfer, Tri-Data offers a version of Avatar Technologies' MacMainFrame called MacMover ($995 for one AppleTalk network of up to 32 users, 16 simultaneously). MacMover is compatible with Switcher, an Apple utility program (supplied with the Netway software) that lets you switch from one application window to another on the Macintosh display without quitting either application. Tri-Data also offers MacWindows 3270 ($125), an optional terminal emulation program for the SNA/SDLC protocol that lets you set up four windows on a Macintosh screen concurrently accessing four different host mainframes.

The MacMover desk accessory, co-developed with Avatar and based on the MacMainFrame desk accessory, lets you transfer text files, Macintosh files (document mode), or binary files to and from the host. As with MacMainFrame, text mode lets you exchange text between any IBM mainframe and a Macintosh connected to the Netway. Document mode file transfer lets you transfer Macintosh files completely (both data and resource forks) to and from the IBM host. The format used to store the file on the host is identical to the MacBinary format described in Chapter 2. Binary mode file transfer lets you transfer PC files such as Lotus 1-2-3 "WKS" files, IBM DCA text files, and IGES graphics files. The companion host file transfer software ($500) runs under TSO, CMS, and CICS mainframe operating systems.

The Netway emulation software provides a set of 3278 function keys you can use by holding down the Option key (Figure 6-15). File transfer (Figure 6-16) is almost identical to that of MacMainFrame. You can use Switcher with MacMover, so that once you start a file transfer, you can switch from the

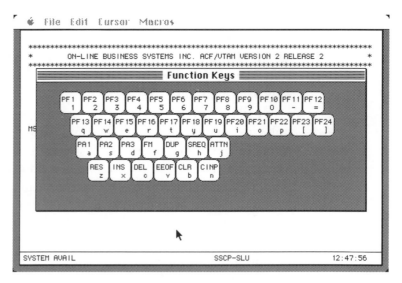

Figure
6-15

Tri-Data's Netway terminal emulation software provides function keys you use by holding down the Option key.

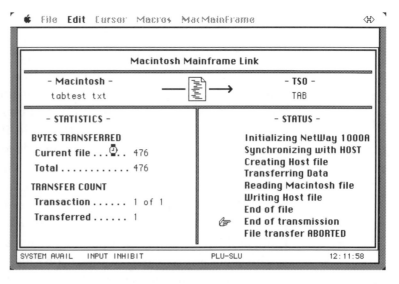

Figure
6-16

288

Using MacMover to perform file transfer, which is a version of MacMain-Frame.

host session back to a Macintosh application while the file transfer continues in the background. You can also copy data

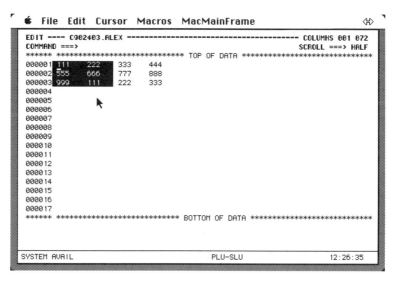

*Figure
6-17*
Using Switcher with Netway's emulation software to copy data from the mainframe before switching to the Macintosh application.

*Figure
6-18*
Switching to the Macintosh application (Excel) to paste the data into spread sheet cells.

from a mainframe session (Figure 6-17) and paste it into a Macintosh application such as Microsoft Excel (Figure 6-18).

MacWindows 3270 lets you display up to four simultaneous mainframe sessions (Figure 6-19), and copy and paste between them as well as perform file transfers. You have full control over resizing windows. Each host needs one Netway device connected to the AppleTalk network; all users on the network can access all four hosts. A Macintosh running Mac-Windows 3270 is an excellent alternative to an IBM 3270 PC.

Tri-Data's Netway package may seem expensive, but if you need to provide access for up to 16 of the Macintosh computers in an AppleTalk, you can't beat the price, which comes down to about $200 per terminal connection.

PBX and Other Alternatives

Another option for connecting one or more Macintosh computers to an IBM mainframe, and also to other mainframes and minicomputers, is to use a private branch exchange (PBX) along with a protocol converter. For example, the Northern Telecom Meridian SL-1 Integrated Services Network, described in Chapter 4, uses the AppleTalk network protocols to extend an AppleTalk Personal Network beyond its physical limitations. You can then connect the PBX to the SL-1/3274 Cluster Controller for an IBM 30xx mainframe, or a 5251 Protocol Converter for an IBM System 36. You can set up automatic log-on and file transfer operations, and call queuing to connect automatically to the next available phone line. Best of all, you can talk on the phone and use the data network at the same time over the same PBX line.

Some IBM systems are non-standard even within the IBM world. For these systems, it is sometimes best to use IBM's gateway connections to SNA/SDLC cluster controllers, or simply connect a single Macintosh to the computer by modem and run communication software that can emulate an appropriate terminal.

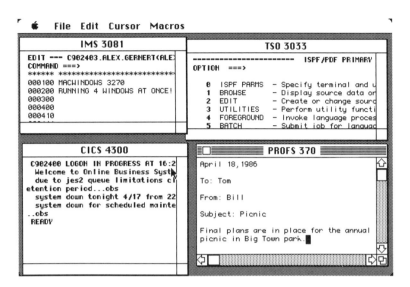

Figure 6-19

Tri-Data's MacWindows 3270 software lets you display up to four simultaneous sessions with different mainframe hosts, and copy/paste data between them.

To connect to an IBM System 34, 36, or 38 (System 3x), you can choose among several terminal emulation programs and protocol converters. The DCF II hardware converter (Wall Data, $3995 to $5995) lets you connect either to System 3x minicomputers or the 370 series of mainframes. The supplied software transforms a Macintosh and ImageWriter printer into an IBM 5251 terminal and IBM 5256 printer, and lets you transfer binary or ASCII text files using Wall Data's FTX software on the host System 3x. You can connect up to six Macintosh computers with one model, 10 with another, and 18 with another.

Another alternative is the Series II Twinax package from KMW Systems Corporation ($1495), which provides similar features with emulation of the IBM 5291 terminal and 5256 printer. KMW's software lets you transfer text and binary files with a host that is running KMW's Emulator Transfer Utility.

As of this writing, Apple Computer is hard at work on a 3270 communications card for the Macintosh II that will let users establish multiple communication sessions for both 3270 and 5250 IBM mainframe controllers. The board will take care of all communication functions, and users will be able to choose file transfer options using the Chooser desk accessory. Apple will also offer an implementation of IBM's Logical Unit 6.2 program-to-program communications protocols which are described in Chapter 5.

More terminal emulation programs are described later in this chapter, since they are useful for communicating with non-IBM mainframes and minicomputers.

Other Worlds

The rest of the world of minicomputers and mainframes can be divided into those computers that can connect to the industry-standard Ethernet network (such as DEC and Sun Microsystems), and those that offer proprietary connections and networks that are addressed only by terminal connection.

Digital Equipment Corporation (DEC) has a large share of the minicomputer market, and the DEC VAX line is the most popular line of minicomputers. Connecting to VAX minicomputers is perhaps easier than connecting to IBM computers because there are more choices.

The physical connection between a Macintosh and the DEC VAX host system can be almost any combination of links: serial cable (directly connected or through use of modems); the Ethernet network, using devices that connect to an AppleTalk network (such as Apple's EtherTalk card for the Macintosh II, or the Kinetics FastPath or EtherSC bridges, all described in Chapter 4); or through an Omninet network from Corvus Systems ($199 per workstation plus $395 for network management software).

After connecting physically to Ethernet or directly to a VAX, your Macintosh still needs communication and file transfer software. Most communication programs emulate DEC VT100 terminals and some also emulate VT220/240,

VT51, Viewpoint 60, Televideo 950, Stratus V102, and Prime PT200 terminals. pcLINK from Pacer Software is one of the most popular terminal emulation and file transfer programs and is closely integrated with Kinetics devices for connecting to VAX host computers.

DEC VAX minicomputers can run a variety of operating systems including VMS, Ultrix (a version of UNIX), and UNIX. Alisa Systems is currently working on a version of AppleShare for the VAX VMS environment that may be available by the time you read this.

The AppleTalk Network System running on an Ethernet backbone, as described in Chapter 4, provides a neat fit into departments running DEC equipment and DEC's network, called DECNet. The combination of Macintosh and DEC computers is sufficiently powerful to challenge IBM in the departmental computing market.

Pacer and Kinetics

You can use any of the methods described in Chapter 4 to connect to Ethernet, including Kinetics' bridge devices and Apple's EtherTalk card for the Macintosh II, and then use Pacer Software's pcLINK or other programs for the Macintosh and VAX environments to accomplish communication.

Pacer's pcLINK lets Macintosh computers communicate over an Ethernet network with DEC VAXes and other computers using the UNIX operating system. Pacer's software supports both the AppleTalk network protocols and the standard TCP/IP (Transmission Control Protocol/Internet Protocol) used in a variety of UNIX systems. The AppleTalk protocols are also supported in the DEC VAX VMS operating environment so that the VAX can provide Macintosh-type printing with PostScript devices, and file sharing services. The TCP/IP protocols can be used to communicate with VAX Ultrix and other UNIX operating environments ranging from Sun Microsystems workstations to Cray supercomputers.

Pacer's host software can communicate with Apple's Ether-Talk card in a Macintosh II, with AppleTalk adaptor cards for PCs, and with Ethernet networks of PCs. You can also establish communication via modem and serial cable.

Pacer's pcLINK offers full emulations of DEC VT100, DEC VT220, DEC VT240, Viewpoint 60, Televideo 950, Stratus V102, and Prime PT200 terminals, with all features supported, including block mode. It also offers complete file transfer including MacBinary files, the ability to set up a virtual Macintosh volumes or even an AppleShare-compatible file server with files on the VAX host's disk storage systems, and host printing on line printers and PostScript-compatible devices.

Pacer pcLINK consists of software installed on both the Macintosh and VAX host computers (the VAX can be running VMS or Ultrix). Pricing is based on the number of host server computers with no additional charges for software on the Macintosh. Host server pricing is based on the number of

Figure 6-20

Pacer Software's pcLINK includes custom scripts, soft key files (with predefined function keys), and terminal emulation and configuration settings documents.

simultaneous users ($2000 for up to five simultaneous users, $5000 for up to 20, $10,000 for up to 50, $15,000 for up to 100, $25,000 for up to 250, and $37,500 for up to 500 simultaneous users), including upgrades and site licenses. This pricing scheme lets you install the software on all computers at the site for even the smallest server license, and upgrade to a higher usage level license only as your needs increase.

Pacer offers graphics terminal emulation (VT241) priced according to the number of Macintosh computers used ($150 each up to 24, $125 each up to 99, $100 each up to 500, and $75 each above 500 microcomputers). Pacer also offers Pacer-Print for using the VAX as a print server, which is priced according to the type of VAX ($1000 for a MicroVAX, $2000 for any other type of VAX, and $4000 for a VAX Cluster). The files supplied with Pacer software (Figure 6-20) help you customize your communication sessions through configuration settings documents, soft key files (containing user-defined function keys), and custom scripts.

The terminal emulation software supports full block mode, and you can leave terminal mode at any time (using Switcher or the MultiFinder) to perform pcLINK or other functions on the Macintosh without logging off the host, with full copy and paste ability. You can set up pcLINK to emulate a specific DEC terminal, communicate with a specific type of host computer running a specific type of operating system, and specifying a soft key file and start-up script (Figure 6-21), then save that particular configuration (called a "personality") in a document that saves those settings for future use.

The program displays soft keys that can be activated by mouse or keyboard, which can be programmed to generate anything from simple commands (for the host) to complex sequences of terminal functions controlled by a script (Figure 6-22). Soft keys can activate other soft key files, so you can use one set of soft keys first to invoke a particular application and then to use that application's associated soft keys. You could easily hide the host application's cryptic commands so that you only need to remember the soft keys (whose names can be descriptive). For example, you could set up a Help soft key

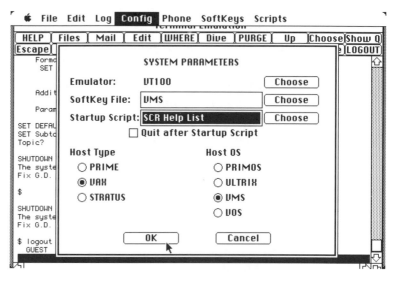

Figure
6-21

Defining the terminal settings for pcLINK, including start-up actions.

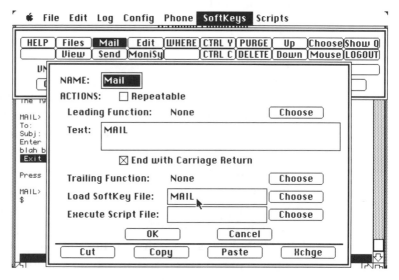

Figure
6-22

Defining a pcLINK soft key to access the mail system on a VAX.

that executes a special script file that controls the VMS help facility (Figure 6-23).

You can use pcLINK to transfer ASCII text files, binary files (such as PC files), and MacBinary files (with full error correction). Text files are converted to the appropriate format depending on the system receiving the file; binary files are left unconverted, and MacBinary files are transferred completely with both the resource fork and the data fork (including icons, fonts, and its name). You select the type of transfer (Figure 6-24) and the file to be transferred. The software is designed to support the creation of archives of Macintosh files on the VAX host, and retrieval of shared documents, spread sheets, and other programs that originated on PCs, on the VAX, and on Macintosh computers. Pacer's proprietary protocol adjusts packet sizes to allow the highest level of throughput for the specific type of connection you are using. You can also select and store a selection of files to transfer as a batch operation.

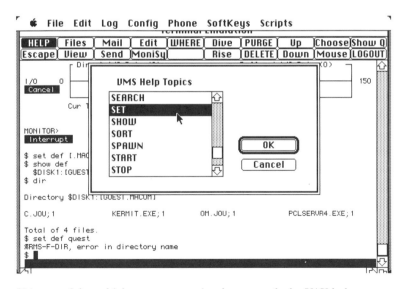

Figure 6-23

Using a soft key which executes a script that controls the VAX help facility, presenting help topics as a Macintosh would present them rather than using the cryptic VAX commands.

You can also integrate the file transfer function with other applications such as word processing translation programs on the VAX. For example, the pcLINK program can be integrated with DEC's ALL-IN-1 office automation package so that when Macintosh users request copies of documents stored in DEC's word processing format, pcLINK is automatically used to convert the documents to the MacWrite format and transfer them over the network.

The virtual disk capability lets you set up an area of a VAX disk to look like a disk drive locally attached to the Macintosh. The virtual disks (any number can be handled) can vary in size from the size of a floppy disk to 30 megabytes or more. Software is also provided to access the virtual disks from the host VAX. The pcLINK software handles sharing the disk over the network and provides command files for setting up an automatic backup from the Macintosh disk to the VAX disk.

Virtual disks can be used as libraries of shared documents, programs, spread sheets, or graphics. You can mount these

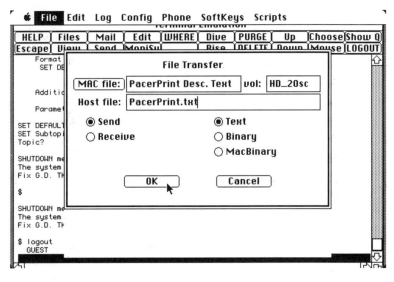

Figure 6-24

Using pcLINK to initiate a file transfer, which lets you supply a host file name as well as the type of file transfer.

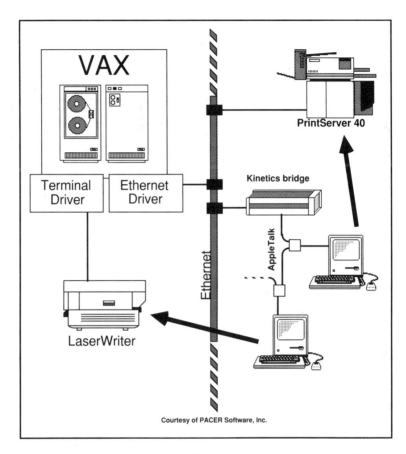

VAX

PrintServer 40

Terminal Driver

Ethernet Driver

Kinetics bridge

AppleTalk

Ethernet

LaserWriter

Courtesy of PACER Software, Inc.

Figure 6-25

PacerPrint lets you connect LaserWriters with serial cable to the VAX for sharing across the network.

VAX-resident volumes as part of starting up the Macintosh each day. The pcLINK program presents the files using familiar Macintosh icons and folders, and provides AppleShare compatibility.

Pacer provides another software package, called PacerPrint ($1000 for MicroVAX license), to directly connect any PostScript-compatible devices, including LaserWriters, to the VAX (using serial cable) for sharing with all VAX users (Figure 6-25). PacerPrint is fully integrated with VMS print services (as a VMS print symbiont) and can be used by any

299

VAX terminal user by means of the PRINT command as well as through pcLINK.

Pacer also offers the pcLINK Spooler which, when used in conjunction with PacerPrint, lets Macintosh users select and spool files to the VAX printers. The host print server software lets any number of Macintosh users spool files to up to 16 PostScript-compatible printers connected on the Ethernet network (Figure 6-26).

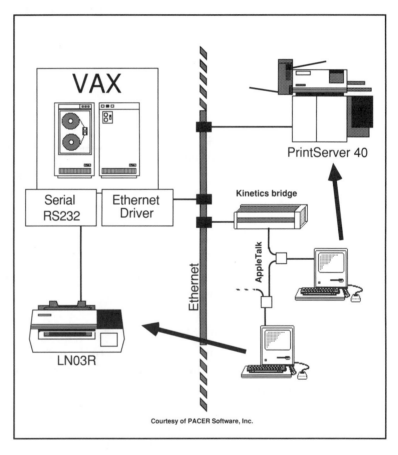

Figure 6-26

Pacer software lets you use the VAX as a print server for PostScript printers on the Ethernet network.

You can select any printer on the network using the Chooser desk accessory, and after you start the print job from the Macintosh (Figure 6-27), the PacerPrint software takes over on the VAX, and pcLINK almost immediately releases the Macintosh for other activities. A VAX can therefore be used as a print server with spooling and queue management ability for an entire Ethernet network and any number of AppleTalk networks. You can also print host files on a LaserWriter connected to any AppleTalk network. The PacerPrint software provides translators to convert Tektronix 4014, ReGIS, Diablo 630, and standard VMS files to PostScript for printing.

Additional features of pcLINK include the ability to let an AppleTalk network coexist with DECNet, LAT-11, XNS, or any other protocol running over an Ethernet network while retaining all VMS security features. The entire VAX family of minicomputers and microcomputers is compatible with pcLINK.

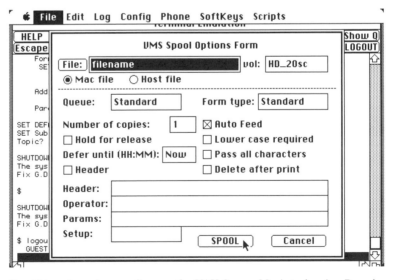

Figure 6-27

Specifying the print spooling on the VAX from a Macintosh using Pacer's pcLINK Spooler.

Pacer's software makes it possible to establish the host VAX as an intermediary for passing data between two Macintosh computers or between a Macintosh and any other computer on Ethernet, including IBM PCs and compatibles. It also lets a VAX function as a file server and print server.

Bridge devices from Kinetics (described in Chapter 4) are often used in conjunction with Pacer software. Kinetics also offers print serving from any UNIX computer.

K-Spool ($495) runs on UNIX systems and acts as an Apple LaserWriter print spooler for both Macintosh and UNIX users. The software lets both systems share common Laser-Writers and spools print jobs. Macintosh printing is spooled immediately to the UNIX system, freeing the Macintosh to do other things. K-Spool is distributed as a UNIX program, and no special software is required on the Macintosh. Connection to Ethernet is established using Kinetics hardware, as described in Chapter 4.

Other Kinetics software products that offer Macintosh-UNIX (over Ethernet) compatibility include K-Talk, an independent implementation of the AppleTalk protocols for the UNIX operating system (including AppleTalk programmers' libraries), and K-Term, a Macintosh program offering multiple windows and terminal emulation for UNIX systems attached to Ethernet.

AlisaTalk

The AlisaTalk package from Alisa Systems is a set of software packages for DEC VAX minicomputers running the VMS operating system to support AppleTalk network services. AlisaTalk is priced according to the type of VAX, starting at $3750 for a MicroVAX II, VAX 2000, VAXStation, 11/730, or 11/750 and going up to $11,500 for a VAX 8800.

With AlisaTalk you can set up a VAX to act as a full AppleShare-compatible file server and provide network spooling, network terminal functions, and file interchange with the VAX environment. AlisaTalk does not require Macintosh users to log into the VAX host, and LaserWriters and other PostScript-compatible devices can be left attached to an AppleTalk Personal Network rather than be connected with serial cable to the VAX. Therefore, Macintosh users do not need accounts on the VAX host, and print jobs can be sent to the printer at the speed of AppleTalk rather than through slower serial cable.

To use AlisaTalk, you connect an AppleTalk Personal Network to Ethernet using either a Kinetics bridge device or Apple's EtherTalk card for the Macintosh II. AlisaTalk can operate with existing DECNet Ethernet hardware, with DECNet and AppleTalk services sharing the same cable.

AlisaTalk's file server lets Macintosh users access Macintosh and VAX files located on VAX storage devices. Macintosh files are accessed by using the File Server Utility that provides text file format conversion and international character translation as well as file interchange between Macintosh and VAX environments. Compared to a virtual disk server (which maps a single VAX file to an entire disk for the Macintosh), the Alisa-Talk file server maps a VAX file to an individual file for the Macintosh. It allows multiple read-write access to each volume so that volumes can be shared among Macintosh and VAX users. Although disk servers may operate faster, the AlisaTalk file server offers full emulation of the Macintosh file system.

Walnut

When Macintosh users mount a VAX volume, they see it as a disk with a special icon that opens just like any Macintosh disk. Many users can mount a volume and read, create, rename, and delete files. A file can have only one writer at a time who can make changes, and a writer can lock a file from further changes. You can mount and dismount volumes from within Macintosh applications or from the Finder using a desk accessory supplied with the package. You can use the Alisa-Talk file server to share Macintosh applications as well as files, but it is not practical to use it for sharing one Macintosh System file among many users.

303

The AlisaTalk network print spooler consists of two VMS processes; no special software is required for the Macintosh users. One process receives the print job (PostScript file) by acting like a LaserWriter; the other process takes care of printing the jobs on the real LaserWriter, which is attached to an AppleTalk Personal Network. The spooler appears as a LaserWriter in the Chooser window (Figure 6-28).

The AlisaTalk Remote Terminal facility lets Macintosh terminal emulation programs communicate to the VAX VMS minicomputer using the DECNet CTERM remote terminal protocol. By using the DECNet terminal services, AlisaTalk minimizes network overhead by keeping most keyboard processing on the Macintosh. The facility works with Mac-240 (White Pine Software) and VersaTerm/Pro (Peripherals Computers & Supplies) which are described later in this chapter.

AlisaTalk can emulate the Macintosh file system and treat each VAX process as a node on an AppleTalk network.

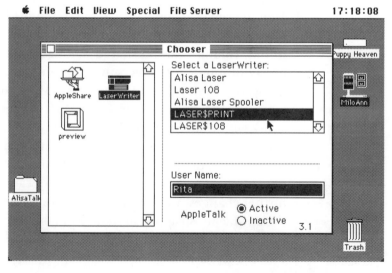

*Figure
6-28*

AlisaTalk includes a network print spooler that uses a DEC VAX to spool print jobs to a LaserWriter on an AppleTalk Personal Network.

Processes (nodes) can communicate with each other using AppleTalk network protocols, and traffic in and out of the VAX is handled by a bridge process, which is a complete implementation of an AppleTalk internet bridge device. For those who have large DECNet networks, AlisaTalk offers bridges on VMS DECNet nodes that use DECNet circuits to communicate with each other and form an AppleTalk internet. You can therefore establish an AppleTalk internet with DECNet handling the low-level details as a backbone network.

Terminal Emulation

To connect Macintosh computers to other mainframes and minicomputers, you have two choices: network connection, in which case the products already mentioned will work as described, or terminal connection as if the Macintosh were a terminal on the system.

With the second choice, you need asynchronous cable and modems for remote connection, and a communication program that can perform terminal emulation. MacTerminal 2.0 from Apple is the most widely used program because it offers DEC VT100 and IBM 3278 emulation as well as the Xmodem and MacBinary file transfer protocols. MacTerminal is described in Chapter 2.

VersaTerm Pro ($295, Peripherals Computers & Supplies) provides the DEC VT100 emulation features plus emulation of the Data General Dasher 200 terminal and the Tektronix 4014 graphic terminal. VersaTerm Pro has the same file transfer protocols, plus Kermit, which is widely used on UNIX and IBM systems. VersaTerm Pro can operate with MultiFinder to provide background communication functions.

Red Ryder, a shareware program available in almost every user group public domain library (you donate money to the developer if you like the program and use it regularly), emulates the VT100 and supports Xmodem, MacBinary, and Kermit. MacKermit (distributed by Columbia University) is another shareware program that offers the Kermit protocol and VT100 emulation.

Blast (Communications Research Group, $250), when running on both the Macintosh and the host computer, uses a proprietary asynchronous protocol designed for high-speed transfer over modems. There are over 80 versions of Blast for different mainframe and minicomputer systems, which makes it one of the most popular common denominators if you need access to a strange computer.

Some programs are designed to emulate, as closely as possible, a specific terminal for mainframe or minicomputer access. For example, MacDasher (Kaz Business Systems, $69), emulates a Data General D210 terminal and lets you set up commands for Data General's CEO software used for office automation. Pacer Software has versions of pcLINK for DEC VAX computers (described earlier), designed specifically for accessing Prime Computer (sold by Prime as Primelink) and providing all the features of the DEC version. White Pine Software offers Mac 240 ($199), which provides full DEC VT-240 terminal emulation with DEC Multinational Character Set (MCS) translations and full ReGIS graphics, plus emulation of the LK-201 DEC keyboard.

To access many different types of mainframes and mini-computers, you might consider Telescape (Mainstay Software, $125), which can emulate over 100 different terminals, including the VT100, Heath H19, Televideo 950, ADM-11, Datamedia 1520, and Tektronix 4014 graphics terminals. Telescape Pro IBM 3101 ($145) emulates an IBM 3101 terminal, with user-defined soft keys and Xmodem (with MacBinary) file transfer capability. Telescape Pro VT100 ($125) emulates both DEC VT52 and DEC VT100 terminals and has the same features. You can also define your terminal control sequences if necessary.

UNIX systems deserve special consideration, since UNIX itself is available for the Macintosh II (A/UX). However, the system has largely been used by programmers and scientists, and its command structure is not easy to learn. Ultra-Office (Lutzky-Baird) is a version of UNIX that links any number of Macintosh computers and PCs to a UNIX host computer in a proprietary method that makes UNIX resemble the Macintosh desktop, with pull-down menus and icons. The network is run from a host computer running the Ultra-Office server software, which provides transparent file service and print spooling to any LaserWriters connected to the proprietary network. The server software runs on a variety of host computers including workstations from Convergent Technology, Sun Microsystems, and Pyramid.

As UNIX becomes available for the Macintosh II, we expect to see a flurry of UNIX to Macintosh file transfer utilities, conversion programs, terminal emulation programs, and applications that can communicate across networks with other applications without user intervention.

7   Planning Your Network

You say you got a real solution
Well, you know
We'd all love to see the plan. —John Lennon/Paul McCartney

Developing a plan to solve your communication needs does not have to feel like a crap shoot. Using equipment you already own as a starting point, you can build a logical structure for communications that fulfills your needs. To be on the safe side, stick to those standards that represent enduring technology breakthroughs.

For example, the AppleTalk Network System is a standard that has passed the test of time and has delivered a method of communicating that can support even the latest advances in network software. You can tell that AppleTalk networks are important to some of the largest network vendors because many have announced future products that will support the AppleTalk system of protocols. Since AppleTalk Personal

Networks are proliferating with the spread of Macintosh computers and LaserWriters, you can expect that future network solutions will incorporate gateways to existing AppleTalk networks.

How do we know this is true? Recently, industry analysts reported that only about 10 percent of the installed IBM PCs and PC-compatible computers are connected to networks. A much higher percentage of Macintosh computers are connected to networks because every Macintosh connected to a LaserWriter uses an AppleTalk Personal Network cable and has the capability to add more Macintosh computers and PCs to share the LaserWriter.

Ethernet is by far the most widely used minicomputer network, and IBM's cluster controllers are the most prevalent mechanism for accessing IBM mainframes. The Macintosh has the ability to connect to both types of mainframes and minicomputer systems, using either conventional terminal emulation and protocol conversion packages, or products that offer the AppleTalk protocols over another network as a backbone.

In addition, recent announcements by Apple point toward a new level of compatibility with IBM's Token Ring network architecture, which has not yet captured a significant market share but is destined to play the most important role in networking IBM's PS/2 line of workstation computers.

3Com and Microsoft announced an agreement to jointly develop and market Microsoft's LAN Manager for PS/2 computers that would also connect Macintosh computers to the Token Ring network.

Apple is also committed to developing a card to link Macintosh II and SE computers to provide the AppleTalk Network System using Token Ring networks as backbones.

Using a Macintosh can no longer be considered a handicap, nor can Macintosh computers be categorized as stand-alone boxes with no network or compatibility potential. Using

Macintosh and AppleTalk technology you can be sure that you are simultaneously protecting your mainframe or minicomputer investment and taking advantage of the newest developments of network technology.

Connection Checklist

We have presented many different network strategies and products. To help you navigate through this information and find solutions to suit your needs, read the following checklist of questions with recommendations on what strategies and products you could use:

1. Why should we connect our computers?

Here are three basic reasons for connecting computers: to share information in a work group or project team, to manage the information flow in a department of a corporation or a business, and to integrate and enhance the presentation of information from other sources (such as mainframes and minicomputers).

The AppleTalk Network System lets you do all of these tasks with both Macintosh computers and PCs. You can also link an AppleTalk Personal Network, or individual Macintosh computers, to minicomputer networks and mainframes. Programs are available for emulating the appropriate terminals, performing file transfers, queuing print jobs, and sharing information between applications.

The Macintosh is especially useful for enhancing your business presentations, using desktop publishing and desktop presentation software. If you already have PCs and other computers, and you want to take advantage of the capability of a Macintosh to enhance information and present it with sophisticated graphics, you will want to find ways to connect PCs and the other computers to the Macintosh computers used by the publishing or presentation group.

2. Do we need a network, or are there other inexpensive ways to share information?

The simplest way to share information is to put it on disk and give it to someone, who then copies it to their disk. You might use "Nike-net" (messengers or runners wearing sneakers). However, a modem may be all you need to communicate with other Macintosh users, mainframes, and minicomputers, and with services such as MCI Mail and CompuServe.

However, the question of adding a network is usually moot if you already have LaserWriters and Macintosh computers, since you already have a network for sharing printers. The question is then whether to expand that network with bridges to other networks, or add services such as file serving, print spooling, and electronic mail. You may also want to replace the relatively slow AppleTalk Personal Network cable with faster Ethernet or less expensive PhoneNET cable (which uses standard telephone cable).

3. Do we use distributed or dedicated file servers to share information between the Macintosh computers on the network?

File servers and disk servers are available for sharing information among Macintosh users (and with PC users who are connected to an AppleTalk or Ethernet network). The question is whether to use a product that distributes the file or disk service over several Macintosh computers and hard disks, or one that dedicates one or more computers or hardware devices with hard disks to performing file service (possibly with electronic mail and network spooling included).

The obvious advantages to using distributed file service are less cost, less restrictions on file sharing, and the ability to shift hard disk resources quickly. The obvious advantages to using dedicated file service are faster throughput on the server, centralized control over file access and spooling, and the ability to isolate the server from unauthorized or inadvertent system crashes. Besides these advantages, it helps to look at the specific features of the servers available.

AppleShare is a dedicated file server that provides sufficient access protection for handling files safely for a corporate department or a large project group. The owner of each folder can set and change file access, which can be selectively granted to individuals and entire work groups. Drop-only folders can be set up with limited access to deposit files but not to get them out or to change them. You can also use the same dedicated server for network spooling and for running the electronic mail message center.

The dedicated file server strategy with AppleShare and with 3Com's 3+Share lets you set up centralized control over file sharing and access. The inherent advantages are department-style control, systematic and organized backup procedures, and faster throughput because you use the entire resources of a dedicated Macintosh or an optimized piece of hardware such as 3Com's 3Server3.

The inherent disadvantages of a dedicated server are higher expense (you have to dedicate a Macintosh or buy hardware), and less efficiency — to share files you have to copy them to the server's hard disk, rather than simply publish an area of *your* hard disk as you would with a distributed server. In addition, if the server disk fails for any reason, and you don't have a hard disk connected to your Macintosh, you are left without any hard disk resource or access to your files.

Distributed file servers are less expensive and offer equal file access without the inherent bureaucracy of centralized management, which can sometimes hinder productivity. Since each user decides which folder to publish (as in TOPS) or which area of a hard disk to devote to sharing (as in MacServe and HyperNet), it is also each user's responsibility to make secure backups and keep sensitive files out of reach. You can control access with passwords and thereby manage work groups without the overhead of maintaining registered user names and group names.

Both methods can be combined on an AppleTalk network and Ethernet, since TOPS currently works in the same network as AppleShare. Electronic mail is compatible with both file server types, and spoolers can work just as well with distributed servers as dedicated servers.

The expense of dedicating a machine to file service may not be necessary if you already have a minicomputer or mainframe, which could act as a file server while handling its usual tasks. The mainframe or minicomputer server could also provide the computing services of a more powerful processor, and a centralized data base.

Expect a well-suited file server arrangement to let you share information effortlessly without breaking your concentration. You should be able to transfer files to and from folders by simply dragging their icons or names.

4. How can users increase productivity with printing?

Spooling files to a LaserWriter is easily accomplished with any one of several spooling programs. The major differences among them are (1) efficient use of your disk space and (2) the ability to spool everyone's files on the network.

You can get individual *client* spoolers for users who do heavy printing, or a multiuser version of a client spooler that lets several users spool to a single disk on the network, or a *server* spooler that runs on a dedicated file server and serves the entire network. There are server spoolers available for running on minicomputers and mainframes that serve the printing needs of one or more AppleTalk networks.

In some cases a spooler will not be able to download fonts for an Aldus PageMaker publication file when using Aldus Prep. However, PageMaker lets you optionally specify Apple's Prep file, which may solve this problem. Also, most spoolers let you bypass the spooler to print directly from your Macintosh.

5. Do we need electronic mail for in-house use only, or also to link with workers in other areas?

You don't use in-house electronic mail packages (such as InBox or InterMail) to connect with public services. To send and receive messages with outside services, use a modem connected to a single Macintosh, a communication program, and an account with MCI Mail, in which you are charged less than a dollar for each message you send, or CompuServe, in which you are charged for the time you spend using it. The same modem and communication software can let you share information with Macintosh users in another town or country.

You may not need in-house electronic mail, especially since you can't use it to communicate with people in other towns and countries unless they also have at least one network and a bridge (such as the Hayes InterBridge) to your network.

However, private electronic mail systems can link office workers together and improve their productivity dramatically. You can send electronic messages and entire files to many other users with a few clicks of the mouse. You can receive your messages and files when you feel like it, and you can choose not to be disturbed without hampering the productivity of others. Electronic mail can also provide reminders for you and others about important events, let you call a group of people to an impromptu meeting, and help you deal with daily emergencies.

6. Do we need to connect IBM-compatible PCs on the local network?

The most common reason for connecting PCs to Macintosh computers is to use information processed on PCs with Macintosh-based desktop publishing and presentation software. Another is to use the PC data with a Macintosh for communicating with other types of computers, since there are so many communication options for the Macintosh.

The least expensive route to connect a Macintosh to a PC or other computer is by using a serial cable and communication software (such as MacLink Plus for connecting to a PC, or pcLINK for connecting to a UNIX system). Another inexpensive route for sharing information with PCs is to use TOPS or PC MacBridge with an AppleTalk adaptor card in a single PC to connect the PC to an AppleTalk Personal Network. Or you may want to buy the Dayna disk drive for your Macintosh Plus, or the Apple disk drive for your Macintosh SE or II, so that you can use your Macintosh to read and write PC disks.

3Com's 3+ network accommodates PCs and Macintosh computers in an Ethernet network. Other mainframe and minicomputer connection products can transfer files to and from the mainframe or minicomputer, which can also perform such transfers with PCs. In fact, if you already use a mainframe or minicomputer as a host for PCs, it may be less expensive to connect a Macintosh by cable or by cluster controller to the host and use the host as a file server for both Macintosh computers and PCs.

7. How many Macintosh computers need to be connected to mainframes and minicomputers?

The answer depends entirely on your application and the equipment in which you have already made an investment. The simplest connection is one Macintosh to one minicomputer or mainframe over a serial cable, with modems for remote access and communication programs emulating terminals. You can also connect a single Macintosh to a cluster controller of an IBM mainframe using AppleLine or MacMainFrame. You can alternatively connect an entire AppleTalk Personal Network to an IBM mainframe with the Tri-Data Netway 1000A, which can be substituted for a more expensive IBM cluster controller and allow 16 users to access the mainframe simultaneously. With more Netways you can link up to four mainframes and minis, and display all four sessions, on each Macintosh screen, then use the copy/paste function to move information from one mainframe or mini to another.

Alisa Systems offers the ability to turn a DEC VAX into an AppleTalk network, with VMS processes mapped to nodes of the network, and complete AppleShare-compatible file service. You can attach any number of AppleTalk Personal Networks with bridge devices to any number of VAX computers, and use DECNet as a backbone for AppleTalk network services.

8. Should we buy high-speed modems for each Macintosh?

Speed is the major issue with modems as technology advances beyond what the phone lines can support. The current standard for the Bell network is 1200 bps, and 2400 bps (defined by an international standards association) is tolerated on the Bell network. Modems at these speeds are relatively inexpensive — under $1000 and as low as $100. So you can afford to connect one to as many Macintosh computers as necessary for users to communicate with electronic mail and information services, mainframes, and minicomputers.

Many higher speed modems (9600 and 19,200 bps) can work with normal telephone lines but require the same modem at both ends of the line; others require dedicated (leased) phone lines. These modems are expensive ($1000 to $3500), and the protocols used are not standard — you can't use another model of modem at the other end, and if AT&T or some other large carrier offers an integrated voice-and-data network in the future with a different protocol, your higher speed modems may turn into doorstops. Finally, services like CompuServe and MCI Mail do not yet offer high-speed service (and when they do, they are likely to surcharge for its use).

However, higher speed means faster operation and higher productivity and can come in handy for use with bridge devices for linking networks, and for communicating with mainframes and minicomputers that already use these types of modems. There are also several methods of sharing a modem over an AppleTalk network, so that you can divide the cost of a high-speed modem (at one end) by the number of users on the network.

9. Which services are worth subscribing to?

Personally, we subscribe to nearly all of them. You can find us on CompuServe, GEnie, MCI Mail, and The Source, to name a few.

Until one large network includes all the users and companies in the industry and offers all the features we need for file transfers, we will continue to subscribe to all these services (and more, if they become available and offer better features). Time is money, but most services are expensive only if you use the data bases and special services a lot. We ran up high bills when we were first learning how to search the Official Airline Guide (OAG), but now we know how to do it quickly.

Here are the features that stand out for each service (note that features may have been added to some of these services by the time you read this):

MCI Mail. You can have messages, and with Desktop Express, entire documents and publications with graphics and fonts, delivered to anyone with a mailbox anywhere in the world, as well as to the largest network of electronic mailboxes (including CompuServe's mailboxes).

CompuServe. The largest service with the most data bases and users also offers MacBinary file encapsulation for transferring entire Macintosh files (with graphics, fonts, icons, and file names), and the Xmodem protocol for transferring files correctly to other types of computers.

The Source. This is the second-largest service, with plenty of helpful Macintosh-related information and a teleconferencing service.

GEnie. This is another large service with lower access charges and the Xmodem protocol.

OfficeTalk. This network uses a version of Desktop Express to let you send Macintosh files with graphics and fonts to other electronic mailboxes.

Sample Applications

Although most of the products described in this book are new, many of them have already been tested in traditional data processing environments and offices by novice users as well as professionals.

For example, the Seafirst Bank in Seattle uses about 2000 Macintosh computers connected by AppleLine to a statewide network of IBM mainframes using the Systems Network Architecture (SNA). Although Seafirst also looked at IBM PCs as substitutes for terminals, the company chose Macintosh computers because they are easier for people to learn how to use.

"The question for us was how to supply our users with the least technical, easiest to use system so they never have to know operating system commands, one in which everything is done graphically," explains Tim Turnpaugh, senior vice president and manager of technical services for Seafirst. Users ship Macintosh documents through the mainframe network using the mainframe network's electronic mail software.

At John Deere Dubuque Works (a division of Deere and Co. in Dubuque, Iowa), Tri-Data Netway 1000A devices are used to connect an AppleTalk Personal Network of Macintosh computers to IBM 3081 and 3083 mainframes and Tandem TXP computers at company headquarters. MacWindows 3270 lets them display four simultaneous 3270 terminal sessions with the four different mainframes. The copy/paste function of the Macintosh program provides engineering data to the mainframes, and engineers use the results of mainframe computations in engineering reports prepared on the Macintosh. They also use the Macintosh computers as engineering workstations, which can connect to the company's DEC minicomputers through serial links and communication programs.

Before using Macintosh computers in a network, design engineers at John Deere had to figure costs by handing information to process engineers for computing, who in turn handed over plans to the accounting department for cost evaluation. Cost data was sent back to the design engineers, again by hand, so that the design engineers could modify their designs and start the process all over again. The AppleTalk Personal Network, connected to the accounting department's mainframe, allowed the company to reduce this three-week process into 2-3 hours.

At Squibb Institute for Medical Research in Lawrenceville, New Jersey, researchers use Macintosh computers to draw chemical compounds and integrate the drawings with graphs and text for reports. They use a DEC VAX 11/750 for molecular design computations, and connected the Macintosh computers as terminals on the VAX system with serial cable and the VersaTerm Pro communication program. VersaTerm Pro emulates a Tektronix 4105 graphics terminal, which is required for the molecular design software on the VAX. Two Macintosh programs used by Squibb researchers are Chem Draw (Cambridge Scientific Computing, Inc.) and Cricket Graph (Cricket Software). Scientists use Chem Draw to draw the chemical structures, and Cricket Graph to produce x-y graphs and pie charts.

Western Industrial Bank of Steamboat Springs, Colorado, uses an AppleTalk network of Macintosh computers to run the one-branch bank, and a Tri-Data Netway 1000A to connect an AppleTalk Personal Network to a mainframe at the Citi-corp service bureau in Denver, using a dedicated phone line. The service bureau handles the bank's transaction processing and accounting, and every transaction is first recorded in the Macintosh data base and seconds later in the mainframe's data base.

Prudential Insurance Company of America has thousands of IBM PCs, several mainframes and minicomputers, and about 70 Macintosh computers used to prepare auditing reports and draw flow charts. The Macintosh users pull information from the company's mainframes using Avatar Technologies' MacMainFrame attached directly to cluster controllers using coaxial cable.

The list of companies putting Macintosh computers and AppleTalk networks to work in environments involving other computers is endless. In one department at Dow Chemical Co. in Midland, Michigan, IBM PC ATs have AppleTalk PC adaptor cards to connect them to an AppleTalk Personal Network, and the AT hard disks are used as file servers for the Macintosh computers on the network. Armco, Inc., of Middletown, Ohio, wired a new building with the DuPont network that supports the AppleTalk network protocols over 4900 feet of fiber optic cable.

The common thread in all these application stories is the use of Macintosh computers to enhance reports and presentations and to integrate information from other types of personal computers, minicomputers, and mainframes for publishing efforts and presentations. The graphic nature of the Macintosh system is the reason for this common thread, and it is also the reason why so many corporate users find the Macintosh easier to learn than other types of personal computers, especially IBM PCs.

General Application Areas

The application areas for networks and well-connected Macintosh computers can be divided into categories of users such as administration workers, information workers, and work groups that need to present or publish information.

The administration worker needs to run multiple applications, and needs to be notified via electronic mail of new work. A file server should always be available to provide shared schedules and a document library.

The information worker usually needs to run large applications with a shared data base on a file server, perhaps on a minicomputer or mainframe. The mainframe or minicomputer might be running a data base management system that allows on-demand access to data, which the information work can copy and paste into reports.

The work group brought together to produce a presentation or publication usually needs to integrate documents and graphics from work group members which must be updated frequently. File servers can share documents and a library of templates for presentations and publications, and electronic mail can notify group members of the most recent changes.

Electronic mail can be useful in all types of applications that link individuals in a coordinated activity. Managers can use messages to remind them of deadlines, requests, and commitments, as well as allow them to freely communicate with each other. Writers in one location can notify a production group in another location that updated documents are available to replace the documents already prepared for publishing.

A document library on a server could be organized so that individual components (regularly used charts, spread sheets, graphics, and boilerplate text) could be assembled quickly for ad hoc publications and presentations. With any file server you can control sensitive documents and with some you can allow members of a work group or just certain individuals to have access.

A Typical Application

To understand how an AppleTalk network of Macintosh computers can improve your productivity, imagine that you are the manager of a marketing department in a large company that manufactures construction material. Early in the morning you realize that you need to calculate revenue forecasts and make a presentation later that day, and that the finance department needs your pricing information two hours before, to prepare their part of the presentation.

You create a shared Presentation folder on your file or disk server, and place in it an outline of the entire presentation, a list of assignments, and a spread sheet already loaded with the functions and assumptions needed to calculate some of the tables. One member of your staff works on the spread sheet, and another starts writing the presentation text. Both work on copies on their own disks and then place their results in the shared Presentation folder.

After learning about last-minute changes in the costs of manufacturing and raw materials, you send an electronic mail message quickly to the staff member working up the numbers on the spread sheet, with a request for receipt notification so that you know when the message was received. The electronic mail software beeps the staff member's Macintosh to let her know about the waiting message, and she can check her mail when she finishes her work.

By late morning you have a Presentation folder containing a finished spread sheet, a written analysis, and charts and graphs depicting alternative manufacturing methods. You can include in a presentation file the information in the Presentation folder along with text and graphics showing last year's marketing survey. You also copy the spread sheet, which is already formatted so that the finance department will immediately recognize the numbers, and drop the copy into a "drop box" folder in finance's server on the network so that it remains confidential (only the appropriate people in the finance department can see it). You also send an electronic message to finance's secretary to let them know the numbers are ready.

Sometime during your lunch break, the finance department finished its section of the presentation and clipped it to a message to your electronic mailbox (where only you can see it). You integrate their section with the rest of your presentation, put some finishing touches on it, then choose the appropriate LaserWriter on the network (one that is not busy with spooled jobs) to print the presentation in time for your meeting.

Later that day you need to send copies of the presentation to offices in New York, San Francisco, Buenos Aires, and to a board member on vacation in Big Sur, California. AppleTalk networks in New York and San Francisco are connected by modem and bridge to your network, so all you have to do is choose a file server on each network (such as one named Inbound) and copy the file to that server, or use electronic mail software to send the presentation file clipped to a message. The Buenos Aires office could also be linked via telecommunications satellite between bridges, or simply linked through a public service such as CompuServe or MCI Mail. Finally, using Desktop Express and MCI Mail's laser printers, you can send the presentation to the Big Sur Post Office, General Delivery, for the board member on vacation. All in a day's work.

Only AppleTalk Personal Networks and Macintosh computers were used in this scenario. At every step, one could have used PCs with AppleTalk adaptor cards, or serial connections to PCs, along with file translation software. The finance department could have used mainframes and minicomputers to prepare its section of the presentation. Ethernet could have been used as a backbone for AppleTalk network services at any location to increase the speed of the network. The file servers could have been any of the ones described earlier in this book.

There are so many possibilities and so few limitations on what you can do with communication products. As we write this, some of the limitations are being lifted and developments are indicating that applications will understand and make use of file servers, communication links, so that eventually a large, full-scale voice-and-data network that will let all computer users have the option to communicate with all other users at high speeds without protocol incompatibilities.

The Future

The most important future developments that will affect your ability to communicate are in the areas of network connectivity, multitasking personal computers, application programs, and telecommunications (cable, satellite link, phone network, etc.).

On the networking front, we expect Apple to introduce Macintosh II and Macintosh SE cards for connecting these computers to IBM's Token Ring network, implementing the AppleTalk network protocols over Token Ring, and offering AppleShare-compatible file service to link PCs and Macintosh computers in a file sharing environment. 3Com already offers a similar type of environment using its 3Server3 hardware and Ethernet cabling.

In addition, Microsoft's LAN Manager will be able to control a network linking Macintosh computers and PCs and providing electronic mail, spooling, file service, and a way for applications to communicate among themselves (called interprocess communications). Eventually we'll see applications that can communicate directly among themselves without involving users (called advanced program-to-program communications). Computers on an AppleTalk network already communicate with each other as peers, not as master computers with slaves; eventually mainframes and minicomputers will also communicate in this fashion (as with AlisaTalk on VAX/VMS minicomputers) with networks of personal computers and workstations.

Multitasking is now becoming available for Macintosh computers. With one application running in a window, you can click in the background behind the application, automatically gaining access to the Finder. You can then launch another application. You can copy or cut text and graphics from one application and paste them into another, without leaving the applications (which are still running). With multi-tasking, a single processor's computing resources are sliced into chunks of time so that each application, while appearing to run simultaneously with the others, is actually awaiting its turn for the processor. The applications are not suspended — they continue to use slices of processor time whether or not you've switched to another application. This capability is not the same as running two or more co-processors, each with a different application. The Macintosh II and Macintosh SE can make use of co-processors as well as do multitasking of Macintosh applications. Multitasking comes in handy, for example, when you want to have your computer call an information service and check your electronic mail while you continue to use it for other operations.

Network-aware applications will soon be developed to offer more capabilities than even those offered with currently-available data base management programs. The applications will handle different data types, with references to data objects in other files. This capability will let you produce documents and data bases that contain rich text and pictures rather than just numbers and strings, even when the individual components are stored on different hard disks. We will eventually see expert systems that draw information from a network, such as an in-house budgeting system that could automatically draw up a budget based on information derived from several different mainframes, minicomputers, and microcomputer network servers.

Advances in telecommunications technology will let us send information more quickly and with accuracy over phone lines and satellites. IBM and large communication companies are in the research and development phase of a project that will link all telephones in the world to an integrated voice-and-data network that can simultaneously communicate both voice and data traffic. You will soon be able to record a voice message, link it to a Macintosh file with graphics, and send both to another Macintosh using a service like MCI Mail. The receiver could play back your voice message and use the file. Such communication could become routine in a few years.

The office of the future is sure to have access to other offices using telecommunications. One day, the sharing of documents with fonts and graphics across networks, through inter-office mail systems involving many different types of computers, will be effortless. One day electronic mail will completely outperform the current methods of hand delivery and be in widespread use. You should not hesitate to get involved in this revolution in communications, and we can hope for the best: that we'll stop cutting down trees to make paper simply for transferring information.

A   File Formats

File formats are usually not a problem for Macintosh networks, since the Macintosh applications already know how to read text and graphics from other applications that use either standard Macintosh PICT files, MacPaint files, QuickDraw instructions, or PostScript instructions.

However, when communicating with PCs, minicomputers, mainframes, and other types of computers, file formats are the single biggest obstacle to establishing proper communications.

Text Files

All personal computers store text using *ASCII* (American Standard Code for Information Interchange). The problem is that ASCII does not include codes for embolding, italicizing, underlining, or other formatting characteristics. Word processing programs usually insert proprietary codes to control text formatting. This is why you can't readily use a file from one word processor with another — unless the file is straight ASCII with no other codes, or the file has been converted to the other word processor's format.

Some word processors and spread sheet programs offer built-in conversion facilities. For example, Microsoft Word can convert a MacWrite file to its own format, and you can then save this Word file as a straight ASCII file, as a PC Word file (for use with Microsoft Word on the PC), or as a file using an Interchange format known as RTF (Rich Text Format). Microsoft Excel on the Macintosh can read a PC-based Lotus 1-2-3 spread sheet directly, and save the spread sheet in the Lotus format.

MacLink Plus, described in Chapter 3, has extensive text file conversion facilities, many of which are shown in the file translation chart in this appendix. Using MacLink Plus, you can, for example, convert MacWrite files to IBM's Document Content Architecture (DCA) files. You can also convert data base and spread sheet files from PC to Macintosh applications and vice-versa.

The text formats considered quasi-standard in the Macintosh world are Microsoft's Rich Text Format (which can include graphics and fonts), MacWrite and Microsoft Word (which can include graphics and fonts), and IBM's DCA (Document Content Architecture — the revisable format). DCA lets you set up document formatting but does not include fonts or graphics.

On the PC side there are DCA and many popular word processor formats, none of which include graphics and fonts at this time; and Rich Text Format for Microsoft Windows applications, which can include graphics and fonts.

Spread sheet programs generally use proprietary formats, but some are interchangeable (such as Microsoft's Multiplan and Excel formats used for both PCs and Macintosh computers). In addition, spread sheet programs have optional formats for transferring data to and from data base programs.

DIF (Data Interchange Format) is the most common format of this type, first used by VisiCalc. The SYLK (Symbolic Link) format was developed by Microsoft for use with Multiplan and Excel (for both PC and Macintosh versions).

Mainframe and minicomputer applications generally employ proprietary formats and use either ASCII or EBCDIC (Extended Binary-Coded Decimal Interchange Code), which was developed for IBM mainframes. Cluster controllers convert EBCDIC to ASCII before the information appears on your Macintosh; otherwise terminal emulation software performs this conversion. Revisable format DCA is very popular in IBM environments. However, most users use ASCII or the format used for Lotus 1-2-3 mainframe files as a standard.

The major difference between Macintosh ASCII files and all other types of ASCII files is that Macintosh ASCII files use a single carriage return code at the end of each line, rather than the carriage return and line feed combination used in most other ASCII files. MacLink Plus performs a simple ASCII-to-Macintosh ASCII conversion, and you can do it yourself by following the instructions in Chapter 3.

Graphics Files

Graphics can be transferred in their native formats across a network of Macintosh computers and PCs. Some PC applications accept MacPaint and PICT graphics files, and others accept PostScript graphics files using the Encapsulated PostScript Format (EPSF). For the most part Macintosh graphics applications do not read graphics from PC files unless they are EPSF files.

Line art and business graphics can also be transported to PCs in a text file using the Rich Text Format. The PICT format is most popular between Macintosh applications, and EPSF is provided by most graphics programs that produce line art and text with fonts, so that you can transfer them to PCs and other computers that support PostScript printers.

Although PostScript is efficient for transferring line art and business graphics (vectors, geometric shapes, and other graphic objects with text), it does not include a compression scheme for *bit-mapped* graphics or scanned images, which are described by dots in a measured space rather than by a language of instructions, as line art usually is described. Files containing bit-mapped graphics and scanned images which are not compressed can occupy a great deal of disk space and increase transmission time, slowing down an entire network.

Bit-map graphics created from paint programs are usually stored as MacPaint documents as well as in a proprietary format (which may or may not be recognized by other programs). Regular MacPaint files, fixed in resolution at 72 dots per inch (equal to the screen of a Macintosh 512, Plus, or SE), are recognized by almost every Macintosh application.

Scanned images and bit-mapped graphics at higher resolutions are most likely to be recognized if they are stored in files using the Tag Image File Format (TIFF). TIFF is capable of carrying compressed gray-scale and color information along with the image. TIFF files can be edited with GraphicWorks (Mindscape,$99.95) and used with PageMaker and other page makeup programs. TIFF has also been adopted by most scanner manufacturers and graphics program vendors for both PCs and Macintosh computers.

TIFF is useful because it is a compressed format, and compression is necessary for efficient transfer of graphics over networks. PostScript by itself (as a text file you can send directly to a printer) or in the EPSF file (ready to be used with other programs that produce PostScript output) is the most useful format for line art, which is usually a set of instructions rather than a large map of dots.

File Translations

The following chart lists popular file formats in the PC world that can be easily matched to Macintosh formats, and the translators you can use to translate them back and forth. Since translators may not convert all features, you should refer to the instructions supplied with the programs for further reference. Note that in all cases you can use TOPS Translators rather than MacLink Plus.

The chart is followed by a summary of formatting characteristics that are changed or ignored during the translation of Document Content Architecture (DCA) text files to MacWrite files, and MacWrite to DCA.

Most Popular Formats

PC Format	Translator	Macintosh Format
ASCII (text)	TOPS	ASCII (text)
ASCII (text)	MS Word	ASCII (text)
ASCII (text)	*MacLink Plus	ASCII (text), MacWrite
ASCII (text)	Apple File Exchange	ASCII (text)
ASCII (any delimiter)	dBASE Mac	dBASE Mac
ASCII (tabs, commas)	Omnis III Plus	Omnis III Plus
ASCII (tabs, commas)	Helix	Helix
dBASE III	dBASE Mac	dBASE Mac
dBASE III Plus	*MacLink Plus	dBASE Mac, Tab Text
dBASE III Plus	Helix	Tab Text
dBASE III Plus	FileMaker Plus	FileMaker Plus
dBASE III Plus	Omnis III Plus	Omnis III Plus
DCA	*MacLink Plus,	MacWrite
DCA	Apple File Exchange	MacWrite
DIF	*MacLink Plus	Excel (WKS), Jazz, Multiplan (SYLK), DIF
DIF	Omnis III Plus	Omnis III Plus
Lotus 1-2-3 (WKS)	Excel	Excel (WKS)
Lotus 1-2-3 (WKS)	Jazz	Jazz
Lotus 1-2-3 (WKS)	*MacLink Plus	Multiplan (SYLK), Jazz, Excel (WKS), DIF
MS Word	MS Word	MS Word
MultiMate	*MacLink Plus	MacWrite
Multiplan PC (SYLK)	Excel	Excel (WKS)
Multiplan PC (SYLK)	Jazz	Jazz

PC Format	Translator	Macintosh Format
Multiplan PC (SYLK)	Multiplan (Mac)	Multiplan (SYLK)
Multiplan PC (SYLK)	*MacLink Plus	DIF,
		Excel (WKS),
		Jazz,
		Multiplan (SYLK)
PageMaker 1.0a	PageMaker	PageMaker 2.0a
SYLK	Omnis III Plus	Omnis III Plus
SYLK	FileMaker Plus	FileMaker Plus
Symphony (WRK)	Jazz	Jazz
Symphony(WRK)	*MacLink Plus	Excel (WKS),
		Jazz,
		Multiplan (SYLK),
		DIF
ThinkTank PC	MORE	MORE
WordStar	*MacLink Plus	MacWrite

* TOPS Translators can be used rather than MacLink Plus.

Apple File Exchange: MacWrite to DCA

The formatting characteristics that are changed or ignored in the translation are:

• Automatic page numbering is shown only at the top right edge of a header or footer.

• If MacWrite text consists of mixed type sizes, horizontal spacing is also changed with type size. Tab spaces in the MacWrite text file should be widened before translation to avoid text going past the next tab stop. If the DCA file has skewed text that goes past a tab stop, widen the tab spaces to fix it.

• Italic, outline, shadow or bold type styles are all changed to bold style.

• Paragraph indents are changed to two spaces (unless you used a tab to begin paragraphs).

• Large type sizes are reduced, and other type sizes and fonts are approximated.

• The underscore character is substituted for unrecognized characters.

• Vertical line spacing is approximated.
• Date and time in headers or footers are omitted.
• Hanging indents are omitted.
• Graphics are omitted.

These differences occur only in MacWrite to DCA file translations. The next step — translating from DCA to a (PC) word processor's file format — may result in additional changes in formatting. For example, line breaks, page breaks, justification or centering of text, and the size of headers and footers may be changed when the file is converted to a particular word processor's file format.

Apple File Exchange: DCA to MacWrite

The formatting characteristics that are changed or ignored in the translation are:

• Automatic page numbering is shown only at the top right edge of a header or footer, unless the DCA header is suppressed, in which case both the header and footer for the page are suppressed in the MacWrite file. If only the DCA footer is suppressed, the footer is not suppressed in the MacWrite file.
• If DCA text consists of mixed type sizes, horizontal spacing changes with type size. Tab spaces in the DCA text file should be widened before translation to avoid text going past the next tab stop. If the MacWrite file has skewed text that goes past a tab stop, widen the tab spaces to fix it.
• Left-justified tabs are substituted for colon tabs, decimal tabs are substituted for comma-aligned tabs, and only the first ten tab stops are accepted by MacWrite.
• Margins and tab stops are used to left-justify MacWrite text that was centered or right-justified in the DCA file. Use MacWrite's Ruler and Alignment commands (from the Format menu) to center or right-justify the text after translation.
• DCA outlines are not indented, but are preceded by mes-

sages giving the level number of each line. Use MacWrite's tabs to indent such lines, substituting a number of tab characters to match the level number of each line.

• Although DCA has no minimum distance between margins setting, MacWrite's minimum setting (two inches between margins) is used.

• Type sizes and fonts are approximated.

• The rectangular box character is substituted for special characters such as backspaces and the null character.

• Vertical line spacing is approximated.

• Carriage returns are substituted for vertical tabs.

• Single underlining is substituted for double underlining.

• The following DCA settings are ignored or omitted by MacWrite:

automatic hyphenation, overstrike type styles, special video attributes (such as blinking, reverse video, and no-display), backspacing in the left margin, character realignment within paragraphs, paragraph keeps, footnote formatting, multiple headers and footers per document, multi-line headers and footers, different header/footer for even pages, page increments other than one, page number reset within documents, line numbering, line end zone (right sub-margin), specified top/bottom margins, maximum/minimum number of lines per page, move/copy column to second column, printer operator messages, stop codes, spell checking, text unit insertion, and text unit numbers.

B   Macintosh Cables

Macintosh cables are available from any authorized Macintosh dealer or directly from Apple Computer; some may be ordered as a finished products from the Apple Support Center.

You can use the following with any Macintosh Plus, SE, or II computer:

• Apple System Peripheral-8 Cable, which connects the Macintosh Plus, SE, or II to the ImageWriter II Printer and the Apple Personal Modem or any modem compatible with the Hayes Smartmodem.

• Macintosh Plus Peripheral Adapter Cable, which lets you connect the Macintosh Plus, SE, or II to popular third-party peripheral devices without discarding your old cables. It can also be used to attach devices previously used with the Macintosh 128K or 512K. This cable is available from the Apple

Support Center. It is also included in the Macintosh Plus Logic Board Upgrade Kit.

• Apple SCSI System Cable, which links the Macintosh Plus, SE, or II to the first SCSI peripheral device in a chain of SCSI devices. Additional devices are linked using Apple SCSI Peripheral Interface Cables. If you need more space between devices, use the one-meter SCSI Cable Extender. A SCSI Cable Terminator is required in every SCSI configuration to help filter the line. SCSI cables can be ordered from your Apple Support Center. (See description of SCSI cabling below.)

• AppleTalk System Connector Kit, which links the Macintosh Plus, SE, or II to the AppleTalk Personal Network. If you are upgrading to a Macintosh Plus, SE, or II from a Macintosh 512, you can choose between the AppleTalk System Connector Kit or the Macintosh Plus Peripheral Adapter Kit.

Part numbers:
Macintosh Plus Peripheral Adapter Cable (M0199)
Apple SCSI System Cable (M0206)
Apple SCSI Cable Terminator (M0209)
Apple SCSI Cable Extender (M0208)
Apple SCSI Peripheral Interface Cable (M0207)
AppleTalk System Connector (M2052)
Apple System Peripheral-8 Cable (M0197)

SCSI Cabling

Up to seven SCSI (Small Computer Systems Interface) devices can be cabled to a Macintosh. Typical SCSI devices are hard disks and scanners. If you are connecting two or more SCSI devices, you need to use SCSI *terminators* as described below. Terminators are small connectors or hardware components built into the devices that make SCSI data transfer more reliable.

The SCSI standard requires two terminators in a daisy-chain of devices: one on the first device and one on the last device. You must consult the manual supplied with your SCSI device to see if it has a built-in terminator; if it does, and you can't remove it, you must use the device as the first or last in the chain, because there can be only two terminators in a chain. Note that the Macintosh SE and II internal hard disks each have a built-in terminator, since each disk is used as the first device for that computer. You can then have only one more terminator — in the last device — when using a Macintosh SE or II with an internal hard disk.

Each SCSI device has a unique identification number between zero and six (the Macintosh itself is number seven). Most devices are factory-set to zero, but you must change that if you use them with other devices. For example, the Macintosh SE internal hard disk is usually set to an ID number of zero; thus, the SCSI disk drive with the highest ID number (from six down to one) performs a system start-up before SCSI drive zero.

Serial Cabling

If you feel you are competent using tiny electrical wiring, you can make your own serial cables to use with modems and printers. All serial cables are either straight modem or null modem cables — straight modem cables connect the Receive Data and Transmit Data pins on one side to the same Receive Data and Transmit Data pins on the other side, and null modems cross connect the Receive Data and Transmit Data pins.

The following diagrams illustrate how you would connect a Smartmodem to a Macintosh 512 (using a DB-9 connector) or Plus, SE, or II (using a Mini DN-8 connector).

Macintosh		IBM PC
Protective ground (PG)	1—1	Protective ground (PG)
Signal ground (SG)	3 — 7	Signal ground (SG)
Transmit data (TxD)	5 — 3	Received data (RD)
Receive data (RxD)	9 — 2	Transmitted data (TD)
	⌈ 4	Request to send (RTS)
Macintosh	⌊ 5	Clear to send (CTS)
DB-9 (male) Connector	⌈ 6	Data set ready (DSR)
	• 8	Carrier detect (CD)
	⌊ 20	Data terminal ready (DTR)

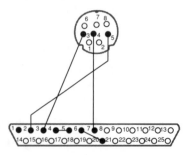

DB-25 (male) Connector
IBM PC

Macintosh Plus		IBM PC
Transmit data (TxD)	3—3	Received data (RD)
Signal ground (SG)	4 — 7	Signal ground (SG)
Receive data (RxD)	5 — 2	Transmitted data (TD)
	⌈ 4	Request to send (RTS)
Macintosh Plus	⌊ 5	Clear to send (CTS)
Mini DIN-8	⌈ 6	Data set ready (DSR)
(male) Connector	• 8	Carrier detect (CD)
	⌊ 20	Data terminal ready (DTR)

DB-25 (male) Connector
IBM PC

Macintosh   Smartmodem II

Protective ground (PG) 1 — 1 Protective ground (PG)
Signal ground (SG)   3 — 7 Signal ground (SG)
Transmit data (TxD)   5 — 2 Transmitted data (TD)
Handshake (HSK)   7·····5 Clear to send (CTS)
Receive data (RxD)   9 — 3 Received data (RD)

Macintosh
DB-9 (male) Connector

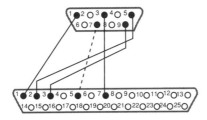

DB-25 (male) Connector
Smartmodem II

Macintosh Plus   Smartmodem II

Input handshake (CTS) 2·····5 Clear to send (CTS)
Transmit data (TxD)   3 — 2   Transmitted data (TD)
Signal ground (SG)   4 — 7   Signal ground (SG)
Receive data (RxD)   5 — 3   Received data (RD)

Macintosh Plus
Mini DIN-8
(male) Connector

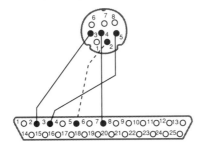

DB-25 (male) Connector
Smartmodem II

C   Products and Companies

3+, $495 for unlimited Macintosh users on a server; 3Com Corporation
3+Mail, $495 (5 users), $990 (unlimited); 3Com Corporation
3+Share, $1790 (for use with 3Server3); 3Com Corporation
3Server3, $5995 (dedicated server); 3Com Corporation
4th Dimension, $695; Acius Inc.

Accelerator, $995; Telcor
AlisaTalk, $3750 to $11,500; Alisa Systems Inc.
Apple File Exchange; Apple Computer Corp.
AppleLine, $1295; Apple Computer Corp.
AppleLine 3270 File Transfer, $99; Apple Computer Corp.
Apple PC 5.25" drive, $528; Apple Computer Corp.
Apple Personal Modem, $429; Apple Computer Corp.
AppleShare, $799; Apple Computer Corp.
AppleTalk PC Card, $399; Apple Computer Corp.
AX/9624c, $1799; Microcom

BLAST, $250; Communications Research Group

Codex 2260, $3495; Codex
CompuServe, CompuServe Information Services
ComServe, $195, Infosphere
C-Server, $595; Solana Electronics

DaynaFile, $595; Dayna Communications, Inc.
DCF II, $3995 to $5995; Wall Data, Inc.
Desktop Express, $149; Apple/Dow Jones & Company, Inc.
Dialog, Dialog Information Services, Inc.
DiskFit, $75 (single), $395 (network); SuperMac Software
Dow Jones News/Retrieval, Dow Jones & Company, Inc.

EtherPort SE, $850; Kinetics, Inc.
EtherSC, $1250; Kinetics, Inc.
EtherTalk, $699; Apple Computer Corp.

FastPath 3, $2750; Kinetics, Inc.
Fedit Plus, $40; MacMaster Systems
Fiber Optic LAN, approx. $300 per Macintosh; DuPont Connector
Systems

GEnie, General Electric Information Services
Glue, $60; Solutions, Inc.

HyperNet, $299 per server; General Computer

InBox/Mac 2.0, $350 (1-3 users), $125 each additional user; Think
Technologies
InBox/PC, $195 each user; Think Technologies
InTalk, $195; Palantir Software
InterBridge, $799; Hayes Microcomputer Products, Inc.
InterMail, $300 (1-4 users), $500 (5-10), $750 (11-20), $950 (21 or
more); Internet

K-Spool, $495; Kinetics

LaserServe, $95; Infosphere
LaserServer, $2295; DataSpace Corp.
LaserShare, $299; Apple Computer Corp.
LaserSpeed, $99; Think Technologies
LaserWriter Plus, $5799; Apple Computer Corp.

Mac86, $599; AST Research
Mac240, $199; White Pine Software
Mac286, $1499; AST Research
MacBuffer LW, $2295 (1M of memory), $2695 (2M); Ergotron Corp.
MacDasher, $69; Kaz Business Systems
MacLink Plus, $195; Dataviz
MacMainFrame DX, $1195; Avatar Technologies
MacMainFrame SE, $795; Avatar Technologies
MacMover, $995; Tri-Data
MacTerminal 2.0, $195; Apple Computer

MacServe, $250; Infosphere
MacWindows 3270, $125; Tri-Data
Maxwell 1200VP, $295; Racal-Vadic
Maxwell 9600VP, $1495; Racal-Vadic
MCI Mail, MCI Mail
MicroPhone, version 1.1, $75; Software Ventures Corp.
Mockwrite, $35; CE Software
ModemShare, Mirror Technologies, Inc.
MultiTalk, $699; Abaton Technology

NetModem, $599; Shiva Corp.
Netway 1000A, $3195; Tri-Data
Network DiskFit, $395; SuperMac Software

OfficeTalk, OfficeTalk Inc.
Omninet Network Interface, $199 ($395 for network management);
Corvus Systems, Inc.
Omnis 3 Plus, (multi-user) $495; Blyth Software

PacerPrint, $1000 for MicroVAX license; Pacer Software, Inc.
PageMaker, $495; Aldus Corp.
pcLink, $2000 to $37,500, $150 for terminal emulation; Pacer Software,
Inc.
PC MacBridge; Tangent Technology
PC MacTxt; Tangent Technology
Personal Modem, $429; Apple Computer, Inc.
PhoneNET, Farallon Computing
Pocket Modem, $259; Migent
Professional 2400, $795; Novation

Red Ryder, $40; FreeSoft

Series II Twinax, $1495; KMW Systems Corp.
Smartcom II, version 2.2, $149; Hayes Microcomputer Products, Inc.
Smartmodem 1200, $599; Hayes Microcomputer Products, Inc.
Smartmodem 2400, $899; Hayes Microcomputer Products, Inc.
The Source, Source Telecomputing
SuperLaserSpool, $150; SuperMac Software

Telescape, $125; Mainstay
Telescape Pro IBM 3101, $145; Mainstay
Telescape Pro VT100, $125; Mainstay
TOPS, $149 ($389 for PC version); TOPS (division of Sun Microsystems)
Trailblazer, $1445; Telebit

Ultra Office, Lutzky-Baird Associates
VersaTerm Pro, $295; Peripherals Computers & Supplies

Acius, Inc.,
20300 Stevens Creek Blvd. #495,
Cupertino, CA 95014.
(408) 252-4444.
Aldus Corp.,
411 First Ave. S., #200,
Seattle, WA 98104.
(206) 622-5500.
Alisa Systems Inc.,
221 E. Walnut St. #230,
Pasadena, CA 91101.
(818) 792-9474.
Apple Computer, Inc.,
20525 Mariani Ave.,
Cupertino, CA 95014.
(408) 996-1010.
AST Research,
2121 Alton Ave.,
Irvine, CA 92714-4992.
(714) 863-1333.
Avatar Technology,
99 South St.,
Hopkinton, MA 01748. (617)
435-6872.

Blyth Software,
2929 Campus Dr., #425,
San Mateo, CA 94403.
(415) 571-0222.

CE Software,
801-73 Street,
Des Moines, IA 50312.
(515) 224-1995.
**Communications Research
Group,** 8939 Jefferson Hwy.,
Baton Rouge, LA 70809.
(504) 923-0888, (800) 242-5278.
**CompuServe Information
Services,** PO Box 20212,
5000 Arlington Centre Blvd.,
Columbus, OH 43220.
(800) 848-8199, (614) 457-0802.
Corvus Systems, Inc., 2100
Corvus Dr., San Jose, CA 95124.
(408) 559-7000.

DataViz, Inc., 16 Winfield St.,
Norwalk, CT 06855.
(203) 866-4944.
Dayna Communications, Inc.,
50 South Main St,
Salt Lake City, UT 84144.
(801) 531-0600.
**Dialog Information Services,
Inc.,** 3460 Hillview Ave.,
Palo Alto, CA 94304.
(800) 334-2564.
Dow Jones & Company, Inc.,
PO Box 300, Princeton, NJ
08543. (609) 452-1511.
DuPont Connector Systems,
515 Fishing Creek Rd.,
New Cumberland, PA 17070.
(717) 938-6711.

FreeSoft, 10828 Lacklink, St.
Louis, MO 63114.
(314) 423-2190.

General Computer, 215 First St.,
Cambridge, MA 02142.
(617) 492-5500.
**General Electric Information
Services,** 401 N. Washington St.,
Rockville, MD 20850. (800)-638-
9636 or (301) 340-4000.

**Hayes Microcomputer Products,
Inc.,** 6610 Bay Circle, Norcross,
GA 30071. (404) 441-1612.

Infosphere, 4730 SW Macadam
Ave., Portland, OR 97201.
(503) 226-3515.
Internet, 20 Amy Cr.,
Waban, MA 02168.
(617) 965-5239.

Kaz Business Systems,
10 Columbus Cir., #1620,
New York, NY 10019.
(212) 757-9566.

Kinetics,
2500 Camino Diablo # 110,
Walnut Creek, CA 94596.
(415) 947-0998.
KMW Systems,
8307 Hwy. 71, West Austin, TX
78735.
(512) 288-1453.

Lutzky-Baird Associates,
5601 Slauson Ave. #222,
Culver City, CA 90230.
(213) 649-3570.

MacMaster Systems,
939 E. El Camino Real,
Sunnyvale, CA 94087.
(408) 773-9834.
Mainstay,
28611B Canwood St.,
Agoura Hills, CA 91301.
(818) 991-6540.
MCI Mail,
PO Box 1001,
1900 M St. NW,
Washington, DC 20036.
(800) 624-2255, (202) 833-8484.
Mirror Technologies, Inc.,
2209 Phelps Rd., Box 304,
Hugo, MN 55038.
(612) 426-3276.

OfficeTalk Inc.,
345 Montgomery Ave.,
Bala Cynwyd, PA 19004.
(215) 664-7440, (800) 345-0133.

Pacer Software, Inc.,
7911 Herschel Ave., #402,
La Jolla, CA 92037.
(619) 454-0565.
Palantir Software,
12777 Jones Rd., #100,
Houston, TX 77070.
(713)-955-8880.

**Peripherals Computers &
Supplies,**
2457 Perkiomen Ave., Mt. Penn,
PA 19606.
(215) 779-0522.

Shiva Corp., 222 Third St. #200,
Cambridge, MA 02142.
(617) 661-2026.
Software Ventures Corp.,
2907 Claremont Ave. #220,
Berkeley, CA 94705.
(415) 644-3232.
Solutions, Inc., PO Box 989,
Montpelier, VT 05602.
(802) 229-9146.
Source Telecomputing,
PO Box 1305, 1616 Anderson
Rd., McLean, VA 22102.
(800) 336-3366, (703) 821-6666.
SuperMac Software,
P.O. Box 390725,
Mountain View, CA 94039.
(415) 964-8884.

Tangent Technologies,
5720 Peachtree Parkway, #100,
Norcross, GA 30092.
(404) 662-0366.
Think Technologies,
135 South Rd.,
Bedford, MA 01730.
(617) 863-5595.
TOPS, 2560 9th St., # 220,
Berkeley, CA 94710.
(415) 549-5900.
Tri-Data,
505 East Middlefield Rd.,
Mountain View, CA 94043-4082.
(415) 969-3700.

Wall Data, Inc,
17769 NE 78th Pl.,
Redmond, WA 98052.
(800) 433-3388.

Index

EtherTalk card for Macintosh II, 142, 170, 183, 184, 270, 292, 293, 303
Excel, 135

Farallon Computing, 171, 176
Farallon Computing's PhoneNET, 15, 175
Farallon Repeater, 179
Farallon StarController, 179
Fastcomm, 64
FastPath, 183, 184, 186
Fedit Plus, 202
fiber optic cable, 141, 166, 171, 181
file
    access management, 233
    and folders, 2, 18, 36
    and print services, 272
    conversion, 2, 66, 135
    encapsulation standard, 58
    exchange, 12
    formats, 135, 144, 329
    interchange, 302
    interchange between Macintosh and VAX, 303
    locking, 22
    management, 115
    menu, 2, 18, 19, 26
    moving, 38
    organizing, 18
    names, 115, 116, 132
    sharing, 257
    servers, 13, 16, 167, 192, 193, 257, 261
    service and print spooling, 143, 307
        background, 265
    sharing, 11, 13, 125, 165, 191, 193, 231, 248, 264, 270
        over AppleTalk networks, 135
    transfers, 120, 122, 125, 126, 279, 283, 287, 294, 303
        batch transfers, 297
        mainframe, 275
        protocols, 96, 275, 305
        software, 278, 292
    translation, 136, 144, 332
        Apple // computers, 149
Financial transaction services, 101
Find File, 31, 32
Finder, 28, 202
Flow control, 62
folder icon, 36
folder window, resizing, 22
folder-level access privileges, 143
font downloading, 207
Font/DA Mover utility, 199, 224
FreeSoft, 96
FTX for System 3x, 291
full and half-duplex operation, 62, 64
function keys, 18

gateways, 143, 188, 189, 272
    to X.400 networks, 209
GE Information Services, 110
gender-changer, 121
General Computer, 265

General Computer HyperNet, 192, 265
General icon, 41
GEnie, 47, 100, 110
Get Info command, 20
glitches, 56, 59
Glue, 68, 82, 86
    ImageSaver utility, 68
    Viewer utility, 68, 87
graphics, 9
    file format and conversion, 331
    terminal emulation (VT241), 295
Grolier's Academic American Encyclopedia, 101, 106, 110
group name, 238

half-duplex operation, 60, 64
handshaking, 58, 63
Hayes Microcomputer Products, 96, 171, 175
    compatibility, 62, 85, 97
    InterBridge, 15, 175, 181
    Smartmodem, 63, 97
        1200, 10, 48, 51, 54
        2400, 10, 175
Headlands Press, 60, 122
Heath H19, 306
Hercules monochrome adaptor, 118
Hewlett-Packard, 141
Hewlett-Packard Plotter emulation, 141
Hierarchical File System (HFS), 233, 266
high-speed modems, 51, 63, 97, 317
    file transfers, 59, 306
    protocols, 60
    sharing, 52
high-speed network cabling system, 166
host, 291
host computer, 274, 279
Host File Transfer (HFT) software, 276, 282, 287
host print server software, 294, 300
host VAX, 298, 302
HyperNet, 192, 197, 257, 258, 265, 266, 268
    installer, 266

IBM
    3101 terminal, 306
    3270 PC, 290
    3274 cluster controllers, 272, 273, 310
    3274-51C or 61C controller, 287
    3274/76 Cluster Controller, 276, 310
    3278, 274, 280, 305
    370 or 308X, 274
    43XX
    5251 terminal, 291
    5256 printer, 291
    Advanced Program-to-Program Communications (APPC), 271
    cabling systems, 179
    Color Graphics Adaptors, 118
    computers, 16
    control unit, 279
    Document Content Architecture (DCA) files, 283, 287
        Revisable Format for Text (RFT), 145

VM/CM, 278
VMPC, 60, 122
VMS operating system, 293, 297, 302
    files, 301
    print services, 299
    print symbiont, 299
voice/data networks, 180, 181
volumes, 193, 234, 241
VT100 terminal, 83, 97
VT220/240 terminals, 292
VT51 terminals, 293

Wall Data, 291
Wall Street Journal, The, 106
Wang Laboratories, 273
White Pine Software, 304, 306
WinPrint, 141
Word, 87, 114, 125, 219
word processing on the PC, 157
word processing programs, 10, 139, 271
WordPerfect, 141

WordStar, 114, 125, 135, 139, 141
    non-document mode, 158
work group, 322

X.25, 60
X.400 networks, 224
X.PC, 60
Xerox, 141, 183
Xmodem MacBinary protocol, 95
Xmodem protocol, 58, 60, 85, 90, 96,
    157,113, 122, 275, 305
XNS, 301
XON/XOFF protocol, 62, 95, 98
XyWrite, 141

Ymodem, 60, 90, 95

zone name, 167
zones, 45, 139, 167, 176, 179, 209, 231,
    232, 240